THE CLASSICAL REPUBLICANS

Great men have been among us; hands that penned
And tongues that uttered wisdom—better none:
The later Sidney, Marvel, Harrington,
Young Vane, and others that called Milton friend.

SECOND EDITION

THE CLASSICAL
REPUBLICANS

*An Essay in the Recovery of a Pattern of
Thought in Seventeenth-Century England*

Z. S. FINK

NORTHWESTERN UNIVERSITY PRESS

To the Memory
of
My Father and Mother

FROM THE PREFACE TO THE FIRST EDITION

THIS book is a chapter in the history of ideas. It is, moreover, concerned with a complex of ideas—the complex which represents in the field of political theory that aspect of the Renaissance which had its motive force in imitation of the classical past. It is based on the assumption that the vast number of references in Renaissance writers to classical political thought and to classical political models and their supposed modern counterparts are not to be dismissed merely as arguments dragged in to support preconceived ideas, though such use was often enough made of them, but are also significant as representing a formative element in modern political thought. It assumes that when seventeenth-century royalist writers in England charged that the reading of the books of the ancient Greeks and Romans made men into republicans, they were stating, certainly not the whole explanation of why some men became republicans, but an important element in the explanation. It claims no more than this; it is not an attempt to deny the operation of other causes, such as men's own experiences and religious beliefs, or to assert necessarily the primacy of the cause with which it deals. The book assumes, in short, that there existed in politics a counterpart to that aspect of the Renaissance which led to classical imitation in literature, architecture, and numerous other fields; that classical writers and models spoke to men in the sixteenth and seventeenth centuries with prestige in the field of politics as they did in the arts. It predicates, however, no blind or slavish adherence to classical precedent in political theory, but rather that kind of free adaptation and modification which in architecture led to St. Peter's being something like a Roman temple, but also something quite different.. That these assumptions are justified and that, because they are, classical imitation must be recognized as a formative element not only in modern political thinking but in modern political evolution, it is the object of the evidence presented to show.

More is intended to be accomplished in the present study, however, than simply a history of a complex of political ideas. The seventeenth-century Englishmen who were influenced by classical political thinking were in several cases men of letters who injected their political ideas into their literary works. It has therefore been my object to study, not only the development of the ideas themselves, but their literary and other ramifications. It is a major purpose of this book to call political theory to the aid of interpreting certain notable literary works and in particular the political phases of the career of the second English poet. This study, indeed, had its inception in an attempt to investigate and elucidate the classical element in Milton's political thinking; it retains that original purpose. It has expanded into the study which it has become because it speedily became apparent to me, not only that the whole background of the classical phases of Milton's political thought was virtually unknown, but that his position in modern political evolution could not be understood unless it was placed in the setting of a comprehensive study of the classical republicanism of the seventeenth century. That the study developed into one which throws light as well on the political ideas of Marvell, Otway, Swift, Addison, and Steele is a development which I originally did not foresee but of which I cannot complain.

Inasmuch as I constantly have occasion to use the terms *monarchy* and *republic* and their derivatives, I should like to make clear the sense in which I employ them. Because the second of these, as John Adams observed, can mean "anything, everything, or nothing," I trust that the reader will be content if I am consistent and will permit me to be somewhat arbitrary in my definitions, the purpose of the definitions being primarily only to secure clarity. I shall avoid the complexities in which modern writers have involved themselves without materially elucidating the differences between two almost hopelessly confused terms and take my criteria from those of the classical republicans themselves. When they spoke of a republic, they had in mind primarily a state which was not headed by a king and in which the hereditary principle did not prevail in whole or in part in determining the headship. A definition based on these *differentiae* is no doubt open to objection, but it is, I suggest, as defensible as any other and will be adequate for our purposes. By a "classical republican" I mean a person who advocated or admired a republic and who took his ideas for such a government in whole or in part from the ancient masterpieces of political organization, their supposed modern counterparts, or their ancient and modern expositors.

Three additional points may be mentioned in the interest of clarity. First, except where otherwise indicated, I use the word *dictator* in the sense in which it was used by the classical republicans as explained in Chapter One and not in its common twentieth-century signification. Second, let the reader remember in passages in which reference is made to Greek and Roman institutions that we are concerned, not with an historical examination to discover what they in fact were, but with what they were thought by various writers to be—two quite different things in numerous cases. Finally, the Machiavelli to whom I refer is the Machiavelli of the *Discourses*, who had, I make bold to assert, far more influence on English political thought in the seventeenth century than the Machiavelli of *The Prince*.

To the Modern Language Association I am indebted for permission to reprint in Chapter IV parts of my article on "The theory of the mixed state and the development of Milton's political thought," which appeared in the *Publications* of the Association in 1942. I am similarly indebted to *Modern philology*, *The modern language quarterly*, and *The journal of English and Germanic philology* for permission to use paragraphs from articles which I have published in them. My thanks are due for many kindnesses to Miss Effie Keith, Acting Librarian, Miss Eleanor Lewis and Miss Dorothy Hutchinson of the Northwestern Library, and to Mrs. Gertrude L. Woodward, who has charge of the Rare Book Room at the Newberry Library. Research grants from Northwestern made possible an extensive use of microfilm.

Z. S. Fink

Evanston, Illinois
December 11, 1943

PREFACE TO THE SECOND EDITION

I AM gratified by the wide acceptance this book has had and the continuing demand for it in the seventeen years since its original appearance. In reviewing it for the present edition I have found nothing of moment that I would wish to alter, and the text of the first edition is accordingly reproduced without change. Some bibliographical additions and other accumulated materials have been incorporated in the existing footnotes in an Addendum at the end. I am indebted to Professor J. H. Whitfield of the University of Birmingham for calling on his vast knowledge of Machiavelli to suggest one or two of these, and I am grateful to Jens Nyholm, Librarian of Northwestern University, for making available to me materials used in some of the others.

Z. S. F.

Evanston, Illinois
January 5, 1962

TABLE OF CONTENTS

CHAPTER ONE

POLITIQUES LEARNED OUT OF HISTORIANS AND DECLAIMERS

All your Politiques are derived from the works of Declaimers, with which sort of Writers, the Ancient Commonwealths had the fortune to abound . . . of whom we can affirm nothing certain, but that they were partiall, and never meant to give a true account of things.—The Censure of the Rota

THAT political theory and religion were still in the seventeenth century closely associated, and that the idealists of the age were dazzled by the vision of a New Jerusalem—these are aspects of the Puritan revolution which have long been recognized. But there were not wanting among the idealists of the time those who saw the New Jerusalem arising as a modern counterpart of the republics of the ancient world. Over these men the spirit of antique republicanism hovered. They would rear a nation whose statesmen would be Catos and Brutuses, whose military leaders, Scipios. They had read "the books of policy and histories of the ancient Greeks and Romans," as Hobbes put it;[1] and as Milton said, were "men more than vulgar bred up . . . in the knowledge of ancient and illustrious deeds."[2] Though Sir Robert Filmer might cry that "it is a shame and scandal for us Christians to seek the Original of Government from the Inventions or Fictions of Poets, Orators, Philosophers, and Heathen Historians,"[3] they would bring "civil virtues" to the modern world from "examples of best ages."[4] And when on the eve of the Restoration the great effort seemed to have failed, one of the chief of them would ask his generation despairingly, "Where is this goodly

---

[1] *Leviathan*, II, xxix. The passage is worth quoting in full: "And as to rebellion in particular against monarchy, one of the most frequent causes of it is the reading of the books of policy and histories of the ancient Greeks and Romans . . . From the reading, I say, of such books, men have undertaken to kill their kings, because the Greek and Latin writers, in their books, and discourses of policy, make it lawful and laudable for any man so to do, provided, before he do it, he call him tyrant."

[2] *Prose works*, ed. Bohn, V, 240. This work is subsequently referred to as *P.w.*

[3] Preface to *The anarchy of a limited or mixed monarchy*. All references to Filmer's works except the *Patriarcha* are to the 1684 edition which came out under the title *The free-holders grand inquest to which are added observations upon forms of government. The anarchy of a limited or mixed monarchy* originally appeared in 1648.

[4] Milton, *P.w.*, V, 240.

1

tower of a commonwealth, which the English boasted they would build to overshadow kings, and be another Rome?"[5]
They would build Rome anew in the West. They knew how they would build it. The ancient historians and orators had analyzed the principles on which the polities of the antique world had flourished and become glorious and had crystallized them into a theory. The theory was that of mixed government.

The idea of the mixed state rested on the notion that there are three "pure" forms of government—monarchy, aristocracy, and democracy.[6] But with the example of the Greek states before them, classical writers were struck with the impermanence of these pure forms. Monarchy, they found, tended to degenerate into tyranny, aristocracy into oligarchy, and democracy into mob rule, which were themselves unstable forms.[7] The conclusion followed easily that forms of government succeeded one another in cyclic progression.[8] The recognition that a state might exist which embodied principles of any two or all three of the simple, pure forms constituted the first step in the formulation of the theory of mixed government. The second one was the development of the idea that if the elements of the three simple forms could be thrown into a balance or equilibrium, the tendency toward degeneration which ultimately brought all pure forms of government to disaster could be arrested and permanence in government secured. The one, the few, and the many would act as effective checks on one another.

The first of these ideas was already old when it was discussed at length by Aristotle, who not only recognized that mixed states might exist,[9] but described three ways in which oligarchy and democracy could be combined[10] and cited Sparta and Carthage as representing such a combination.[11] Indeed, what Aristotle described as the best of practical states, as opposed to the pure aristocracy which he considered ideally best,[12] itself represents this combination.[13] The second basic idea in the theory of mixed government developed more slowly. Aristotle recognized that the mixing of democratic and oligarchic elements made for stability, citing Carthage as evi-

---

[5] *Ibid.*, II, 114.
[6] Cf. Plato's classification of the forms of government in *The statesman* and Aristotle, *Politics*, III, vii.
[7] Aristotle, *op. cit.*, III, vii and IV, ii.
[8] Plato, *Republic*, VIII, 546 *et. seq.*; Aristotle, *op. cit.*, III, xv; Cicero, *The republic*, II, xxv; I, xliv.
[9] *Op. cit.*, II, xi; IV, viii; V, vii, viii; VI, ii.
[10] IV, ix.   [11] II, xi; IV, ix.   [12] IV, vii.   [13] IV, xi; cf. III, xi.

dence of the fact,[14] and recommended this procedure in his list of means of rendering governments permanent.[15] He thought also that the stability of mixed states was due to the fact that they rested on a balance of the different components.[16] Yet though Aristotle set forth many of the elements out of which the theory of mixed government was made, he can hardly be regarded as having formulated the developed theory, for though he mentions in one place that some thought that the constitution of Solon represented a mixture of oligarchy, aristocracy, and democracy,[17] his own specific references to mixed constitutions as such are largely confined to those which represented a blending only of oligarchy and democracy.[18] Moreover, though he employed the principle of balance as a means of securing stability in government, he did not give it the characteristic form which it later assumed, his use of it being principally confined to the idea of a large and prosperous middle class as a balancing medium between the very rich and the very poor, and to the notion of a balance between the rich few and the many being attained by giving supreme power to the many but choosing great officers of state from among the few.[19] It is also true that Aristotle did not give to the principle of mixed forms the same emphasis or importance which it later assumed. It was not, for him, the grand secret for rendering governments stable, but rather one among a dozen means of securing stability.[20] Nor did Aristotle think that mixed governments were not subject to change, even though he considered them more stable than some other forms, for he discusses the causes of impermanence in them as he discusses those of other forms.[21]

It was the Greek historian Polybius who, by bringing into conjunction the three ideas of divided power, balance, and permanence in government, and applying these principles specifically to the mixture of monarchy, aristocracy, and democracy, was mainly responsible for giving the theory of mixed government its characteristic form.[22] Writing just before the century of civil strife which ended

[14] II, xi.   [15] V, viii; cf. VI, iv.   [16] IV, xi, xii.   [17] II, xii.
[18] In V, vii we are told that a mixture of oligarchy and democracy was what all free states aimed to achieve.
[19] III, xi.
[20] V, viii–ix. Aristotle's idea that governments often continued firm from the wise conduct of magistrates when there was no inherent stability in the form of government is quite the opposite of the ideas of seventeenth-century theorists who sought stability by well-devised political institutions which would compensate for the natural evil in man (see Harrington, *Oceana*, ed. S. B. Liljegren [Heidelberg, 1924], p. 185).
[21] V, vii.
[22] *Histories*, trans. Evelyn Shuckburgh (London and New York, 1889, 2 vols.), I, 466 ff.

in the collapse of the Roman republic, Polybius saw in Rome and Sparta the grand masterpieces of political organization. In each state, in Rome through gradual adjustment, in Sparta through the surpassing wisdom of Lycurgus, a constitution had been arrived at in which monarchial, aristocratic, and democratic elements were not only present and shared in the power, but existed in a perfect equilibrium or balance. The result was a mixed state in which the degenerative tendency which led every pure form of government to destruction had little room to operate, and a stability which for practical purposes approached permanence was attained. A passage on Lycurgus epitomizes his leading ideas:

That statesman was fully aware that all those changes which I have enumerated come about by an undeviating law of nature; and reflected that every form of government that was unmixed, and rested on one species of power, was unstable; because it was swiftly perverted into that particular form of evil peculiar to it and inherent in its nature. For just as rust is the natural dissolvent of iron . . . so in each constitution there is naturally engendered a particular vice inseparable from it: in kingship it is absolutism; in aristocracy it is oligarchy; in democracy lawless ferocity and violence; and to these vicious states all these forms of government are, as I have lately shown, inevitably transformed. Lycurgus, I say, saw all this, and accordingly combined together all the excellences and distinctive features of the best constitutions, that no one part should become unduly predominant, and be perverted into its kindred vice; and that, each power being checked by the others, no one part should turn the scale or decisively out-balance the others; but that, by being accurately adjusted and in exact equilibrium, the whole might remain long steady like a ship sailing close to the wind.[23]

In such a state Polybius thought that the monarchial element might or might not be represented by kingship. In Rome, for example, he saw this element as represented by the consuls.[24] Two important consequences followed. In the first place, a mixed state might be in superficial form either a monarchy or a republic. In the second place, this notion and the fact that Polybius described in Rome a state in which the monarchial element was not in the form of kingship facilitated the identification of this element in later political thought with the executive branch of government whether conceived of as king, consul, council, doge, or president. By consequence it was also easy to identify the aristocratic element when conceived as a council or senate with the legislative power. These identifications, however,

[23] I, 466–67.   [24] I, 469.

though compatible with the theory in its original form, were not made until long afterward.

The extent to which Polybian ideas influenced subsequent Roman republican political theory is strikingly illustrated by Cicero's *Republic*. If Polybius was the historian who was chiefly in mind when seventeenth-century royalists accused exponents of the mixed state of having taken their theories from ancient historians, there is little reason to doubt that Cicero was the chief of the "declaimers" aimed at by the royalist whose phrase suggested the title of this chapter. The superiority of a government which is a mixture of monarchial, aristocratic, and democratic principles is the central contention of the *Republic*, the glorification of the Roman commonwealth in the days of its perfection as a supreme example of such a state, its leading motif.[25] Cicero restated all the principal ideas of the Polybian theory, giving particular emphasis to the notion that stability was secured through the principle of balance in the mixed state. Some passages, indeed, might have been written by Polybius himself:

> For the primary forms already mentioned degenerate easily into the corresponding perverted forms, the king being replaced by a despot, the aristocracy by an oligarchical faction, and the people by a mob and anarchy; but whereas these forms are frequently changed into new ones, this does not usually happen in the case of the mixed and evenly balanced constitution, except through great faults in the governing class. For there is no reason for a change when every citizen is firmly established in his own station, and there underlies it no perverted form into which it can sink.[26]

So spoke Scipio Africanus the Younger, Cicero tells us, in the memorable conversations which he imagines as having taken place in Scipio's garden. When we find seventeenth-century exponents of the mixed state hailing those to whom they looked for the realization of their ideals as modern Scipios, we can be sure that the Ciceronian dialogues were lurking in the background in their minds.

Cicero's discussion of mixed government is also notable for the exposition which, professing to follow Polybius,[27] he gave of the steps by which Rome attained its perfection. Romulus, he found, not following Sparta but discovering the same principle which Lycurgus had used, associated the state's most eminent men in what

[25] I, xxxv–lxxi; II *passim*. Key passages are I, xxviii–xxix, xxxv, and xliv–xlv; II, xxiii, xxxix.

[26] I, xlv. I quote from the Loeb edition by C. W. Keyes. On the general question of Cicero's indebtedness to Polybius, see the bibliographical note in this edition, p. 8.

[27] II, xiv.

later became the Senate to participate with himself in the government.[28] By thus dividing authority between the monarchial and
aristocratic powers, he provided an excellent basis for the future
development of the state. He gave some power to the people also.[29]
Next the Romans perceived a fact which had escaped the Spartans—
that the true foundation of kingly power was virtue, not membership
in a royal family; hence, passing over their own citizens, the people
in an assembly of the *curiae*, with the advice of the Senate, chose the
Sabine Numa Pompilius to be their king. Thus the popular element
entered more prominently into the government. To provide for the
interval between the death of a king and the choice of a new one,
the wise men of the Senate devised the Interrex.[30] Subsequent kings,
notably Tullius Hostilius, wisely granted certain rights to the
people, providing a meeting place, not only for the Senate, but also
for the popular assemblies.[31] Lucius Tarquinius doubled the size
of the Senate, divided the senators into greater and lesser according
to their families, and established the knights.[32] Servius Tullius divided the citizens into five classes in such a way that, though no one
was deprived of the suffrage, the greatest number of votes belonged,
not to the common people, but to the rich, putting into effect the
principle which, says Scipio (Cicero's spokesman), "ought always
to be adhered to in the commonwealth, that the greatest number
should not have the greatest power."[33] From this account Laelius
concludes that the constitution of Rome was the product of a series
of gradual adjustments.[34]

This discussion is followed by the drawing of a specific parallel
between the Roman and Lacedaemonian governments and also that
of Carthage. Cicero found, however, that Sparta and Carthage and
also Rome as it was under the kings were all defective as examples
of mixed polities because they lacked that equilibrium or balance
on which the success and stability of mixed states rested. The reason
for this was that they all had kings who held office for life. Where
there are kings, he argued, the royal power will inevitably become
supreme, and the state will turn into a pure monarchy, which will
degenerate into a tyranny since all pure or unmixed forms of government are unstable and tend to succeed one another in cyclic progression.[35] The proof in Rome's case was the tyranny of Tar-

---

[28] II, ix; cf. xxiii.   [29] II, xxviii.   [30] II, xii–xiii; xvii.
[31] II, xvii.   [32] II, xx.   [33] II, xxii.   [34] II, xxi; cf. i.
[35] II, xxiii, xxv–xxvi. There is further criticism of the Lycurgean and Romulean versions of mixed government for containing kings in II, xxviii. It is symptomatic, however,

quinius Superbus, from which the city was rescued by the preëminent wisdom and courage of Lucius Brutus—a name destined to become famous indeed among classical republicans. The chapter in which Cicero describes the constitution as it existed after the expulsion of the kings is in some ways the most important in the entire work. He saw the state as one in which the consuls, though holding office for only one year, truly represented the monarchial element and the Senate the aristocratic, but in which the people, though free, performed few political acts. Furthermore, the principle essential to the preservation of the aristocratic power prevailed that no act of the popular assembly was valid without ratification by the Senate. At the same time was instituted the device of the dictatorship as a formal feature of the constitution which provided for the exercise of vast power in times of crisis and emergency.[36] Then indeed was Rome great when "the whole government was kept, with the people's consent, in the strong hands of the aristocracy, and in those times mighty deeds of war were done by the brave men who held the supreme power either as dictators or consuls."[37] The suspicion is irresistible that it was at this time that Cicero saw the balance of the state as most perfect. One defect, however, he was constrained to admit, still existed—the rights of the people were inadequately provided for because of the existence of enslavement for debt. The remedy for this was found when the Senate abolished such enslavement, but this remedy was not applied until after the pressure of debt had driven the people to insurrection with the resultant creation of the plebeian tribunes. The result was some curtailment of the power of the Senate, but it "remained great and respected, because the wisest and bravest still guarded the State by arms and counsel, and their influence continued to be supreme because, while they surpassed the masses in preferment, they had a smaller share of the pleasures of life, and in property were not, as a rule, better off than their fellows."[38] Passing silently over the strife which preceded the Decemvirate, Cicero tells us that some years after the institution of the tribunes the plan was adopted whereby the consuls and tribunes gave up their offices, and a board of decemvirs was appointed to exercise power and draw up a code of laws. These men duly performed their functions, but the board which they caused to be elected

---

of the virtues of mixed government in Cicero's mind that though he found the Romulean state imperfect, he found it stable for two hundred and twenty years until the time of Tarquinius Superbus (II, xxxi).

[36] Cf. Cicero's views in De legibus, III, iii, ix.   [37] II, xxxii.   [38] II, xxxiii–iv.

for the following year usurped power for the two following years until their misrule aroused the army against them.[39] At this point the account is broken off; in the lost pages Cicero probably recounted how the overthrow of the decemvirs restored the previous state of things. When the text resumes, we find Scipio observing that in his account he has given an adequate response to Laelius's inquiry about the ideal state and asserting once more the superiority of mixed polities.[40]

A writer who was no less impressed with the superiorities of mixed government, but who saw the history of Rome in somewhat different terms from those of Cicero was Dionysius of Halicarnassus, who avowedly wrote for statesmen and philosophers as well as simple readers of history. The *Roman antiquities*, an account of the earliest periods of the Roman state, was intended to fill the gap left by Polybius, whose *Histories* begin with the Punic Wars. In Dionysius to an even greater extent than in Cicero we see the triumph of an idea at the expense of fact. It is scarcely too much to say that in his hands history was moulded to prove and illustrate the theory of the superiority of mixed government. It was Dionysius's contention that the Romans were the descendants of Greeks who migrated to Italy centuries before the Trojan War,[41] that their government was based on Spartan and other Greek models,[42] that it was instituted in almost perfect form at the beginning of the history of the state by Romulus, whom Dionysius saw as a Lycurgean legislator,[43] and that it lasted in its original Romulean balance without any internal strife or bloodshed, for six hundred thirty years, until the tribuneship of Gaius Gracchus destroyed its equilibrium.[44] These contentions involved another, that the Senate held from the beginning its great powers and did not gradually acquire them,[45] a point on which he agreed with Cicero.[46] Later writers did not usually adopt Dionysius's notion that Rome came into existence all at once as a mixed state, but followed the more common idea in Polybius and Cicero that the Roman government acquired perfection gradually. They were, however, without being troubled by the inconsistency in which they involved themselves, prone to repeat Dionysius's notion that Rome lasted as a mixed state without essential change for five or six centuries. It was easy to do this if one viewed the overthrow

[39] II, xxxvi–xxxvii.   [40] II, xxxix.
[41] Trans. Earnest Cary (London and Cambridge, Mass., 1937—), I, xi ff.
[42] II, viii, xii, xiii, xiv.   [43] II, vii ff., especially xi and xiv.
[44] II, xi.   [45] II, xiv; VI, lxvi.   [46] *Republic*, II, ix, xii.

of the kings and the substitution of the consuls simply as a change in the form of the monarchial element in the state and not as one which affected its basic mixed character further than to improve it.

When Plutarch wrote his account of Lycurgus in the *Lives*, a work which enjoyed a celebrity during the Renaissance rivalled by few antique works, he gave an exposition of the principles embodied in the Spartan constitution. According to Plutarch, Lycurgus's master-stroke was the creation of the Senate, "for the state which before had no firm basis to stand upon, but leaned one while towards an absolute monarchy, when the kings had the upper hand, and another while towards a pure democracy, when the people had the better, found in this establishment of the Senate a central weight, like ballast in a ship, which always kept things in a just equilibrium."[47] The implication of this statement that a successful mixed state could not be made out of only two of the three elements is one in which earlier theorists, from Polybius on, would have concurred; what is notable about it is the suggestion that the stability of mixed polities arose from the fact that what we may call the middle element held the balance *between* the other two. Of both this idea and the older notion of the three elements checking one another, much in later times was to be heard.

The fact that Plutarch's account of mixed government is found in his account of Lycurgus may serve to call our attention to one of the notable features of the theory of mixed polities—its close connection from the beginning of its history with the idea of the legislator or law-giver. The Greeks typically thought of governments less as gradually evolved than as instituted by a single constitution-maker, a view which was suggested both by their legends and by their own experience, Solon, Zaleucus, Charondas, Philolaus, and Tellecles having functioned in this capacity.[48] The conception appears prominently in Plato, especially in the *Laws*, and it colors the whole of Aristotle's *Politics*, a work which was conceived essentially as a handbook for institutors.[49] Closely connected with this conception was the notion of the constitution-maker as a great and wise man who instituted a government without himself aiming to become its head. Indeed, Plato contends in *The Republic* that good constitutions can be made only when the law-giver does not aim to become the ruler himself. The mere fact that Sparta was seen at once as the

[47] Trans. Dryden-Clough, Modern Library ed., p. 53.
[48] Aristotle. *Politics*. II. xii: IV, xiv.
[49] See II, ix, xi, xii; III, ix; IV, i, xii, xiv; V, viii; VI, i, vi; VII, xiv.

creation of Lycurgus and as a great example of mixed government tended to give the idea of the institutor prominence in the thought of proponents of such polities. How the notion could be carried over and affect even the interpretation of Roman history, we have the example of Dionysius of Halicarnassus to show us.

Another important aspect of the theory of mixed government is that though political writers held that the success of such a state resided in attaining and then maintaining a balance or equilibrium among the three elements, this idea was not thought of as being inconsistent with some one of the three having a preponderance of power. Aristotle, indeed, had asserted that mixed states in which one element was dominant tended to turn into pure oligarchies or democracies,[50] but, as we have seen, he was thinking primarily of states mixed of only two elements, and his remark in no sense is representative of the usual view. Quite to the contrary, there was a distinct tendency to suggest that the equilibrium on which mixed governments rested could be attained only if one of the three elements had a preponderance of power, a conclusion which meant, of course, that the theory of mixed polities could be given either an aristocratic or a democratic interpretation. In the case of Cicero and Dionysius there can be no question as to where they wished the greater part of the power to be placed, for we have seen that both of them pointed their accounts of Roman history in such a way as to bring out the dominance of the Senate in the periods of which they approved most highly.

II

In that epitome of Renaissance political theory, the *Six livres de la république* (1576), Jean Bodin names Machiavelli, Sir Thomas More, and Cardinal Gasparo Contarini as the principal writers who had taken up the antique theory of the superiority of mixed polities and diffused it in the modern world.[51] Machiavelli's exposition of the idea appears in the so-called *Discourses on Livy*, a title which is somewhat of a misnomer as far as indicating the sources of his political ideas is concerned.[52] His point of departure is clearly

[50] *Politics*, V, vii.

[51] II, i, p. 184. I use the translation by Richard Knolles which appeared in London in 1606 as *The six bookes of a commonweale*.

[52] Whatever Machiavelli may have owed to Livy for his history, his great debt in political theory was to Polybius. Villari goes so far as to suggest that in the opening chapters, especially I, ii, Machiavelli not only deliberately imitated Polybius but perhaps even translated from some Latin version of him (*Niccolò Machiavelli and his times*, trans. Linda Villari [London, 1878, 4 vols.], III, 283). The *Discourses* are not a close com-

indicated in his remarks prefatory to the First and Second Books. Greece and Italy had once been glorious, but he found them in "extreme misery, infamy, and degradation" in a period "stained by every species of the lowest brutality" and devoid of the "observance of religion, law, or military discipline." He intended, therefore, "boldly and openly" to say what he thought of "the former times and of the present, so as to excite in the minds of the young men . . . the desire to avoid the evils of the latter, and to prepare themselves to imitate the virtues of the former."[53] The "former times" which were glorious, it appears from the *Discourses*, were the days of the antique Roman republic in Italy and of Sparta in Greece. In thus taking the ancients as his guides in political wisdom, Machiavelli asserted that he was opening "a new route . . . not yet . . . followed by anyone"—a fact at which he could only wonder when he contemplated the general respect for antiquity and the large sums paid for fragments of antique statuary.[54] The "new route" is no sooner opened than it becomes apparent that Machiavelli's central contention was to be the superiority of mixed government. His Second discourse is at the same time an epitome of the main ideas of the classical theory and one of the best statements of it ever made. We learn of the three simple forms of government, their tendency to degenerate into the three corrupt forms corresponding to them, and the way in which in cyclic progression one form succeeds another unless a state is so fortunate as to evolve a mixed government out of its own experience and wisdom or to have a legislator who bestows such a systen. Machiavelli's account is distinguished, however, by the emphasis of his recognition of the idea, by no means new even with him, that mixed states might come into existence through a social compact, and his contention, developed more fully in the two following discourses, that the quarrels and dissensions of the nobles and the people in ancient Rome, which some saw as cause for condemning the Roman commonwealth, were actually the very thing out of which it finally attained its greatness as a mixed polity. Machiavelli reached this conclusion by ignoring the attempts of writers like Dionysius of Halicarnassus to make Romulus into a Lycurgean legislator and to see the democratic element as present in the original Romulean settlement of the state. Romulus,

mentary on Livy. Sometimes a single remark of the Latin historian provided the starting point for a discussion of some aspect of political theory in which Machiavelli not infrequently set out to prove Livy wrong. See, for example, I, lviii, in which he dissents from Livy's view of the people.
[53] Preface to Book II.   [54] Preface to Book I.

he found, though he gave many good laws, aimed to establish, not a mixed polity, but a monarchy, and the result was that even after the expulsion of the kings and the creation of the consuls, Rome still had only two of the three elements of a mixed government—the monarchial and aristocratic. The state lacked balance, with the consequence that the oppressions of the nobles induced the people to rise. Out of the struggles of these two groups came the creation of the tribunes, by means of which the democratic element was added to the constitution and the state achieved perfection.[55] That violence continued in Rome after the setting up of the tribunes was, Machiavelli declared, an erroneous notion.[56] It may also be observed of his theory of mixed government that he had those exaggerated notions of the length of time which mixed states lasted without material alteration which are a notable characteristic of the theory of mixed polities in the period. Sparta, we are told, lasted eight hundred years "in the most perfect tranquillity."[57] By seeming to provide actual examples, notions of this sort afforded powerful support to the idea that mixed states attained a stability denied to other forms of government. Machiavelli, however, did not think, as some later theorists were to think, that absolute perfection could be attained in even a mixed state or that such a state could be rendered everlasting by the exactness of its balance, for he found even the best of things subject in time to the universal human tendency toward corruption,[58] a circumstance which led him to advocate as a device for the retardation of this process the frequent renewing of states by reducing them to their original principles.[59] The excellence of mixed government was a relative excellence, but it was so much greater than that of other forms that it was the only really desirable government.

Three aspects of Machiavelli's views demand more detailed examination. Though he shared the belief that Rome was not made in a day, he was strongly under the influence of the idea of states as being best contrived when instituted all at once by a single great legislator. The Ninth discourse is devoted to the proposition that "To found a new republic, or to reform entirely the old institutions of an existing one, must be the work of one man only." Here the implications inherent in the traditional praise of Lycurgus and other Greek legislators are made explicit. The passage in which this occurs is so important, not only in Machiavelli's thought, but in the subsequent history of classical republicanism, that it demands quotation:

[55] I, ii.   [56] I, iv.   [57] I, ii.   [58] I, vi.   [59] III, i.

But we must assume, as a general rule, that it never or rarely happens that a republic or monarchy is well constituted, or its old institutions entirely reformed, unless it is done by only one individual; it is even necessary that he whose mind has conceived such a constitution should be alone in carrying it into effect. A sagacious legislator of a republic, therefore, whose object is to promote the public good, and not his private interests, and who prefers his country to his own successors, should concentrate all authority in himself; and a wise mind will never censure any one for having employed any extraordinary means for the purpose of establishing a kingdom or constituting a republic.[60]

A consequence of these views, of course, was that though the institutor gathered all power into his hands in the establishment of a state, he would have to resign his supreme power after the government was set up or, if he retained it for life during the infancy of the state, he should not attempt to pass it on to his successors.[61]

Though in a mixed government, once it was established, no one would possess arbitrary power, Machiavelli believed that there were times when extraordinary power had to be exercised. This led him to adopt the device of the dictator. He meant by it, not a person who attains power by irregular or supra-constitutional means and then maintains himself as long as he is able, but a constitutionally provided body or institution, consisting of one person or a council of several, which functioned with great power for limited periods of time in cases of national emergency, and which might, or might not, be accountable at some regularly provided subsequent period to the bodies which controlled the government under normal conditions. In this sense the dictator had been a feature of the Roman constitution from 501 to 213 B.C. The Thirty-fourth discourse is devoted to proving that "the authority of the dictatorship always proved beneficial to Rome, and never injurious" and that "it is the authority which men usurp, and not that which is given them by the free suffrages of their fellow-citizens, that is dangerous to civil liberty." In support of this contention, he argued that no one could seize supreme power in a state without the support of a faction, and that factions had little room to operate while the Roman people were still uncorrupted; that the severe temporal limitation of the dictator made him powerless to bring about great changes; and that even if this were not so, he was rendered unable to change the constitution by the fact that his power was limited to the specific situation which

[60] I, ix. I suggest that this passage offers a clue to the relationship between the *Discourses* and *The prince*.   [61] I, ix.

he was created to deal with and that he had no authority to alter any
existing institutions of the state. A constitutionally-provided and safe
dictatorship being possible, therefore, in a mixed state, Machiavelli
went further to assert that in all such states provision for the exercise
of extraordinary authority in times of emergency was an absolute
necessity. The customary proceedings of republics, he found, were
slow because no magistrate or council was permitted to act inde-
pendently, and much time was usually necessary to harmonize conflicting opinions. Hence in a situation requiring quick action, such a
state had either to adhere to regular processes and run the risk of
ruin or resort to a frank disregard of the law. The necessity for
a constitutional dictator arose in Machiavelli's eyes from the fact
that these alternatives were equally bad. "In a well-ordered republic," he declared, "it should never be necessary to resort to extra-
constitutional measures; for although they may for the time be beneficial, yet the precedent is pernicious, for if the practice is once
established of disregarding the laws for good objects, they will in a
little while be disregarded under that pretext for evil purposes."
Thus at the basis of Machiavelli's views we find the concept of the
necessity for the universal rule of law. No republic, he declared,
would be successful if it had not "by law provided for everything,
having a remedy for every emergency, and fixed rules for applying it."[62]

The last of the major problems of mixed government with which
Machiavelli concerned himself in the *Discourses* led him to some of his
most significant and influential conclusions. He devoted the Fifth
and Sixth discourses to the question of where the preponderance
of power in a mixed state should be placed. Sparta, he found, placed
it in the hands of the aristocratic element; Rome in the people.
Results, he remarked, indicated that a law-giver should incline in
favor of the former practice, for Sparta lasted longer than Rome.
The observation is significant as showing the importance attached
by political writers in this period to the supposed length of time that
actual examples of mixed government had managed to maintain
themselves. This initial conclusion, however, he almost immediately
modified, for he found that the question was inseparable from a consideration of the end for which a state was instituted. Some states
aimed to extend their domain, others only to preserve their original
boundaries. Governments, in short, were made for either expansion
or preservation. Sparta was an example of the latter. In such a state
strangers must either be excluded altogether, or, if they are admitted,

[62] I, xxxiv.

must not be employed in any matters that would tempt them to seize authority. They must not, for example, be permitted to have arms or engage in military affairs. By following these principles Sparta secured an internal tranquillity which lasted for centuries and attained the "first degree" of happiness. But such a state, Machiavelli concluded, is weak because of its lack of people. It can succeed only where people are few or a fortunate geographical situation gives it security. Moreover, continual tranquillity is enervating and eventually renders a people unfit for great deeds. Rome, by contrast, aimed at extending its empire, and to this end neither excluded strangers nor kept them out of its armies. The result was the development of a people numerous and warlike, but so strong that they held the preponderance of power and caused many internal disturbances. Hence, though Rome attained security, it arrived at only the "second degree" of happiness. As between the first and second degrees of happiness in an imperfect world there was to Machiavelli's utilitarian spirit no question as to where the choice should lie. He would have his legislator constitute his state for expansion. That this involved a government in which preponderant power was held by the people, since the strength requisite for such a state · could be secured only by giving them arms and many privileges, was a conclusion which Machiavelli was fully ready to accept.[63]

In 1519, in his *Discourse on reforming the government of Florence*, he undertook to embody his ideas in a set of constitutional proposals for his native city. Pope Leo X and Cardinal Giulio de' Medici had requested Machiavelli to compose this work; what they found in it was an invitation to play the rôle of law-givers and institute a mixed government over which they would have control as long as they lived, but which would thereafter function wholly by itself. With fervid eloquence and appeals to the examples of Lycurgus and Solon, Machiavelli urged on them the consideration that "no man is so much raised on high by any of his acts as are those who have reformed republics and kingdoms with new laws and institutions." "After those who have been gods," he declared, "such men get the first praises."[64] The regal element in Machiavelli's government would be represented by a council of sixty-five citizens who were over forty-five years old and who would hold office for life. One of their number would be chosen gonfalonier for a term of two or three years or possibly for life. The remaining sixty-four would be divided

---

[63] I, vi. Cf. I, xxi, which develops the proposition that "Princes and republics who fail to have national armies are much to be blamed."

[64] Trans. Allan H. Gilbert in his edition of *The prince and other works* (Chicago, 1941), pp. 87, 88, 91.

into two equal groups which would alternate annually in governing
with the gonfalonier. The thirty-two serving in any given year
would be further divided into four groups of eight each, each of these
groups successively living in the palace of the gonfalonier and participating with him in the transaction of business. In matters of importance, the remaining twenty-four would be consulted, as might
also be the thirty-two who were not serving at the time, and who
would normally be employed in committee-work. For the aristocratic element in his state, Machiavelli proposed a senate or council
of the "selected," two hundred in number and composed of citizens
over forty years of age. The democratic element would be represented by a grand council consisting of six hundred or a thousand
members, which would have the function of choosing the officers of
the state except for the councils of sixty-five and two hundred and a
few other officials who were to be appointed by the Pope and the
Cardinal. After their deaths, these also would be chosen by the
popular council. In conformity with Machiavelli's view that in a
mixed state preponderant power should be placed in the people,
this council would have final authority, its decisions over-riding those
of all other bodies in the state.[65] If this system seems complicated
to the modern reader, it did not seem so to Machiavelli. He achieved
it by the wholesale abolition of existing or traditional councils,[66]
and declared that he had contrived a government which had the requisite three elements and no more.[67] These proposals, however,
do not complete Machiavelli's system, nor would we expect them to
when we keep in mind his praise in the *Discourses on Livy* for the
Roman institution of the dictator. This device, indeed, does not

[65] Pp. 55–59. The reader should keep in mind the fact that "the people" in Machiavelli's works, in those of the Italian theorists generally, and, as we shall see, in those of
some of their English followers meant those who were citizens, that is, entitled to participate in the government. In Florence at this time they numbered about 3200. One
should not, however, jump to the conclusion that Machiavelli approved of the size of the
Florentine citizenship, for he opposed the practice of tightly closing the citizenship
and praised the Romans for not doing so (*Discourses*, I, vi). Moreover, his concept of a
state for expansion predicated a large body of citizens.

[66] He mentions among the bodies with which he would dispense the councils of seventy,
one hundred, the commune, the people, the eight of Practica, and the twelve good men.
See pp. 85, 86.

[67] P. 86. One statement in the *Discourse on Florence* which is likely to mislead the reader
and obscure the essential correspondence between the theory of the *Discourses* and the
proposals for Florence is that which Professor Gilbert translates as follows: " . . . no
government can have stability if it is not a true principality or a true republic, for all the
constitutions between these two are defective" (p. 83). As the context makes unmistakably clear, this observation refers to the government as it had existed under Cosimo
de' Medici when what was in fact a principality had masqueraded as a republic, and not
to the necessity for mixing the three elements of a state.

appear in the proposals for Florence in its Roman form, but something not wholly unrelated to it does. Among the officials to be chosen by the grand council, or by the Medici as long as they lived, would be sixteen gonfaloniers of the companies of the people, chosen for terms of four months. Once a month, the sixteen would choose four head men, so that by the end of their term all would have served in this capacity. The four chosen for any given month would take weekly turns residing in the palace with the nine resident members of the signory and attending all meetings of that body, which would be powerless to act without them. They would have no vote, but could prevent the signory from taking a decision which they deemed counter to the interests of the state by appealing the matter to the whole group of thirty-two. The thirty-two, in turn, could decide nothing without the presence of two head men, who again had no vote but could appeal the matter to the council of two hundred. Machiavelli would require six gonfaloniers including two of the head men to be in attendance before the senate could give a decision, and any three of these could take the matter from that body and appeal it to the great council, the decision of which would be final. The popular council, however, could not itself act unless twelve of the sixteen gonfaloniers were present. The object of this elaborate device, Machiavelli explained, was two-fold: to prevent any one group in the state from taking action detrimental to the whole or to the other groups, and to prevent time-consuming deadlocks which would rob the government of the power to act.[68]

We notice among the officials who would be temporarily appointed by the Medici two commissioners of brigades who would have charge of the armed forces. These represented in Machiavelli's constitution not a new element but the retention of one for the introduction of which into Florence in the period from 1500 to 1506 he had himself been mainly responsible. Together with the militia which they headed they represented one of his favorite projects and one which was the natural counterpart of the conviction expressed in the *Discourses on Livy* that unless favored geographically, states were strong enough to survive only when they placed arms in the hands of their citizens and did not rely on mercenaries.[69] Machia-

---

[68] Pp. 88–89. Machiavelli proposed also a legal system which would retain the existing Eight of Guard for the administration of the ordinary courts and supplement them with a court of appeals of thirty drawn from the grand council and the senate. See pp. 89–90.

[69] See I, xxi on the subject that "Princes and republics who fail to have national armies are much to be blamed," and II, xx, "Of the dangers to which princes and republics are exposed that employ auxiliary or mercenary troops." On Machiavelli's militia see J. A. Symonds, *Renaissance in Italy*, Modern Library ed., 2 vols., I, 157–58.

velli's views on military matters, in short, were the direct expression not only of his political philosophy, but of the lessons which he had learned from his examination of the ancients, for though the example of the Italy of his own day was enough to teach him that the system of employing mercenaries was disastrous, it was ancient Rome whose example suggested the appropriate correction for the current evil.

The idea of following the ancients and the adoption of the Polybian theory of mixed government were by no means so original with Machiavelli as his own statements would suggest. The views of Polybius had been diffused in Italy in the fifteenth century. By the time Machiavelli wrote, they had become the accepted creed of a notable group of Florentine political theorists, which he rather expressed and represented than invented.[70] Though they differed among themselves over details, especially over the question of where the preponderant power should be placed, from Soderini to Giannotti these writers were champions of the mixed polity. Whether they fought the Medici or served them, their ideal was the creation of such a state in Florence. Savonarola, who appears in this group for all his opposition to classical precedent and the "chains of antiquity," set the theory forth at great length in his *Trattato circa il reggimento e governo della citta di Firenze*. Guicciardini gave it an even more notable exposition in his *Del reggimento di Firenze*.[71] Moreover, the specific proposals made by these writers, like Machiavelli's own, represent attempts to embody the principles of *governo misto* in an actual constitution. The plan of government, for example, which was adopted at Florence in 1495 under the influence of Savonarola and Soderini after the expulsion of the Medici, a plan notable as the first attempt in the modern world to initiate a government deliberately formed on the principles of mixed polities, provided a signory to represent the regal element, a council of *ottimati*, eighty in number, for the aristocratic branch, and for the popular, a grand council to which all citizens who were *beneficiati* or possessed of the right to participate in the government were eligible. To prevent the last of these bodies from being unwieldy, the 3200 citizens were divided into three groups who were to serve successively for terms of six months.[72]

---

[70] Amadeo Crivellucci, *Del governo popolare in Firenze, 1494–95, secondo il Guicciardini* (Pisa, 1877), pp. 102 ff. See also Villari's comments, III, 283, 247.

[71] *Opere inedite* (Florence, 1857, 10 vols.), II, 60 ff., especially pp. 129, 130, 139–41 *et seq*. Cf. II, 262; I, 6.

[72] On Savonarola's constitution see Guicciardini's *Storia Fiorentina*, cap. xvii. This work may be found in the *Opere inedite*, vol. I, in which it first appeared. See also Guicciardini's

The plans for Florence proposed by Savonarola and Machiavelli both gave great power to the people. Guicciardini, who proposed a plan with the same essential parts—a gonfalonier and signory, a council or senate of one hundred sixty to one hundred eighty members, and a grand council to elect magistrates[73]—wished, however, to concentrate power in the *ottimati*, contending that the excessive power given the people was the cause of the ruin of Savonarola's constitution,[74] and taking Machiavelli to task for advocating the same mistake.[75] His views are significant as illustrating the appeal of the theory of mixed government to those whose conception of government was essentially aristocratic. He approached his panegyric on mixed polities through an analysis of the defects of tyranny and democracy.[76] "Liberty" to him and to others of his stamp was not a matter of putting political power in the hands of the people, but of securing the well-born or the rich or the virtuous from the encroachments at once of tyrants and people. These were the great enemies of "liberty." Guicciardini was as unsparing in analyzing the defects of the one as of the other. His ideal presumably would have been a pure aristocracy. But a realist before everything else and convinced that the facts of human nature made such a government unstable and short-lived, he saw the mixed state as creating that situation in which the few with the greatest stability and the greatest chances of success had the largest range of political freedom.

Guicciardini's interpretation of the mixed state was shared in large measure by the Venetian political theorist, Paolo Paruta.[77] He too was a champion of the dominance of the *ottimati*, asserting that though mixed government was the best form, not all mixtures were equally perfect, and that the too great power of the popular ele-

---

comments in the *Reggimento di Firenze* in the same edition, II, 27–30, and the extended account in the *Historie of Guicciardini, conteining the warres of Italie*, trans. G. Fenton (London, 1579), pp. 77 ff. and p. 177. Cf. Benedetto Varchi, *Storia Fiorentina* (Florence, 1721), I, 169. Admirable modern scholarly treatments may be found in Villari's *Machiavelli*, I, 334, and in his *Life and times of Girolamo Savonarola*, trans. Linda Villari (London, 1899), pp. 269–305.

[73] *Opere inedite*, II, 262 ff.   [74] *Historie*, p. 177.

[75] *Considerazioni intorno ai Discorsi del Machiavelli* in *Opere inedite*, I, "Considerazione on I, v."   [76] *Opere inedite*, II, 34–39, 50–60.

[77] From the evidence of editions and translations, this writer must be regarded as of some importance in the diffusion of the theory of the mixed state. His *Della perfettione della vita politica* had at least four Venetian editions between 1579 and 1600 and a French translation, Paris, 1582. His *Discorsi politici*, in addition to Venetian editions in 1599 and 1629, appeared at Geneva in 1600, at Bologna two years later, and in an English translation by Henry Earl of Monmouth, London, 1657. The *Historia Venetiana* appeared at Venice in 1605 and 1645 and was translated into English by Monmouth in 1658.

ment was the cause of the ruin of the Roman republic.[78] He added to this analysis the idea that Rome fell also because of the bestowal of too much authority on the regal element,[79] giving expression to that strong distrust of executive power which characterizes so many advocates of mixed polities.[80] In conformity with these views, Paruta found Sparta to be the most perfect of the antique mixed states. He found a further cause of its success in the fact that it was made all at once by a legislator instead of growing by accident and imperfect adjustment as Rome had grown.[81] For the rest, his views need not detain us. We may notice in passing his acceptance of the notion that a state unprovided with a constitutional dictator for emergencies would come to ruin.[82]

One more continental figure we must look at before we turn to the diffusion of the idea of mixed government in England—Jean Bodin. Unlike the Italian theorists, Bodin was no champion of the mixed state. By the time he wrote, the concept had made its way into France, and French theorists had been busy applying it to their interpretation of the French constitution.[83] To it Bodin flatly opposed the theory of sovereignty with which his name is so inseparably connected. Sovereignty being indivisible,[84] he argued, there could be but one place in a state where it resided. If it was placed in one, the state was a monarchy; if in the few, an aristocracy; if in the many, a democracy.[85] A mixed state, therefore, had no existence in nature and was a logical absurdity. Such a state had never existed and, he thought, could hardly be imagined.[86] Having made these pronouncements, he set about the task of showing that the formidable list of supposed mixed states were all in fact one or the other of the three simple forms. Sparta was a pure aristocracy; the Roman commonwealth one in which the sovereign power and majesty of the state were in the people; France was a pure monarchy.[87] Evidently, Bodin was not too sure of his success in demonstrating this point, for presently we find him admitting that though sovereignty itself could not be divided, the rights of sovereignty could be. States in which this condition prevailed, however, were not properly common-

---

[78] *Politic discourses*, ed. 1657, pp. 3, 12. [79] *Ibid.*, p. 3.
[80] Cf. his statement on p. 5: "Certainly to grant but a limited power, and but for a short time, to Magistrates are excellent precepts of such Legislators as will constitute a free city."
[81] *Ibid.*, p. 6. Cf. the high praise of Lycurgus on pp. 11–12. [82] *Ibid.*, p. 21.
[83] Claude de Seyssel, *La grande monarchie de France* (Paris, 1558), p. 13; Bernard de Girard du Haillan, *De l'estat et succez des affaires de France* (Paris, 1580), p. 154.
[84] *Op. cit.*, I, viii ff., pp. 84 ff. [85] *Ibid.*, II, i, pp. 184–85.
[86] *Ibid.*, II, i, p. 194. [87] *Ibid.*, II, i, pp. 186–91.

wealths at all, but corruptions of government in which the elements
sharing in the power contended through endless civil broils for all of
it until the whole system collapsed.[88] Though Bodin's book was one
of the most widely read works of the sixteenth and seventeenth
centuries,[89] it did not demolish the theory of the mixed state; quite
to the contrary, it seems probable that it helped to give it currency
among men of liberal views. What the book did do was to supply
in the doctrine of sovereignty a concept which could be made and
which was made by succeeding absolutists in both France[90] and
England[91] into an argument against attempts to limit the royal
power.

III

In England, the history of the mixed state as a Renaissance idea
formed in conscious imitation of the classics begins early. It begins,
in fact, with no less a work than Sir Thomas More's *Utopia*. Though
More did not specifically elaborate the theory, even a cursory examination of the constitution of his ideal state as set forth in the
section "Of the magistrates" is sufficient to show that it was intended to represent an embodiment of the principles of mixed government, and that Bodin was quite right in seeing in More one of those
who were impressed with the advantages of such a system. Every
thirty families, we are told, chose annually an officer known as a
philarche or syphograunte. Over every ten syphograuntes and the
families under them was a chief philarche[92] or tranibore, whose grant

[88] *Ibid.*, II, i, pp. 194–95.
[89] Editions tell the story. The book appeared in French or Latin at Paris in 1576, 1577,
1578, 1579, 1580, 1583, 1586; at Lyon in 1579, 1580, 1593; at Geneva in 1608 and 1629;
Frankfurt, 1591, 1609, 1622. In addition to the English translation of 1606 already referred to, an Italian translation appeared at Geneva in 1588 and a Spanish rendering at
Turin in 1590.
[90] The French phase of this development is brilliantly treated by W. F. Church in his
Constitutional thought in sixteenth century France (Cambridge, Mass., and London, 1941),
pp. 308 ff. Bodin did not himself push the theory to the extreme lengths arrived at by
some of his followers, for he saw the king as limited by various restraints such as the law
of nature. See Church, pp. 225, 226–27, 229–35.
[91] The point is illustrated by the notions of Sir Robert Filmer, who, quoting Bodin,
argued that monarchy and mixed government were wholly incompatible, since a monarchy was the government of one. See *The anarchy of a limited or mixed monarchy*, ed.
1684, pp. 238–39 *et seq.*
[92] More borrows the term, of course, from the Greek, a philarche having been in the
ancient Athenian system the head of the largest political subdivision in the state. Cf. Dionysius of Halicarnassus's account of the Romulean divisions in Rome: "He [Romulus]
divided all the people into three groups, and set over each as leader its most distinguished
man. Then he subdivided each of these three groups into ten others, and appointed as
many of the bravest men to be the leaders of these also. The larger divisions he called
tribes, and the smaller *curiae*, as they are still termed even in our day. These names may

of authority was renewed yearly but who was not changed except for the weightiest reasons. The chief philarches, of whom there were ten, formed a council which met every third day and in which all matters had to be debated for three days before being decided. The prince, who sat with them, was chosen for life from four candidates nominated by the people in each of the four quarters of the city, the selection being made by secret voting by the syphograuntes, who were represented also by two of their number, constantly changed, at every meeting of the chief philarches. Matters of great weight and importance were brought to the meeting-place of the syphograuntes, who laid them before their families. All discussion of governmental affairs was limited to the councilar meetings, it being an offense punishable by death to violate this rule. Sometimes matters were laid before a great council of all the citizens. It is clear that in this system the prince and the council of ten chief philarches, whom More describes as acting together, represented the monarchial element and the council of two hundred syphograuntes the aristocratic, and that the democratic principle was recognized in the great council of all the citizens and the popular nomination of the prince. It needs only to be pointed out to complete the resemblance of Utopia in main outlines to the constitutions of mixed state theorists that More envisioned a state in which not all who were adults and native-born were citizens and entitled to participate in the government. Indeed, under the influence of Greek conceptions, his non-citizens, who do all the drudgery and vile forms of labor, turn into bondmen, though he repudiated the idea of a class of hereditarily disenfranchised inhabitants like that in the Italian republics.

The theory of mixed government did not long remain among Englishmen on the utopian plane on which More employed it. It had been clear to theorists of mixed government from the beginning that in such a state the monarchial power might or might not be represented by a king, and there was, therefore, nothing to prevent a state which was a monarchy from being seen also as a mixed polity. Moreover, the theory accorded well with the actual form of the English constitution. The application of the theory to the interpretation of that constitution was made, at least by implication, by

---

be translated into Greek as follows: a tribe by *phyle* and *trittys*, and a *curia* by *phratra* and *lochos*; the commanders of the tribes, whom the Romans call tribunes, by *phylarchoi* and *trittyarchoi*; and the commanders of the *curiae*, whom they call *curiones*, by *Phratriarchoi* and *lochagoi*. These *curiae* were again divided by him into ten parts, each commanded by its own leader, who was called *decurio* in the native language" (*op. cit.*, II, vii).

John Ponet, Bishop of Winchester, Greek scholar, Marian exile, and friend of Ascham, in his *Short treatise of politike power*. In this work, with allusions to Rome, Sparta, and Lycurgus which leave no question as to the sources of Ponet's ideas,[93] we are told of the three simple forms of government, monarchy, aristocracy, and democracy, and of the superiority of that form which is mixed of all of them and in which affairs are in the hands of "a king, the nobilitie, and commones." The advantage of this form Ponet found to reside in its stability. "Wher that mixte state was exercised," he wrote, "ther did the common wealthe longest continue."[94] After reading these sentiments, no one need be surprised to find Sir Thomas Smith in his *De republica Anglorum*, posthumously published in 1583, not only specifically describing England as a mixed monarchy, but declaring that nearly all actual states were mixed in character.[95] Similar ideas were entertained by Sir Walter Raleigh—if we may discern his views beneath what appear to be intentional contradictions. Though he might on occasion declare that kings are made by God and are not subject to law,[96] we find him elsewhere describing the theory of mixed government,[97] declaring that though the prince had power in England to make laws, treaties, and wars, yet "to give contentment to the other degrees they have a suffrage in making laws,"[98] and asserting that "in every just state some part of the government is or ought to be imparted to the people: as in a kingdom a voice or suffrage in making laws."[99] Moreover, if we can generalize from two of his remarks about the great historic examples of mixed polities, Raleigh had definite notions as to where preponderant power in a mixed government should be placed. In one of these, we find him declaring that in all such systems one of the three elements held more power than the other two, and that in Rome it was the aristocratic element which was predominant. This is so contrary to the usual view of Rome in the political writers of the time that it seems reasonable to suppose that it affords a clue as to where Raleigh thought the greater share of power ought to be placed.[100] At any rate, in a second passage in which he gives the customary opinion that the popular element was dominant in Rome, we find him exalting

[93] (London, 1556), sigs., A4v, A5, A6r. Cf. sig. Kr.   [94] *Ibid.*, sig. A5r.
[95] I, vi. It is possible that Ponet learned about mixed government from Smith, whose pupil he was, but whatever he learned from Smith was certainly supplemented by continental writers with whom he came in contact during his exile.
[96] *Works* (Oxford, 1829, 8 vols.), III, 144.
[97] *Remains* (London, 1675), pp. 9–11, 21.
[98] *Works*, VIII, 2.   [99] *Works*, VIII, 155.   [100] *Remains*, p. 9.

Sparta over Rome on the ground that by its nobility it enjoyed freedom longer, and declaring that "Politicians do affirm, that nobility preserves liberty longer than the commons," statements which he accompanied with the observation that "Solon's popular state came far short of Lycurgus's by mixed government; for the popular state of Athens soon fell, whilst the royal, mixed government of Sparta stood a mighty time."[101]

Raleigh's caution in setting forth his ideas was doubtless dictated both by the exigencies of his personal situation and the aristocratic interpretation which he gave to the theory of mixed polities. Smith, however, had not advanced his views as either revolutionary dogma or an ideal, but simply as a statement of fact. Even after the distinct cleavage between king and parliament had begun, it is remarkable how long writers who upheld extreme claims for the royal prerogative were willing to assent to the proposition that England was a mixed monarchy. A striking illustration is afforded by Henry Ferne, the most redoubtable of the royalists before Filmer, who in 1643 undertook to find no other term to describe the English government.[102] More remarkable still, if we can believe Tyrrell, is the fact that King Charles I himself on one occasion declared: "This Kingdom is mix'd of Monarchical, Aristocratical, and Democratical Government; and that so wisely, that we have all the Conveniences, and none of the Inconveniences of any of those Forms taken single."[103]

It was inevitable, however, that in the great dispute between king and parliament, the theory of mixed government would become a weapon in the hands of the king's opponents. Two things made this a natural development. The first of these was that the concept *ipso facto* placed great limitations on royal power, particularly in the crucial matter of the right to make law. All that men read of mixed government in the classical masters and their Renaissance exponents told them that in mixed polities the monarchial element was subject to greater limitations than royalists could admit. The champions of mixed polities had debated over whether predominant power should be placed in the democratic or aristocratic elements; it had not even occurred to most of them to think of putting it in the regal element; the constitutions they had drawn up had all been

101 *Works*, VIII, 296.

102 *A reply unto severall treatises pleading for the armes now taken up by subjects in the pretended defence of religion and liberty* (Oxford, 1643), p. 12.

103 James Tyrrell, *Bibliotheca politica. In fourteen dialogues* (London, 1718), p. 241.

characterized by weak, strictly limited monarchial elements. In the second place, the theory afforded a plausible justification of resistance, even of armed resistance, to the royal will. These points are well illustrated by the *Treatise of monarchie* which Philip Hunton published in 1643, "not . . . to foment or heighten the wofull dissention of the Kingdome; but if possible to cure, or at least to allay it."[104] After a classification of government into the three simple forms and a declaration of the superiority of the mixed form which might have been written by a Polybius or a Machiavelli,[105] Hunton proceeded to find that England was "acknowledged to be a Monarchy mixed with an Aristocracy in the house of Peeres, and Democracy in the house of Commons."[106] It followed by consequence that power in England was in its very nature divided among the three elements of the government. But if this was true, not only did Charles not have all the power which his supporters claimed for him, but subjects might seem to have an undoubted right to resistance and rebellion. How this consequence followed was illustrated clearly by Hunton when he proceeded to argue that in the event of fundamental disputes arising among the three elements of a mixed state, the king could not be permitted to decide the issue, for in the act of doing so he would necessarily exercise arbitrary power. "In this case," Hunton declared, "which is beyond the Government, the Appeale must be to the Community, as if there were no Government; and as by Evidence mens Consciences are convinced, they are bound to give their utmost assistance."[107] In three cases particularly the other

---

[104] Preface, sig. A2r.

[105] "The third division is into simple and mixed. Simple is when the Government absolute or limited is so intrusted in the hands of one, that all the rest is by deputation from him; so that there is no authority in the whole Body but his, or derived from him: And that One is either individually one Person, and then it is a simple Monarchy: Or one associate Body, chosen either out of the Nobility, whence the Government is called a simple Aristocraty: or out of the Community, without respect of birth or state, which is termed a simple Democracy. The supreme authority residing exclusively in one of these three, denominates the Government simple, which ever it be.

"Now experience teaching People, that severall inconveniences are in each of these, which is avoided by the other: as aptnesse to Tyranny in simple Monarchy: aptnesse to destructive Factions in an Aristocracy: and aptnesse to Confusion and Tumult in a Democracy. As on the contrary, each of them hath some good which the others want, viz. Unity and strength in a Monarchy; Counsell and Wisedome in an Aristocracy; Liberty and respect of Common good in a Democracy. Hence the wisedome of men deeply seen in State matters guided them to frame a mixture of all three, uniting them into one Forme, that so the good of all might be enjoyed, and the evill of them avoyded" (pp. 24–25).

[106] P. 40. Cf. his remark on p. 39 that it was a "cleare and undoubted Truth, that the Authority in this Land is of a compounded and mixed nature in the very root and constitution thereof."   [107] P. 28.

estates could "lawfully assume the force of the Kingdome, the King not joyning, or dissenting": when foreign invasion was imminent or had occurred; when an internal faction undermined or openly assaulted the laws; and when "the Fundamentall Rights of either of the three Estates be invaded by one or both the rest." In the last case especially, the wronged could "lawfully assume force for its own defense; because else it were not free, but dependent on the pleasure of the other."[108]

In Hunton's hands, then, the theory of mixed government became a justification of resistance to the royal will. It was inevitable that it either would lead some men still further or become a weapon in their hands, for though since the time of Polybius himself it had been recognized that the monarchial power in a mixed state might or might not be represented by a king, a fact which the inclusion of Sparta in the list of mixed polities illustrated, there was much in both the history of the theory and its inherent implications which led straight to republicanism. The idealization of the Roman republic at the hands of Polybius, Cicero, and Machiavelli, the republican sentiments which are strewn through Machiavelli's *Discourses*,[109] Englished in 1636, and the republican character of the constitutional experiments at Florence in the preceding century, about which Englishmen had been reading at least since the first translation of Guicciardini's *Storia d'Italia* in 1579,[110] illustrate the point. Moreover, the idea that mixed government was incompatible not only with absolutism, but with monarchy in any form because of its tendency to degenerate into tyranny and thus ruin the balance on which mixed polities depended, had, as we have seen, made its appearance among champions of such systems as far back as Cicero. Finally, both the concept of the Roman government as having achieved perfection through frequent man-made alterations and the notion of other mixed states as having been made by legislators encouraged the belief that men were free to set up whatever government they pleased. When royalists began to realize these republican implications of mixed government, they ceased calling England a mixed monarchy in the sense of being a state in which power was itself divided,[111] elaborated

[108] Pp. 66–67.

[109] See especially I, x, xvii, xix, xx, xxix, lviii, lix. For an admirable discussion of Machiavelli's republicanism see Gilbert's edition, pp. 12–13.

[110] There were other editions in 1594 and 1618.

[111] Robert Sheringham wrote in *The king's supremacy asserted, or a remonstrance of the king's right against the pretended parliament:* "The Author of the Treatise of Monarchy, the fuller Answerer, and other Pretended Parliamentarians, have invented a new form of Government to delude the People, which they tell them is the Government established in

the theory of the divine right of kings in its most extreme forms,[112] and began to listen to Sir Robert Filmer, who, symptomatically, published in 1648 *Observations upon Mr. Hunton's Treatise of monarchy: or, the anarchy of a limited or mixed monarchy*.[113] When exponents of mixed government came to the same realization, they became republicans. These facts considered, we need not be surprised to find appearing in the 1650's men who, steeped in "politiques" learned out of historians and "declaimers" and fired with admiration of the mixed polities of the ancient world, had in some cases begun by attempting to see England as a mixed monarchy, but had ended by rejecting monarchy, and who aimed to create in England an ideal mixed polity. These men were the classical republicans. Before we look at them, however, we must examine the development of a political reputation which was in part an outgrowth of the theory of mixed government and in part an influence on it, and which was intimately connected with it at all stages of its history in England.

England; namely, a mixed Monarchy, consisting of three Estates, independent for their authority upon one another, all of them being coordinate, and having several shares in the rights of Sovereignty, by the fundamental lawes of the land. A strange kind of Monarchie, not so much as heard of until these times, much lesse established in England: for Monarchy is the Government of one alone" (ed. London, 1660, p. 80).

[112] The origin and development of this theory are treated by J. N. Figgis in *The divine right of kings* (Cambridge, 1896).

[113] This work contains all of the views associated with Filmer's name, including that of the patriarchal origin of the state (ed. 1684, pp. 244 ff.). Like Sheringham, he asserted that Hunton's doctrine of mixed monarchy was "an opinion but of yesterday, and of no antiquity, a meer innovation in Policy, not so old as New England, though calculated properly for that Meridian" (p. 238). Filmer grounded his defense of absolutism fundamentally on two propositions. The first of these was that God gave absolute parental power to the father of a family, a notion for which he cited Genesis iii, 16; that states originated out of the expansion of a family; and that kings by inheritance derived their authority from the original divine grant (p. 244). The second of his basic contentions rested on an appropriation from Bodin, whom he quotes (p. 239), of the indivisibility of sovereign power (Preface, sig. S2r., pp. 240, 243, and especially pp. 279–81). Filmer's views have been too often dismissed as merely the personal aberrations of Filmer. He had the good sense to see that Charles's acts had been absolutist in character and demanded an absolutist theory to defend them. It is symptomatic of the truth of this statement that the second Stuart attempt at absolutism, that in the 1680's, saw a great revival of his doctrines and was carried on frankly under his banner. Locke, Tyrrell, and Algernon Sydney wrote long and detailed answers to him. We cannot suppose that men of their abilities devoted their energies to replying to ideas which were considered inconsequential or not widely held. In taking over the Bodinian doctrine of the indivisibility of sovereignty, he merely supplied for an English absolutism that failed the same basic defense that the French theorists supplied for one that succeeded in establishing itself. Furthermore, the patriarchal theory, though Filmer pushed it to absurd lengths, is when considered simply as a theory of the origin of government and stripped of its Biblical impedimenta, historically a more likely theory than that of the social compact.

CHAPTER TWO

THE MOST SERENE REPUBLIC

Rome men, Venice the Gods did trace.
            —Sannazaro.
Till Nature and the Univers decline,
Venice within her Watery Orb shall shine.
            —Thuanus.
Venice, the eldest Child of Liberty.
She was a maiden City, bright and free;
No guile seduced, no force could violate.
            —Wordsworth.

SPARTA and the Roman republic were great examples of mixed government. But they belonged to the past. When the theorists of the Renaissance looked about in the contemporary world for a mixed polity, they discovered in the republic of Venice a supreme illustration of their concept. Several factors entered into the development of this idea, but foremost was the actual form of the government itself. This is of such great importance in subsequent attempts to create mixed constitutions that it is necessary to describe it in some detail. At the top of the pyramid to which the writers of the age were fond of comparing the Venetian government[1] was the Doge, elected for life and assisted by six councillors, one from each of the six tribes into which the city was divided, who were chosen for terms of eight months.[2] It is significant of how weak the authority of the Doge was that a majority of the councillors could act without him, but that he could not act unless at least four of them were present. Even with this safeguard on the power of a "single person," his powers were redefined at each new election by a committee of the Grand Council, the *Inquisitori sopra il doge defunto*, and were either increased or decreased as experience seemed to indicate. By the *Promissione ducale* he swore to observe the charter

---

[1] A not uninteresting article could be written on the uses of this simile by political writers. Though it is a Renaissance commonplace, C. M. Walsh curiously seems to think that Sir William Temple invented it, alluding to his use of it in the *Essay upon the original and nature of government* as his "famous simile" (*The political science of John Adams* [New York and London, 1915], p. 360).

[2] On the Doge and the councillors see Gasparo Contarini, *The commonwealth and government of Venice*, trans. Lewes Lewkenor (London, 1599), pp. 42 ff.

28

of his powers. He had one vote in the Senate and two in the Great
Council. With the councillors he decided only the most minor matters
on his own authority. In all matters of importance, the ducal council
sat with the College of Sages or Preconsultors, which was essentially
a committee of the Senate consisting of sixteen members chosen for
terms of six months. Of these, five were *Savii di terra firma*, and five
Savii di gli ordini or *Savii di mare*, forming specialized smaller councils, and six were *Savii grandi*, having superior jurisdiction over
both the Sages of the Sea and those of the Land.[3] When the Doge,
the Council of Six, the Sages, and the Triumvirs, heads of the
judicial organization, sat together, a body of twenty-six members
was formed which constituted the full *Collegio*. The Sages, with
or without the Doge and the Council of Six, gave matters a preliminary hearing and then laid them before the Senate or Council
of *Pregadi*, the main deliberative and legislative body of the state.
Since the Senate could not initiate a measure or consider it until the
Sages collectively or individually, or some member of the *Collegio*,
all of whom had the right to propose, had laid it before the *Pregadi*,
the twenty-six were in effect the chief ministers of the state.[4]

The Senate consisted of sixty ordinary senators elected annually
by the Great Council, and sixty members chosen by the first sixty.[5]
In addition to these, various officers and dignitaries of the state had
membership, though not in all cases with voting privileges—the
Doge, the Council of Ten, the *Quarantia* or forty judges of criminal
causes, the Prefect of the Arsenal, and the Procurators of St. Mark,
who were senators for life. The full membership was well over two
hundred.[6] The powers of this body were vast. "The whole manner of
the commonwealths government," wrote Contarini, "belongeth to
the Senate. That which the Senate determineth is held for ratified
and inviolable. By their authority and advice is peace confirmed and
war denounced. The whole rents and receipts of the Commonwealth
are at their appointments collected and gathered in, and likewise
laid out againe and defrayed. If there be any new taxations or sub-
sidies to be laid upon the citizens, they are imposed & likewise levied

[3] *The maxims of the government of Venice* (London, 1707), p. 24. The notes added by
the translator to this edition of a work erroneously attributed to Paolo Sarpi (see below,
p. 141) contain much information on many features of the Venetian constitutional
system.   [4] *Maxims*, pp. 23–24.

[5] Contarini, pp. 65 ff.; James Howell, *A survey of the signorie of Venice, of her admired
policy and method of government* (London, 1651), p. 13.

[6] Contarini gives the membership as about two hundred twenty (p. 66); the annotator
of the *Maxims* as about three hundred (p. 23).

by the Senates decree. And if at any time it shall seem necessary for the good of the commonwealth, to create a new officer or magistrate upon any sodaine urgent occasion, he is by the Senate elected. Besides, the senate by a perpetuall prerogative, hath authority to chuse such Embassadors as are to bee sent to forraine princes, and likewise to create the colledge of those, whose office is to assemble the senate, and to report unto them."[7]

At the base of the pyramid was the *Gran Consiglio* or Great Council, which met every eighth day and sometimes oftener. In it sat all male citizens or patricians whose families were entered in the *Libro d'Oro* and who had attained the age of twenty-five. A certain number of those eligible, however, were admitted by lot upon attaining the age of twenty. In 1581, 1843 out of a total population of 134,890 were eligible to sit.[8] This body ratified laws, but its great function was the choice of many of the magistrates of the state. In the choice of the Doge an elaborate system combining choice by lot and election was employed. On such occasions, all the members over thirty years old assembled and cast their names into a pot. In another pot was the same number of balls, of which thirty were gilt. A child then drew from the two pots until the thirty gilt balls had been drawn, with thirty corresponding names. The process was then repeated, the thirty names being put into one pot and thirty balls in the other, of which nine were gilt. The nine picked by this lot nominated forty, out of whom twelve were selected by lot, who nominated twenty-five. Nine of these were then picked by lot and proceeded to nominate forty-five, who were reduced by lot to eleven. The eleven chose forty-one leading members of the Senate, who then did the electing of the Doge, twenty-five votes being necessary for an election.[9] Contarini explains that the element of lot made it seem that the choice was by the whole people, that is, the whole body of patricians, but that the element of lot was overbalanced by that of election in a system in which the choice really rested mainly with the wise and the virtuous.[10]

In addition to these bodies was the famous Council of Ten, in-

---

[7] P. 68. Cf. Howell: "They treat of peace and warr, their power extends to lay taxes, to make extraordinary levies and erogations of moneys: They make choice of Ambassadors to be employed to forren Princes; they have power allso to summon the Sages of Land and Sea, with all the chief Magistrats" (*op. cit.*, p. 13).

[8] Symonds, I, 100. Lewkenor gives the number in the Great Council as 3000 (p. 155); Lassels, as 2000 (*The voyage of Italy* [Paris, 1670], Pt. II, p. 368); the annotator of the *Maxims* as formerly 1500 or 1600 but in his own time as not exceeding 800 or 900 (pp. 22–23).   [9] Contarini, pp. 53–56. Cf. Howell, p. 34.   [10] P. 56.

vested with great powers and charged with maintaining the safety of the republic. In the minds of most people today the Ten pass for an infamous institution, a reputation acquired at the hands of nineteenth-century writers who based their opinion of it on the later history of the republic, when it did indeed become the malodorous organ by which a decayed aristocracy maintained a tyranny over the state. But nothing is more certain than that sixteenth-century writers did not see it in this way. They saw it as an organ in a delicately-poised and perfectly-functioning government which contributed to the balance of the whole by acting as a check and being itself subject to other checks. Normally it sat with the Doge and the Council of Six, and was really a committee of seventeen. On grave occasions, it might be increased by an addition (*giunta*) of twenty or more of the principal men of the state. The Ten were elected annually by the Great Council and were responsible to it. Indeed, for long they were held to such strict accountability upon leaving office that it was frequently difficult to get anyone to serve. Symonds quotes a statement by Giannotti that so great was this difficulty that a law had to be passed declaring that the existing members had not completed their term of office until their successors had been chosen.[11]

The machinery of the state was completed by various officials and tributary councils. We need notice only the three councils of forty judges each, one for criminal and two for civil affairs, which had charge of the judiciary of the republic. Members of these bodies were first chosen for terms of eight months to the *Quarantia Civile Nuova*, which administered the lower courts; then they were translated for successive terms of equal duration to the *Quarantia Civile Vecchia* and the *Quarantia Criminale*, after serving on which they were not eligible for reëlection until a further period of eight months had elapsed.[12]

The system of succession employed among the judges may serve to call our attention to the fact that one of the most striking features of the Venetian constitution was that of rotation. The Doge was chosen for life and the Great Council was perpetual, but in almost every other aspect of the government either a full or a partial rota-

[11] *Op. cit.*, I, 111. See also Jacob Burckhardt, *The civilization of the renaissance in Italy*, trans. S. G. C. Middlemore (London, 1892), p. 66. The best account of the Ten is Contarini's, pp. 76 ff. See also Howell, pp. 13–14, and *Maxims*, pp. 43–45.

[12] See Lewkenor's notes appended to his translation of Contarini, p. 163, and *Maxims*, p. 28.

tion prevailed, the principle commonly observed being that an official was ineligible for reëlection until a period equal to the term of his office had passed. The Ten and the sixty senators chosen by the Great Council held office for only one year, the Ten being ineligible for being chosen again until a period equal to twice their term of office had elapsed.[13] The Ducal Councillors were changed every eight months, the Sages every six months, the three *Capi di dieci*, who headed the Ten, every month. The result of these provisions was that although the entire administration did not change at any one time, one part or another of it was changing almost all the time. Back of this system lay the idea that human nature is such that men cannot be trusted with long continuance in offices of great power, but it was motivated also by the idea that in a society of equals it gave many a chance to learn both how to rule and how to be ruled and thus supplied the state at all times with a large body of trained and able statesmen. To seventeenth-century travelers it seemed that the system came close, at least, to achieving its purpose. In 1670 Lassels wrote that in Venice he saw "five hundred gentlemen walking together every day, everyone of which was able to play the Embassador in any Princes court of Europe."[14]

Another notable feature of the Venetian government was that it was in no sense a party system. We cannot suppose that the "five hundred gentlemen walking together every day" did not on occasion consult with one another informally, but the Venetians had a keen sense of the disasters which factional feuds had brought to other Italian cities,[15] and three features of the constitution not only were designed to prevent the rise or existence of political parties, but effectually operated to do so. One of these was the element of lot or chance which was introduced into the election of the Doge. Another was the use of the secret ballot in the form of a box with white and red balls[16] in the voting on measures in both the Senate and the Great Council. Under a system in which no one could tell how another had voted on any matter, it was impossible to enforce on occasion or assert consistently that party discipline without which

---

[13] On the rotative aspects of the Ten see *Maxims*, p. 45.

[14] *Op. cit.*, Pt. II, p. 378.

[15] Cf. Machiavelli's opinion that the aristocratic republic set up at Florence in 1393 had come to ruin because "no check was laid on powerful men to keep them from forming parties, which are the ruin of a state" (*Discourse on Florence* in Gilbert's ed., p. 79).

[16] This system, which had Greek and Roman antecedents and counterparts in some of the other Italian states, was a world's wonder to the travelers of the time. Lassels gives a good description of it (Pt. II, pp. 368–69).

political parties do not readily maintain themselves. The third provision was the enactment of the most severe penalties for anything resembling electioneering or canvassing for votes.[17] Under the Venetian system, a gentleman voted, not as a party member intent on carrying out a political program, but as an individual exercising his own best judgment on the affairs of the state.

With an eye on the 133,047 who had no share in the government, there would be few today who would not unhesitatingly pronounce the Venetian republic a close oligarchy.[18] But here again, as in the case of the Council of Ten, it is important to point out that it was not so viewed by Renaissance writers. Though they held that a democratic element should have expression in the life of the state, and though Machiavelli thought that it was undesirable to follow the Venetian practice of closing tightly the citizenship to newcomers, few indeed of the Italian political theorists thought of the "people" other than in terms of citizenship. Even Machiavelli remarked of Venice that newcomers had nothing to complain of in the government of the state, for, never having possessed anything, they had lost nothing.[19] Moreover, the theorists of the age were encouraged in such views by the prevalence of a similar situation in the antique polities. It is also true that they tended to think of the Venetian citizenship as being comprised of the descendants of all of the original members of the state. From this point of view, any system that gave recognition to the whole body of citizens contained a democratic element. These considerations kept in mind, it is not difficult to see how the Venetian constitution was seen by the theorists of the age as an example of *governo misto* and to understand why one of them climaxed a dissertation on the superiority of mixed polities with a eulogy of Venice[20] and another lavished his time and energy on the analysis and exposition of the ways in which

[17] Preface to *Maxims*, p. xix.

[18] The modern reader should remember, however, that no system of government, even democracy itself, is truly and fully democratic except as it widens the base on which it rests. This widening through extension of the suffrage did not come in even England and the United States until the nineteenth century, and was not wholly completed until the twentieth. Though the base was, of course, much wider in seventeenth-century England than in sixteenth-century Venice, the difference was one of degree, and restrictions were such that it was still possible for Filmer to estimate that not one-tenth of the commons possessed the suffrage (*Anarchy of a limited or mixed monarchy*, ed. 1684, p. 256). Keeping these facts in mind will help one to understand, not only how sixteenth-century Italian theorists looked at Venice, but also why seventeenth-century Englishmen of even republican tendencies found it easy to look at it in the same way.

[19] *Discourses*, I, vi.

[20] Guicciardini, *Opere inedite*, II, 139–41.

it embodied the principle.[21] The Signory, it was thought, represented the monarchial element, the Senate the aristocratic, and the Grand Council the democratic, consisting as it did of all the adult citizens of the state.[22] Because of the dominance of the Senate, the republic was considered to be a mixed state of the aristocratic sort, and because of the rigid limitation of the citizenship, a commonwealth like Sparta made for preservation rather than expansion.[23] The Council of Ten not only afforded no difficulty in the way of viewing Venice as a mixed government but actually illustrated one of the favorite ideas of proponents of such polities—that it was necessary to have some body possessed of extraordinary powers in times of emergency. Machiavelli saw the Ten as the Venetian equivalent of the Roman constitutional dictator;[24] Contarini compared them to the Spartan Ephors.[25] It also contributed to the reputation of the city as a mixed state that it not only embodied the principles of divided authority and equilibrium secured by checks and balances, but had developed these to extraordinary degrees of elaboration and refinement. Contarini put the general view of the political theorists of the Italian Renaissance when he declared: "This only citte retayneth a princely sovereigntie, a government of the nobilitie, and a popular authority, so that the formes of all seeme to be equally balanced, as it were with a paire of weights."[26]

Along with the idea that Venice was the most perfect example of *governo misto* in the modern world went the parallel notion that it was the modern counterpart of the antique polities. Machiavelli[27] and Contarini[28] discussed it in the same breath with Rome and Sparta. The idea was, in fact, implicit in the traditional origin of the republic. The eulogists of the city told how it had been founded by remnants of the antique nobility who fled to the islands in the Adriatic on which it is situated when the barbarians over-ran all the rest of Italy, and who preserved there and put into operation the princi-

[21] Donato Giannotti, *Libro de la republica de Vinitiani* (Rome, 1542 etc.).

[22] The citizens formed the patriciate or nobility with respect to the whole population (Contarini, p. 16); with respect to the government the whole body of them constituted the people.   [23] Machiavelli, *Discourses*, I, vi.   [24] *Ibid.*, I, xxxiv.

[25] P. 78. Elsewhere (p. 65) he lumped the Ten together with the Senate as constituting the aristocratic element of the state. The two remarks are not really contradictory, for the Ten simply assured in times of crisis the same aristocratic dominance which the Senate secured under normal conditions.

[26] P. 15. See also p. 65. Machiavelli thought Venice the best of all modern states, inferior to Rome only in giving the dominance to the aristocratic element and being a commonwealth for preservation, a defect partly compensated for by its geographical location (see *Discourses*, I, xxxiv; v–vi).   [27] *Ibid.*, I, v–vi.   [28] P. 6.

ples of ancient political wisdom at a time when all the rest of Europe fell under the sway of barbarous and ill-contrived Gothic governments. Venice, in short, by a fortunate accident of history, perpetuated into the modern world those principles of government which had made Rome and Sparta famous and which the ancient philosophers had enshrined in their works.[29] The idea was implicit also in the rather striking similarity observable between some features of the Venetian system and such semi-utopian antique works as Plato's *Laws*.[30]

It is, however, not merely the notion that Venice was an outstanding example of mixed government and that it preserved antique political wisdom into the modern world with which we have to deal. The idea appeared in various writers that it was superior to Rome and Sparta—that it was, in fact, the supreme example of the mixed polity. Contarini asserted that the republic "surpasseth all antiquitie."[31] His opinion was shared by Trajano Boccalini, who admired no modern government but the Venetian and chose to live under it.[32] The line at the head of this chapter which I quote from Sannazaro's "Hexastic" on the city was another expression of this point of view.[33] This idea was especially characteristic of theorists who favored the variety of mixed government in which the aristocratic element was dominant, it being their opinion that the Roman republic fell because it gave too much power to the popular element and that this defect was corrected in the Venetian constitution.[34]

Such views would have been quite sufficient in themselves to account for the political fame of the republic, but other things conspired to swell its reputation. There was the obvious fact that the government seemed to work. Comparatively speaking, the Venetians enjoyed an internal tranquillity greater than that of any other Italian state. When Brabantio in *Othello* says to Roderigo,

> What tell'st thou me of robbing? this is Venice;
> My house is not a grange,

[29] Giannotti, *op. cit.* (Venice, 1548), p. 7; Contarini, p. 4; Paruta, *Politick discourses*, p. 77; Machiavelli, *Discourses*, I, vi.

[30] Common to the two, for example, were the principle of checks and balances and the mixture of lot and election.   [31] P. 5. See also p. 7.

[32] *The new-found politicke* (London, 1627), p. 197.

[33] I quote from Howell's version in the *Survay*, sig. Ar.

[34] Paruta, *Politick discourses*, pp. 3, 7, 12; *The history of Venice*, p. 3. Cf. Paruta's criticism of the Florentine constitution of 1495 and the contrast he drew between the quiet of Venice and the turbulence produced in Florence by excessive "popularity" (*Pol. dis.*, p. 54).

he expresses an attitude which the facts of the time seemed to warrant. The republic was, moreover, the only one in Italy which had not fallen before the despots. To those, therefore, who either openly or secretly hated tyranny—and these included some of the leading theorists of the age—she appeared as the one state in which something approximating liberty had been achieved. Nor was there any clear perception in the sixteenth century that the republic had declined in either internal or external matters. Though the political reputation of the city offers the paradox of a state becoming a model in the days of its decline, the blows which had been dealt the republic by the war with the League of Cambrai and the maritime discoveries of the last decades of the preceding century were not seen in the historical perspective with which we view them today. The writers of the age saw, not a state in decadence, but a happy creation of the hand of man which was, if anything, more flourishing than ever. The superior perceptions of a Machiavelli, indeed, discovered in events a proof of the military weakness of the republic,[35] but others saw Venice destined for a future more glorious than its past.[36] Giovanni Botero praised Venice for "the gloriousnes of her present and magnificent estate,"[37] and in his *Relations* expressed the opinion that after maintaining herself for thirteen centuries, she was more potent than ever before.[38]

It is clear that the political reputation of the republic owed much to the works of Venetian historians and scholars. Every native of the city wrote as a patriot. Paolo Paruta illustrates the point perfectly. When he prepared his *History of Venice*, he undertook also to represent "the form of our Republick . . . wherein may be seen the true Image of perfect Government, for those things to which the wit of man hath not been able to attain, in their fancying the Government of an excellent commonwealth, are all seen to be confirmed by time and experience, in the City of Venice."[39] He was similarly laudatory in his *Politick discourses*. Venice, he asserted, was born free and did not labor under the difficulties of states which suddenly attain liberty after tyranny and know not how to use it.[40] Hence from the

---

[35] *Discourses*, I, vi.

[36] Paruta, *History of Venice*, p. 3. Cf. Guicciardini's opinion that the Venetians aspired to the rule of all Italy (*Historie*, p. 3).

[37] *Treatise concerning the causes of the magnificencie and greatnes of citties* (London, 1606), p. 10.   [38] (London, 1630), pp. 341, 359.   [39] P. 3.

[40] Cf. Machiavelli on the difficulties attending a people who suddenly become free after living under a prince (*Discourses*, I, xvi, xvii).

very beginning, she ordered herself "according to the true Civil end, to wit, to Peace and Concord, and to the Union of her Citizens."[41] The government originally set up differed in some respects from that later used, but it was from time to time improved upon by the wisdom of the citizens until it attained "a height of perfection."[42] Since reaching this point, he continued, Venice "not having given way to such corruptions as use to trouble the quiet of civil life, nor afforded means to any who should goe about to plot against the publick Liberty, hath been able for a very long space of time to maintain herself in one and the same condition, and free from those dangers, unto which other Commonwealths have faln, for not having a Government of equal temper with that of hers."[43] One defect, indeed, he was constrained to admit that the state had: its military orders were "not altogether such as are requisite for the acquiring of a large Command." The republic had been instituted for civil ends, not for war, and had long pursued maritime affairs. Then later, when territorial expansion had seemed desirable, she had trusted in hired soldiers and commanders who had served her ill. In this respect, the Romans had done better in using their own citizens, for the Roman militia overcame the numerically-superior hired soldiers of Carthage. Paruta thought it was true that the introduction of a state's own citizens into the land-forces made for turmoil in the state, and he asserted that this had caused great disturbances in Rome, but he was confident that in Venice the superior understanding of political wisdom and the perfection of the governmental institutions would obviate this difficulty.[44]

The reputation of the republic owed even more to Cardinal Gasparo Contarini, a son of one of its most distinguished families,[45] whose *De magistratibus et republica Venetorum* first appeared in 1543. It is not merely the fact that Contarini praised the Venetian constitution which makes him important. He did that. He wrote indeed in such superlatives as to make his English translator conclude that the

[41] P. 12.   [42] *Ibid.*, p. 13.

[43] *Ibid.*, p. 54. See further his statement on p. 121 that in many centuries the republic had never been troubled with any domestic discords.

[44] *Ibid.*, pp. 121–22. It is clear that Paruta would have liked to have what Machiavelli had said could not be had—a state which had a dominant aristocratic element and at the same time the strength of a citizen army. The point is interesting, for, as we shall see, Harrington attempted to construct a state which would have a citizen army but neither an aristocratic nor democratic dominance, a state, furthermore, which would have the power of Machiavelli's system with the internal tranquillity of Paruta's.

[45] No fewer than eight of its members were doges.

Great Council rather "seemeth to bee an assembly of Angels, then of men."[46] What gives Contarini his unique significance is the fact that by asserting the changelessness of the Venetian constitution and developing the conception of the state as dominated by an aristocracy of virtue, he not only put the finishing touches to the elaboration of what we may call the Venetian myth, but provided an important basis for seventeenth-century utopianism. Contarini achieved the former of these objects partly by treating lightly the historical evolution of Venetian institutions and partly by outright misrepresentation. That the power of the Doge and of the people had once been greater than it later became, that the *Consiglieri Ducali* and the *Pregadi* had come into being about 1032 as a means of checking the power of the Doge, that the Senate was not originally the dominant power in the state, that the Great Council as an elected body came into existence in 1172 and supplanted the *Concione* or general assembly of the people, that the *Promissione Ducale* dated from 1198, that the closing of the Great Council by the decree for the *Serrata del Maggior Consiglio* had occurred in 1297, that the *Golden Book* was an innovation of 1315 and the Council of Ten of 1311—these are matters which in Contarini's account were either omitted or obscured in the interest of establishing the fiction that the whole developed system as it existed in the sixteenth century dated from the institution of the government at the founding of the republic thirteen centuries before and had worked flawlessly and essentially without change for a longer period of time than any other government ever contrived by man. Contarini's remarks about the limitations on the power of the Doge illustrate the point. He tells us that "the Duke of Venice is deprived of all meanes, whereby he might abuse his authoritie, or become a tyrant: which ancient and long continued custome from the first beginnings of the citie, even to these times, hath now taken such foundation and roote, that there is nothing whereof the citie of Venice need stand lesse in feare, then that their prince should at any time be able to invade their liberty."[47] Similarly, Contarini made the Council of Ten a wise provision of those who had ordained the government.[48] It is, I think, beyond question that in adopting and developing this view of the Venetian constitution, he was influenced, not only by patriotism but by the idea of the state as something made all at once by a single great institutor or group of legislators, an idea which we have seen

[46] Sig. A2r. I quote, as previously, from Lewkenor's translation.
[47] P. 42. The idea is repeated on p. 51.   [48] P. 77.

to have always been closely connected with the theory of mixed government, and which was particularly acceptable to the Renaissance mind because it accorded well with the tendency of the age to reduce all phases of human endeavor to an art—with that tendency which produced such works as Castiglione's *The courtier*, Machiavelli's *The arte of warre*, and the endless *Arts of poetry* of the sixteenth century.

Contarini's second great contribution to the idea that the Venetian republic was a masterpiece of politics came in his development of the conception of the state as a mixed polity in which an aristocracy of wisdom and virtue was dominant. He met Machiavelli's criticism, which had bothered Paruta also, that Venice was a commonwealth for preservation, and turned it into a further argument for the supremacy of Venice. Rome and Sparta, he found, had been organized for war. The result in Rome was that when Carthage was detroyed, the citizens, being nurtured in war, turned their arms against one another and produced the internal dissension which brought about the collapse of the republic. But the true end of civil government was not war, but peace. The things of war, he declared rather finely, are only to be desired for the things of peace. Venice had ordained her institutions for the true end of civil government, the happiness and prosperity of men. But happiness rests on virtue, and in virtue only the few excel. The Venetians had wisely, therefore, contrived that dominant power should rest with the few who were wise and good.[49]

The clue to this way of writing about Venice is to be found in Contarini's comparison of the republic with the ideal states of the antique philosophers. Though he gave one of the best accounts of the age of the organs and functions of the republic as they existed in his own time, it is impossible to regard him in his more extravagant aspects as other than an utopian writer. In one of the most widely read of all books on Venice, a work which attained international celebrity,[50] he performed the extraordinary feat of bringing the real and the ideal together and described a miracle. He conjured up before the dazzled eyes of men the vision of an ageless state per-

---

[49] Pp. 5 ff., 95.

[50] In addition to the original edition of 1543, I have noted Latin editions at Venice in 1589 and 1592, at Paris in 1543, and at Basel in 1544 and 1547. The Elzevirs brought out editions in 1626, 1628, and 1722. The Italian version by E. Anditimi had editions at Venice in 1544, 1548, 1551, 1564, 1591, 1630, and 1650. A French translation by Jean Charrier appeared at Paris in 1544 and at Lyon in 1557. To these must be added the English version of 1599 from which I cite.

fect in its balances, flawless in its working, immune from the ravages of time. Venice seen thus both owed something to the theory of mixed government and contributed something to it. If Venice had lasted unchanged and uncorrupted for centuries, the fact invited the conclusion that it would last for centuries more—even to the very end of the world. Presently we find Thuanus predicting the immortality of the republic in the couplet quoted at the head of this chapter.[51] The way was open for the rise of the conception that by mixed government the cyclic changes and decays to which all other forms of government were subject could be not only arrested—which was all that Machiavelli had claimed—but wholly eliminated. The perpetually healthy state, in short, was not a dream of the poets and philosophers, but a possibility.

That the Florentine historians and theorists, though more critical than Contarini, subscribed to the praise of the Venetian constitution and helped to swell its fame will be apparent from the allusions already made in this chapter to such writers as Guicciardini and Giannotti.[52] The Florentines, moreover, possess a special importance, for in them we see Venice appearing as a model for other states. Champions as they were of the mixed polity, they turned naturally to the republic as possessing a government worth imitating. The whole series of constitutional experiments and proposals at Florence to which the expulsion of the Medici gave rise and which we have noticed in the previous chapter owed much to the Venetian model. Essentially the constitution of Savonarola and Soderini and the plans of government suggested by both Machiavelli and Guicciardini represented variant simplifications and modifications of Florentine institutions after the Venetian pattern of a signory, senate, and great council. This is apparent from the very form of Machiavelli's proposals; it is clear from Guicciardini's eulogy on Venice in the very tract in which he undertook to discuss the reform of Florence;[53] and it is clear in Savonarola's case from his own specific acknowledgment. In the sermon of December 12, 1494, which marked his entry into the field of political discussion, he said: "The form of government best adapted to this city would be that of a Grand Council on the Venetian plan."[54]

---

[51] I quote Howell's version in the *Survay*, p. 3. The original runs:
"Venetiae non nisi cum Rerum natura
Et Mundi machina periturae."

[52] Giannotti's *Libro de la republica de Vinitiani* had its first edition at Rome in 1540. There were subsequent ones in Latin, Italian, French, German, and Dutch in 1542, 1557, 1570, 1574, 1591, 1631, 1650, and 1667.   [53] *Opere inedite*, II, 139–41.

[54] In his *Savonarola* Villari gives large extracts from this sermon from which I quote, p. 263. See also the same idea in a later sermon (Villari, p. 265).

Not the least remarkable thing about the more extravagant aspects of the political reputation of Venice is the fact that they for long survived all attacks. One of the most notable of these was made by Bodin. Challenging Contarini directly, he denied both that the republic had continued without change since its institution and that through the centuries it had never been disturbed by internal strife. Giannotti, he found, afforded evidence that Venice had been a pure monarchy not many centuries previously, and the older Venetian historian, Sabellicus, counted thirteen dukes who had abused their authority or lost their lives in popular tumults. Moreover, Bodin undertook to controvert the idea that Venice was a mixed polity. It was rather, he asserted, a pure aristocracy.[55] It is rather remarkable that his views did not have more influence than they apparently had on the established reputation of Venice. How little that influence was is strikingly illustrated by a seventeenth-century writer who quoted Bodin's views on one page and then proceeded to fill a whole book with eulogies of the mixed constitution of the republic.[56] No doubt, Bodin's lack of appreciable effect on the reputation of the city is to be partly explained by the fact that he wrote late, at a time when the political renown of Venice had been growing for many decades. Partly, too, we may attribute the disregard of his views in some quarters to the circumstance that his ideas on the indivisibility of sovereignty became, as we have seen, one of the foundations of absolutist theory, a fact which caused liberal-minded men to repudiate his authority generally.

II

Tudor-Stuart Englishmen suffered from no paucity of information about Venetian institutions. Not only the editions of Contarini, Paruta, and Giannotti which came steadily from the continental presses circulated freely,[57] but there is ample evidence that even the minor historians who had treated of the city and new writers like Mauroceni[58] were well known.[59] But even if accounts of Venice in Latin and Italian had not been current in England, there were ample sources of information in English from the closing years of

[55] *Op. cit.*, II, i, pp. 190–91.   [56] Howell, *op. cit.*, pp. 182, 10 ff.

[57] Harrington begins the first section of the *Oceana* with a reference to "Janotti, the most excellent describer of the Commonwealth of Venice" (ed. Liljegren, p. 12).

[58] *Historia Veneta* (Venice, 1623).

[59] A copy of Bembo's *Historiae Venetae* (Venice, 1551) in the British Museum is in a binding with the arms of Edward VI (see the so-called "Bibliography of Venice" by Edith H. Cobb in the *Bulletin of bibliography*, III, No. 3 [1902], 40). Lassels quotes Sabellicus, the oldest of the Venetian historians (*op. cit.*, Pt. II, p. 370). Under date of 23 September, 1637, Milton wrote to Diodati asking for a copy of "Giustiniani, the historian of the Venetians" (*P. W.*, III, 495).

the sixteenth century. In 1599 Lewkenor translated Contarini and published an edition with lengthy extracts from Giannotti, Giustiniani, Bardi, Sansovini, and Sebastian Munster. In 1612 Shute translated Fougasses' *Generall history of the magnificent state of Venice* with a laudatory address "To the reader." About the same time, the appearance of the English versions of Botero's *Treatise concerning the causes of the magnificencie and greatnes of cities* (1606),[60] D'Avity's *Estates, empires, and principallities of the world* (1615),[61] and Boccalini's *The new-found politicke* (1626)[62] made extended and laudatory descriptions of the republic readily available. Other translations, the works of English political writers, and descriptions of the Venetian government by the travelers of the age continued throughout the seventeenth century.[63]

With such stores of information available, the political reputation of Venice had established itself in England by the latter part of the sixteenth century.[64] The council scene in *Othello*, in which the wise Venetian senators see through the deceptions of the Turks, gives a picture of the functioning of the Senate which Elizabethans well understood. When the Duke in this play promises Brabantio that the abductor of his daughter will be punished even though the culprit should turn out to be the Duke's own son, Shakespeare was writing

[60] Pp. 10 ff.   [61] Pp. 526 ff.   [62] P. 197.

[63] John Raymond, *Itinerary contayning a voyage made through Italy in the years 1646 and 1647* (London, 1648), p. 188; *Reliquiae Wottonianae* (London, 1672), pp. 247 ff.; James Howell, *Instructions for forreine travell*, ed. Arber (London, 1895), p. 42; *Familiar letters*, ed. Joseph Jacobs (London, 1892), I, 69 and II, 586; *Dodona's grove* (London, 1644, 2nd ed.), pp. 59–63; and Battista Nani, *The history of the affairs of Europe in this present age, but more particularly of the Republick of Venice*, trans. Sir Robert Honywood (London, 1673). To these should be added the translations of Paruta and Machiavelli and the works of Howell and Lassels previously cited.

[64] The reputation of Venice in England has been almost wholly neglected. There is no such comprehensive study as Béatrice Ravà's *Venise dans la littérature française* (Paris, 1916). When the subject has been noted at all, some curious pronouncements have been made. A. E. Levett, for example, is of the opinion that the Venetian constitution was "usually quoted in England as an awful example" ("Harrington," in *The social and political ideas of some great thinkers of the sixteenth and seventeenth centuries*, ed. F. J. C. Hearnshaw [London, 1915], p. 176), a pronouncement which will, I believe, in the light of the evidence I present, itself stand out as an "awful example." Equally strange is Gooch's twice repeated statement that Harrington was the first real student of the Venetian constitution in England (*The history of English democratic ideas in the seventeenth century* [Cambridge, 1898], pp. 288–89; *Political thought in England from Bacon to Halifax*, [London, 1915], p. 112). Even when more accurate statements have been made by Sir Charles Firth (*The last years of the Protectorate, 1656–58* [London, 1909, 2 vols.], I, 68), and by such students of Harrington as Liljegren (*Oceana* [Heidelberg, 1924], p. 236) and H. F. Russell Smith (*Harrington and his Oceana* [Cambridge, 1914], p. 38) whose attention was of necessity directed towards Venice by their author's repeated references to it, no attempt has been made to examine the subject in any detail.

in the spirit of that inexorable administration of justice which was a prominent feature in the contemporary reputation of the republic.[65] Further evidence is afforded by the extravagantly laudatory complimentary sonnets which are prefixed to Lewkenor's translation of Contarini, and by Lewkenor's own remarks, which show a strong admiration for the republic.[66]

But not only did the political reputation of Venice early make its appearance in England. It reached there and was diffused in its extravagant form. Not merely was the republic described as a great example of mixed government[67] and compared with Rome and Sparta,[68] but we find appearing the notion of its superiority to the Roman commonwealth[69] and the idea that the constitution had continued without change since the original founding of the city.[70] No doubt the fact that it was Contarini who was chosen by Lewkenor for translation in 1599 had much to do with this. But had Contarini never been translated or even circulated in England, it is clear that much the same result would have been attained, for the conclusion is inescapable that by the latter part of the sixteenth century the Contarini myth had so colored the view of Venice as to leave its mark on almost all descriptions of the republic.[71]

[65] This reputation is also reflected in, and gave added significance to, *The merchant of Venice*. In this play Shylock is punished by the Duke under the law. In this fact, indeed, we need see nothing more than that Shakespeare was fond of rulers who observed the law—the Duke, for example, in *The comedy of errors*. But it is impossible to believe that as Shakespeare wrote this play in which everyone (Shylock, Antonio, Portia) except the irresponsible Salarino assumes that the laws will be adhered to, in which the laws are adhered to, and in which Shylock reaches for his triumph and arrives at his doom at every step in accordance with the law, and in which his case breaks down, not because the Duke refuses to enforce the law against a patrician, but because the law is discovered to be against Shylock—it is impossible, I say, to believe that as Shakespeare portrayed these things he was unaware of the contemporary reputation of Venice for justice and that it did not color to some extent his handling of his materials. See also Richard H. Perkinson, " 'Volpone' and the reputation of Venetian justice," in *Modern language review*, XXXV (1940), 11–18.

[66] See especially sig. A2.

[67] Lewkenor, sig. A2; Sir Walter Raleigh, *Remains*, p. 9. Howell wrote: ·"The Venetian Government is a compounded thing, for it is a mixture of all kinds of governments, if the division of the Philosopher into Monarchy, Aristocracy, and Democracy be allowed to be perfect" (*Survay*, p. 10).

[68] See Shute's prefatory "To the reader" in his translation of Fougasses; Howell, *Survay*, Table of contents; *The excellencie of a free state: or the right constitution of a commonwealth* (London, 1656), p. 62 *et passim*. Cf. John Harrington's sonnet prefatory to Lewkenor's translation.   [69] Raleigh, *Works*, VIII, 296.

[70] Lewkenor, sig. A2; Raymond, p. 188; Lassels, Pt. II, p. 377.

[71] This influence is clear in Botero (*Relations*, p. 341), Boccalini (*op. cit.*, p. 197), and D'Avity (*op. cit.*, p. 530) with their assertions of the longevity of the Venetian system and its superiority over that of Rome.

It is clear that the political fame of the republic was aided by various extraneous circumstances. The city itself held for Tudor-Stuart Englishmen a peculiar fascination, an attraction the more striking because it appears as a persistent counter-current to the marked anti-Italianism in much of the literature of the period. "Whosoever that hath not seene the noble citie of Venis hath not sene the beewtye and ryches of thys worlde," exclaimed Andrew Borde in 1542,[72] setting the tone in which most Englishmen for more than a century and a quarter wrote of the city.[73] Coryate outdid himself in ecstasy on the subject,[74] and a later traveler described Venice as a "place where there is nothing wanted that heart can wish . . . the admiredst City in the World."[75] For this admiration there were various causes—the unique location of the city, the mellowing beauty of its buildings, its position as the safeguard of the West,[76] as Wordsworth was later to phrase it. Also influential was the fact that for a time, as a result of the great dispute between Venice and Pope Paul V, which began in 1605–06, the republic appeared to Englishmen as the anti-papal champion in Italy.[77] This celebrated controversy turned on the question of civil supremacy in civil matters and led to the flat and successful defiance of papal authority. The issues involved were themselves of a sort to recommend the republic to the favorable attention of Protestant Englishmen, but the dispute produced in Paolo Sarpi a Venetian champion whose prestige and writings carried the fame of it to the whole of Europe.[78] This able controversialist, the correspondent of Galileo, Bacon, Harvey,

[72] *The first boke of the introduction of knowledge*, ed. F. J. Furnivall (London, 1869–70) p. 181.

[73] There were, of course, some exceptions. Ascham condemned Venetian immorality (*The scholemaster*, ed. Arber [London, 1897], p. 84); and it was in Venice that Sir Philip Sidney formed some very unfavorable opinions of Italy (*Correspondence with Languet*, ed. S. A. Pears [London, 1845], p. 48). W. R., the author of a curious tract published in London in 1588, *The English ape, the Italian imitation*, wrote that the vanities of Venice presented a "world of woes" (p. 19).

[74] Venice was "this incomparable city, this most beautiful Queene, this untainted virgine, this Paradise, this Tempe, this riche Diademe and most flourishing garland of Christendome" (*Crudities* [Glasgow, 1905], I, 427). He would take a journey to Venice in preference to four of the richest manors in Somersetshire. Cf. Fynes Moryson, *Itinerary containing his ten yeeres travell* (London, 1617), pp. 74–90.

[75] Howell, *Familiar letters*, I, 70.

[76] [Matthew Wren], *Considerations on Mr. Harrington's commonwealth of Oceana* (London, 1657), sig. A4v.

[77] On the sympathy aroused in England for Venice on this occasion see Logan P. Smith, *The life and letters of Sir Henry Wotton* (Oxford, 1907), I, 81, and the *Calendar of state papers, Venetian*, X, 495.

[78] In 1626 Potter translated Sarpi's *History of the quarrels of Pope Paul V with the state of Venice*.

and Gilbert, a man eminent among his contemporaries as a philosopher, statesman, historian, astronomer, and mathematician,[79] adopted on many questions positions which seemed to men of the age more Protestant than Catholic and encouraged Protestants to believe that under his guidance Venice might actually become Protestant.[80] Sarpi's fame remained great in England throughout the entire seventeenth century[81] and perpetuated with it the reputation of Venice as an anti-papal champion.[82]

Until the 1640's, Englishmen could admire Venice without regard to which side they favored in their own political differences. But as that decade advanced, it was inevitable that the republic should come to have a particular interest for Parliamentarians. There were obvious reasons for this. The conception of the Doge or monarchial element which the Venetian constitution exhibited was fundamentally at variance with the increasingly great claims for the royal prerogative which were being made by the king's supporters. We have seen, moreover, that as republicanism developed in this decade, men's thoughts turned back to the mixed polities of the antique world for their ideal, and that this ideal influenced the form that their thinking took.[83] In an England in which the con-

---

[79] Sarpi is credited with the discovery of the contractility of the iris. Galileo called him "my father and my master" and asserted that no man in Europe excelled him in mathematics (Alexander Robertson, *Fra Paolo Sarpi* [New York, 1894], p. v). There is probably no good basis for the claims of enthusiastic champions that he anticipated both the sensationalism of Locke and the discovery of the circualtion of the blood by Harvey, but enough is known of his lost scientific treatises to make clear that his attainments were great.

[80] R. G., apparently the translator of Giovanni Diodati's *Pious and learned annotations upon the Holy Bible* (London, 1648, 2nd ed.), says in a prefatory address "To the reader" that Diodati began the work at the time of the quarrel between Venice and Paul V, when "all Christendome" was expecting that "famous Commonwealth" to shake off the papal tyranny. It was the settled policy of Sir Henry Wotton during his first Venetian ambassadorship to bring Venice into an alliance with the Protestant powers of Europe (L. P. Smith, *op. cit.*, I, 75 ff.).

[81] See the translation of Micanzio's *Life of the most learned Father Paul* (London, 1651), and the many translations and editions of Sarpi's works. *The history of the council of Trent* had English editions in 1620, 1629, 1640, and 1676; *The history of the Inquisition* in 1655; the *Letters* in 1693; *The free school of war* in 1625; and *The rights of sovereigns and subjects* in 1722. The spurious *Maxims of the government of Venice* had English editions in 1689, 1693, and 1707. Milton several times refers to Sarpi (*P. W.*, II, 60, 397, 405) and drew from him in his account of the rise of licensing in *Areopagitica*. Dr. Johnson is said to have projected a life of Sarpi.

[82] See Henry Nevill, *Plato redivivus* (London, 1681, 2nd ed.), p. 24.

[83] See above, pp. 1–2. The fact is strikingly attested also by the discussions of classical governments which fill an anti-republican tract of 1647, *A parallel of governments: or a political discourse upon seven positions*. Nothing in my statements is to be construed as an attempt to deny the importance of men's own experiences and other factors in both the development and form of seventeenth-century republicanism.

ception had been developing for half a century that Venice was the
modern counterpart of the antique republics, turning back to Rome
meant turning also to Venice. Moreover, since the days of Sir
Walter Raleigh, Venice had appealed to that notable group of Protestant Englishmen of birth and position in the seventeenth century
whose forerunners were the Leicesters and Sidneys of the age of
Elizabeth, and whose political ideal was an England in which an enlarged and revivified and virtuous aristocracy played the dominant
rôle. The earlier members of this group were the Raleighs whom
James I threw into prison and the Sir Henry Nevills who during that
king's reign drew up papers recommending a surrender of James's
absolutist pretensions. A later generation supplied more than one
outstanding figure of the Puritan Revolution. For these men, Venice,
with its character as a mixed state with a dominant aristocratic
element and a limited executive, had a special interest. Events, therefore, were merely following an almost inevitable development
when in 1644 a group of Parliamentary leaders requested the Venetian ambassador to supply them with a description of the Venetian
constitution. In 1647, significantly, we find much attention being
given to a criticism of Venice in an anti-republican tract, *A parallel
of governments: or a political discourse upon seven positions*.[84] Under
date of December 25, 1648, John Laurens in a letter to Secretary
Nicholas expressed the opinion that the Independent leaders were
attempting to reduce Charles's power to the point where he would
be no more than "a Duke of Venice, which I hear is the hard condition they intend to impose on him."[85] If the parallel between the
Venetian Doge and what was apparently the program of at least
some of the Independent leaders was apparent to Laurens, who was
a royalist agent, we can be sure that it had occurred also to men on
the other side. Englishmen had long cherished the idea that their
king was more like the Doge of Venice than like any other Continental sovereign—in Elizabeth's time the notion had been expressed
by no less a figure than Sir Thomas Smith[86]—and it is clear that in
1648 there were some who wished to make the parallel actual at
least as far as the king's power was concerned.

The same interest in Venetian precedents is observable after the
instituting of the republic. We find Sir Oliver Fleming, Master of

[84] P. 5.

[85] *The writings and speeches of Oliver Cromwell*, ed. Wilbur C. Abbott (Cambridge,
Mass., 1937–), I, 718.

[86] *Op. cit.*, II, iii; I, vii. Smith, however, with perfect correctness, of course, found the
King far more powerful than the Doge.

Ceremonies under the Council of State, citing Venetian practices before those of all other states in a memorandum on the forms to be observed in his office.[87] Moreover, with the appearance of the republic and the fluidity of government consequent upon its instability,[88] the way was open for more ambitious projects of patterning the state on the Venetian model. Had we no other evidence, we could surmise that such plans were in the air in the early 1650's by the detailed attack which that redoubtable champion of lost causes, Sir Robert Filmer, made on Venice in his *Observations upon Aristotle's Politiques* (1652). Following Bodin, Filmer attacked every premise on which the contemporary reputation of the republic was founded. The city, he asserted, owed what success it had achieved, not to its government, but to its location. But even its success was more a matter of reputation than of reality. It lived in constant fear of attack from without and conspiracy from within. The "intricate Solemnities" of its constitution, in which champions of the city saw evidence of its supreme political wisdom, were merely testimonies to the fact that the Venetians lived in perpetual jealousy of one another. Those who founded the city were guilty of desertion of, and rebellion against, the Roman emperors to whom they were originally subject. Moreover, wrote Filmer, "it is a strange Errour for any man to believe, that the Government of Venice hath been always the same as it is now." First it had been an oligarchy; later under the Dukes it became an absolute monarchy, at which time it had flourished most and gained its greatest victories.[89] In the last two hundred years, the loss of royal power had been accompanied by a cessation of great achievements. Nor was Contarini correct in describing the government as a mixture of monarchy, aristocracy, and democracy. It had neither true monarchial nor democratic elements. It was a pure aristocracy, and an oppressive one. Taxes were so heavy that ordinary men lived better under the Turks than under

[87] *Cal. state papers, domestic, 1649*, pp. 113–14; see also *ibid.*, *1648–49*, p. 412.

[88] There was nothing settled about the government set up in 1649. After the battle of Worcester Cromwell called together a number of members of Parliament to consider what form of government should be adopted (Gooch, *Political thought*, p. 93).

[89] The assertion reminds one of that great subject of controversy between republicans and royalists—whether Rome had attained its most flourishing condition under the republic or the empire. Filmer maintained that Rome began its empire under a monarchy, had its longest peace under Augustus, and reached its greatest "exaltation" under Trajan (*Patriarcha* [London, 1680], pp. 56–57). G. S. advanced similar opinions in *The dignity of kingship asserted* (New York, 1942), pp. 97, 99–100. For the opposite view see Nevill, *op. cit.*, p. 43, and Algernon Sydney, *Discourses*, II, xii. Earlier the question had been discussed by Paruta in his *Politick discourses*, pp. 2 ff.

the Venetians. The very revenues which the courtesans alone paid for toleration maintained a dozen galleys.[90]

We do not have to rely on the certainty that whatever Filmer attacked was precisely what at least some republicans were thinking, for specific evidence is at hand in various works which now began to appear. In 1651 James Howell published his *Survay of the signorie of Venice, of her admired policy and method of government.* He had long been a great admirer of the Venetian constitution and its most persistent panegyrist. He knew Bodin's views on the republic,[91] but they had very little, if any, effect upon him. Venice as Howell saw her was the Venice of Contarini. In his *Instructions for forraine travell* (1642) he had described the city as a "thing of wonder, an Impossibility in an impossibility," and declared that "she hath continued a Virgin . . . nere upon twelve long ages, under the same forme and face of Government without any visible change or symptome of decay, or the least wrinkle of old age." And even at that date he had expressed the opinion that "there are many things in that Government worth the carying away."[92] Much the same sentiments were repeated in *Dodona's grove,* in which, under the title of "A character of Adriana," he had produced an extended eulogy of the timeless perfection of the Venetian constitution,[93] and in the *Familiar letters.*[94] The ostensible purpose of the *Survay* was to exhort the Parliament to go to the aid of the Venetians against the Turks. But this avowed purpose is curiously out of accord with its contents. Instead of a long exhortation to help the Venetians, we find one whole section devoted to an elaborate description of the republic's governmental institutions, the most detailed description, in fact, which had appeared in English since Lewkenor's version of Contarini. Another lengthy section is devoted to "A parallel twixt the government of Old Rome and Venice," and what this was intended to show is made perfectly clear by the Table of Contents, in which the section is referred to under the heading "Of her imitation of old Rome in most things." What stronger appeal could have been made to republicans with their admiration of the Roman commonwealth?

---

[90] Ed. 1684, pp. 137–40.   [91] P. 182.   [92] P. 42.

[93] Pp. 59–63. The comparison of Venice to a virgin is repeated here as in all of Howell's works referring to Venice. The figure fascinated him as it did indeed many other writers. For Coryate's use of it see above, p. 44. See further J. Ashley's sonnet prefatory to Lewkenor's *Contarini,* and Lassels, Pt. II, p. 377. The figure survived the political reputation which gave rise to it. Wordsworth's "maiden city" in his sonnet "On the extinction of the Venetian republic" is no doubt to be viewed as a late variation on it.

[94] I, 69–70; II, 586.

The exhortation to help the Venetians against the Turks gets, in the end, just three and a half pages at the very conclusion of the book—as if Howell had almost forgotten the purpose for which he had professed to be writing. Finally, it may be noted that Howell is at pains to develop a parallel between England and Venice, the two great island sea powers of the modern world,[95] that he asserts that if one were to attempt to set up a perpetually healthy government, "the Republic of Venice were the fittest pattern on Earth both for direction and imitation,"[96] and that in the Table of Contents the first main section is described as being "upon her Constitutions and Government, wherin ther may be divers things usefull for this Meridian." It seems clear that whatever other aims he may have had, it was Howell's intention to recommend the Venetian constitution to his countrymen. That he proceeded with some caution is to be attributed to the fact that he was suspected of royalist sentiments, had been imprisoned for a considerable period before the appearance of the book, and was under bond for good behavior at the time of its publication.[97]

In 1653, George Wither published *A poem concerning a perpetuall parliament*. The tendency of the modern reader, unaccustomed to the spectacle of political ideas set forth in verse, is no doubt to view as a poetical fantasy this work of one who described himself as,

> on the hills of contemplation,
> A voluntary watchman for the Nation.[98]

But nothing is more certain than that this "poem" is not to be so regarded. Wither's whole career as a political pamphleteer and his habit of using verse to express his views on all sorts of subjects combine with the content of the work itself to make clear that the *Perpetuall parliament* was intended to be a serious proposal for the settling of the government. It appeared with another poem *The dark lantern*, which is supposed to record the author's musings on November 3, 1652 "about Midnight," and it is clear from Wither's address "To the reader" that both poems were written before Cromwell's abrupt dismissal of the Long Parliament. Wither begins by vindicating his right to set forth his views on the constitution of the government. God, he says, sometimes reveals himself to "poor and simple persons" to enable them to give advice to "Counsells grave and

[95] Sig. Bv.   [96] P. 1.
[97] Jacobs, Preface to his ed. of the *Familiar letters*, I, xliv.
[98] *Miscellaneous works*, Spenser society ed., III, 48.

mighty Potentates."[99] The central proposition which he proceeds
to set forth is contained in the following lines:

> In England, and in Wales, there is a Shire,
> For ev'ry week that's numbred in the year.
> By twelve, according to the moneths divide
> The Counties, with their persons qualifi'd
> For Knights and Burgesses, proportioning
> As neer as may be, to an equalling
> The number of the whole, so, or so many
> Unto each moneth, without omitting any.
> Ascertain, then, the moneth and the day, wherein
> Each twelfth part an election shall begin:
> (The middle of the week, appearing best
> As being furthest from the day of rest)
> On each first Wednesday, of each moneth, let those
> By whom their Deputies are to be chose,
> Respectively convene in ev'ry Shire,
> Upon that moneth, and Wednesday ev'ry year,
> Which is to them assign'd; and having chosen,
> (At moneths end) let each twelfth part, of the dozen,
> Send up their chosen men, to represent
> Their Shires and Boroughs in the Parliament:
> And on that very day, in which they come,
> Let all their Predecessors give them room.
> Thus one moneth some; and moneth by moneth forever,
> Let each twelfth part, still orderly persever
> To take a turn, till ev'ry share hath had
> A moneth in ev'ry year; and having made
> Their choice, let them still enter and withdraw
> Successively, by a perpetuall Law,
> No man a place of trust, supplying there,
> At one election, longer then one year.[100]

The advantages of this system, Wither went on to explain, would
be that Parliament, like the Thames, by an annual supply would
continue "everlastingly" and yet some part of it would be continually changing. It is impossible to read these proposals and the
ones which follow without seeing that Wither had Venice in mind
as he made them. His central conception of a government which
would be perpetual, yet constantly changing in one or another of
its parts, was of the very essence of the Venetian system. A further
striking parallel occurs in his suggestion that the choice of members

[99] P. 46.   [100] Pp. 51–52.

should be by a combination of lot and election. His proposal to change the speaker monthly had its Venetian counterpart in the practice of changing monthly the heads of the Council of Ten and of various other governmental bodies. The Councils of Sages which he recommends remind one, not only in organization and function but in their very name, of nothing so much as the Councils of Sages or Preconsultors in the Venetian system. Finally he himself makes specific the source of his inspiration when we find him proposing to build an arsenal in imitation of one of the most famous institutions of the republic,[101] and citing the example of Venice to support his contention that the Parliament should meet on Sundays as well as on other days of the week.[102]

Wither and Howell afford two striking illustrations of the kind of thinking which Filmer was aiming at when he assailed the city in 1652. But the history of the political reputation of the republic in England and the attempt to model institutions upon it is not concluded with their works. Far greater men and far more ingenious ones than either of them were to attempt in the name of mixed government to introduce Venetian institutions into the country.

[101] Most of the travel accounts of the time dwell on the Arsenal as one of the wonders of the city. For a typical description see Lassels, Pt. II, pp. 392 f.
[102] P. 60.

CHAPTER THREE
IMMORTAL GOVERNMENT: OCEANA

Mr. Harrington hath by transcribing her Orders very wisely put himself under the Protection of the most serene Republique of Venice.—Matthew Wren (1657)

Oceana is the only valuable model of a commonwealth that has yet been offered to the public.—Hume

Oceana is as the Rose of Sharon, and the Lilly of the Valley. As the Lilly among thorns, such is my Love among the Daughters. She is comely as the Tents of Kedar, and terrible as an Army with Banners.—Harrington

I

JAMES HARRINGTON was perhaps the outstanding seventeenth-century prophet of the great rôle of Britain in world affairs. Comparing England and Venice, he declared: "The Sea giveth law unto the growth of Venice, but the growth of Oceana giveth law unto the Sea."[1] But he was at the same time one of the most enthusiastic of admirers of the ancients, a man who saw all moderns as men who either came but haltingly in the footsteps of antique civilization or had woefully blundered in striking out on paths of their own. It was, he declared, due to the Romans that modern nations had "given over running up and down naked and with dappled hides, learn't to write and read, to be instructed with good Arts." It was due to the ancients that "we are as it were of Beasts become Men." And by their means, he went on to assert, "we might yet of obscure and Ignorant men (if we thought not too well of our selves) become a wise and a great People."[2] Harrington, in short, would reform the land by antique wisdom that it might play a great rôle in the future.

The author of *Oceana* saw what he called "prudence" or political wisdom as divided into two great periods, the classical and the modern. Ancient prudence was first given by God to the Israelites; the Greeks and Romans got it by following God's footsteps in nature and based their commonwealths upon it. It was ended by the usurpation of Julius Caesar, which ushered in the "execrable raign of the Roman Emperours." Modern prudence dated from those inundations

[1] *Oceana*, ed. S. B. Liljegren (Heidelberg, 1924), p. 11. See also pp. 84, 94, 117, 188, 193, and 197.   [2] P. 43.

of Goths, Vandals, Huns, and Lombards which overwhelmed the Roman Empire and "deformed the whole face of the world with . . . ill features of Government."[3] The governments of Europe, including that of Oceana down to the Puritan Revolution, rested on modern prudence. Exemplifying as they did what Harrington was fond of calling the "Gothick ballance," they were defective in their institution and had become worse with the passage of time. Seeing his own century as representing a political crisis in the history of the world, he declared them to be in a state of dissolution. In showing how they might be remade when they utterly collapsed, he would follow ancient prudence and the states which had exemplified it—Sparta, Rome, and the Hebrew Commonwealth. "The people of the world," he declared, "in the dregs of Gothick Empire, bee yet tumbling and tossing upon the bed of sickness . . . nor is there any means of recovery for them, but by ancient prudence."[4]

But he would follow something else also. He would follow the *Discourses on Livy* of Machiavelli. He had no praises too high for the Florentine statist. He accepted the claim in the *Discourses* that Machiavelli was the first of the moderns to seek to recover antique political wisdom for the guidance of the modern world, and indeed declared that before himself Machiavelli was the "sole retriever" of ancient prudence.[5] He would follow Machiavelli, "the onely Polititian of later Ages," and abjure Hobbes, whose *Leviathan* sought to destroy what ancient prudence had to teach.[6]

Harrington would, moreover, follow Venice, which, because of the happy accident of its impregnable situation, he saw as having escaped the ravages of the barbarians and preserved the principles of antique commonwealths into the modern world.[7] He had all the common notions about the Most Serene Republic. Not only did he parallel it with the masterpieces of ancient political wisdom, but he asserted its superiority. By keeping its eye upon ancient prudence it had attained to an excellence beyond its copy.[8] Though it came

[3] P. 12.

[4] P. 197. See also pp. 12, 39, 60, 124–25, and 187. On the "Gothick ballance" see pp. 15, 43, 119, 124.

[5] Pp. 12–13, 30. Harrington, of course, was no more the second retriever than Machiavelli was the first. Nor can his statement be taken as confirmation of the correctness of the widespread view that Machiavelli was all but uniformly execrated in seventeenth-century England, a notion which rests on the assumption that the "murderous Machiavel" of the Elizabethan dramatists represented the universal opinion. Political writers support no such conclusion. The *Discourses* were translated in 1636, and the evidence is beyond all dispute that even before this time Machiavelli had begun to exert a powerful influence on English political thinking. [6] P. 13. Cf. Hobbes's remarks cited above, p. 1.

[7] Pp. 13, 39. [8] Pp. 13, 137–38; cf. pp. 185–86.

short of that ideal perfection which was to be reserved for Oceana, and though its situation limited it to being what Machiavelli had called a commonwealth for preservation, as distinguished from a commonwealth for empire or expansion,[9] it was the most perfect government which the whole history of the world up to his time had to show.[10] Harrington, moreover, was completely under the sway of the Contarini myth that the government had been made all at once at the institution of the republic and had never undergone any essential change. Venice, he declared, "at this day with one thousand years upon her back" continued "as fresh, and free from decay, or any appearance of it, as shee was born."[11] No sedition had ever disturbed her ageless internal tranquillity.[12] What made the republic particularly attractive to Harrington was the fact that he found in it a balance of the democratic principle of equality and an aristocratic predominance in administration. Taking up the notion that the Venetian constitution, at the time of its creation, had embraced all who were then in Venice, an idea which earlier exponents of mixed polities had used to show that there was any democratic element at all in the government, and disposing of the large number of inhabitants who had no political privileges by treating them under the head of a foreign colony within the limits of the possessing state, he declared not only that a democratic element was present in the republic, but that the Venetian system was "the most Democratical or Popular of all others."[13]

Three main bases, then,—ancient prudence, Machiavelli the retriever, and Venice the exemplifier—supplied the foundations on which Harrington proposed to remake the constitution of Oceana. We should note in addition that he had traveled on the Continent and had observed closely the Swiss and Dutch republics. These states, however, are to be regarded more as useful to him as affording parallels than as efficient agents in the formation of his thought. He considered them to be far inferior to Venice, Sparta, and Rome and as tinged with those defects of the "Gothick ballance" which he confidently expected would shortly prove the utter ruination of the great monarchies of Europe.[14]

[9] Pp. 11, 33.   [10] Pp. 32, 33, 137.   [11] Pp. 185–86.   [12] P. 31.   [13] P. 19.
[14] Pp. 119, 124, 189. The sources of Harrington's thought have been most inadequately dealt with. Though his indebtedness to the classics and to Venice has been recognized by H. F. Russell Smith, *op. cit., passim;* Liljegren, pp. 236, 309; Levett, *loc. cit.,* p. 177; Gooch, *Political thought,* p. 112; and T. W. Dwight, "Harrington and his influence on American political institutions," in *Political science quarterly,* II (1887), 18, none of these writers has investigated the matter adequately or given a satisfactory account of it.

What ancient prudence taught Harrington was the superiority of mixed government.[15] He begins the preliminary essay on the principles of government in the *Oceana* with what is essentially an epitome of the theory of the mixed state as it appears in the classical writers and in Machiavelli. We meet once more the familiar Polybian doctrine that as the one, the few, or the many rule, we have monarchy, aristocracy, or democracy, and that these tend to degenerate into tyranny, oligarchy, and anarchy. The mixed state alone is good. This, Harrington tells us, was the doctrine of the ancients.[16] How completely it was also his own doctrine can be seen by taking his account of the natural principles on which government rests. If we take a group of twenty men, he explained, it will be found that about a third part of them are "wiser, or at least lesse foolish" than the rest. The six will fall to discoursing and arguing with one another, and as a result of their discussions the fourteen will find many things made clear which had previously perplexed them. Hence they will turn to the six for guidance and advice. From this circumstance, it may be concluded that there is "a naturall Aristocracy diffused by God throughout the whole body of mankind," and of this natural aristocracy the people have by nature not only a right, but an obligation to make use. There should, therefore, in a commonwealth be a senate composed of men holding office, not by hereditary right as in a house of lords or by virtue of their wealth, but by election for their "excellent parts," with the function of advising, rather than commanding, the people. The duty of a senate is to debate and recommend. But though "the wisdom of the Few

It is also unfortunately true that the subject has fallen into the hands of persons who have not approached it from a scholarly point of view. Smith (p. 154) quite properly complains of the bitterness toward England and the gross over-statement of the Dutch influence which characterizes Campbell's *The puritans in England, Holland, and America*. Even less defensible is Christian Wershofen's *James Harrington und sein wunschbild vom germanischen staate* (Bonn, 1935).

[15] Smith appears wholly to have missed this fact in his study of Harrington. Not only does he make no reference to Harrington as a believer in mixed polities or to Polybius and the whole train of speculation which proceeded from him, and fail to see what Machiavelli and Venice might have suggested to him, but he curiously makes Algernon Sydney's adherence to mixed government a reason for largely excluding him in his discussion of contemporaries of Harrington who had ideas similar to those in the *Oceana* (p. 134). A consequence is that his discussion of Harrington's influence is somewhat impaired by his failure to see that the idea of balance was not a notion peculiar to Harrington, but merely one common to all believers in mixed polities. He concludes, for example, when he finds William Penn defining government with emphasis on balance, that Penn was directly under Harrington's influence (p. 139). It is indeed likely that such was the case, but the weight which Penn gave to the principle of balance does not in itself justify the conclusion.   [16] Pp. 13–14.

may be the light of mankind . . . the interest of the Few is not the profit of Mankind, nor of a Commonwealth." Hence a senate should not have the power to decide and thus to make law. The natural reason for this Harrington illustrated by the case of two girls who are given an undivided cake. If the one who is to cut the cake has also the right to choose which part she will take, the cake will be unequally divided, but if one cuts and the other chooses, an equal division will be made and each will get her just share. In order that a commonwealth may be similarly equal, the senate should debate and propose and the people choose. Hence the fourteen should constitute a second council. But if a state is populous, the whole people cannot very well perform this function. Hence the council should consist of "such a Representative as may be equall, and so constituted, as can never contract any other interest then that of the whole people." The few debating and proposing and the many choosing take in the interest of the whole. Thus emerges one of Harrington's basic principles: that no single-council government or unicameral legislature can ever be "equal" or just, and that the legislative power must be divided between two bodies representing the wisdom and the interest of the commonwealth.[17]

But since laws are but words and paper, there must to the two orders of a commonwealth be added a third "to be executive of the laws made, and this is the Magistracy." The magistracy might differ in different commonwealths as to both number and function, but there was "one condition of it, that must be the same in Every one, or it dissolves the Common-wealth where it is wanting: And this is no lesse then that as the hand of the Magistrate is the executive power of the Law, so the head of the Magistrate is answerable unto the people, that his execution be according unto the Law."[18]

Such is Harrington's outline of the orders of a commonwealth as deduced from nature. How this scheme fits in with the theory of mixed government becomes apparent when we find him declaring that a commonwealth consisting of "the Senate proposing, the People resolving, and the Magistracy executing" and "partaking of the Aristocracy as in the Senate, of the Democracy as in the People, and of Monarchy as in the Magistracy . . . is complete."[19] The essential identity of his basic conception with that of the theorists of the mixed polity becomes apparent, too, when we find him declaring that Machiavelli showed, and the ancients held, that there was no other commonwealth in art or nature, and when we observe the

[17] Pp. 23–25.   [18] P. 25.   [19] P. 25.

examples which he cited of such commonwealths as he found accorded in whole or in part with his theory—Sparta, Carthage, Athens,[20] Israel, and Venice.[21]

Harrington, however, did not produce in the *Oceana* merely a repetition of the theory of mixed government. He elaborated, refined, and in various ways modified the conception. This aspect of this thought can be seen in his views on the rôles of the aristocratic and democratic elements in mixed governments. To the casual reader, his remarks on this subject may well seem to be confusion itself. Passages can be found which suggest that he envisioned a mixed polity with a dominant aristocratic element; others, that he was anti-aristocratic and intended to give preponderant power to the democratic element. We find him declaring, for example, that an over-balancing nobility or gentry "is the utter bane and destruction" of a state,[22] and condemning the sort of government in which a nobility holds the greatest share of power as one totally foreign to ancient prudence and the concept of an equal mixed polity.[23] Such a system he found, rather, to be one of the "ill features" of modern prudence, and he accordingly pilloried it as the "Gothic ballance," a consequence of the feudal system of land tenure.[24] We also find him speaking of the government which he proposed for Oceana as a "popular" state, or a "free" state, or a "democratic" one,[25] placing sovereignty in the hands of the people,[26] putting the power to make law in the hands of the popular assembly,[27] suggesting that that body should be the court of highest appeal,[28] and proposing a state in which no hereditary titles or dignities would be conferred.[29] But apparently quite different sentiments appear when we find Harrington declaring

[20] The case of Athens in the writings of exponents of mixed government is an interesting one. Earlier writers like Machiavelli saw the city as a democracy and as short-lived and accordingly compared it unfavorably with Rome, Sparta, and Venice (*Discourses*, I, ii), but some seventeenth-century writers like Algernon Sydney contrived to discover that it, too, was a mixed state and admired it accordingly (*Discourses*, II, xvi). Harrington clearly thought of it as a mixed polity, but he agreed with Machiavelli in finding it far inferior to Sparta and Venice (pp. 29, 119).

[21] Pp. 25–29.   [22] P. 18. See also p. 119.

[23] He believed, however, that it was the gravitating of excessive power into the hands of the nobility, as a result of defects in the constitution, which brought about the ruin of the Roman republic (p. 139).

[24] Pp. 42 ff., 119.   [25] Pp. 117, 119, 123, 146.

[26] P. 108. Harrington's views on sovereignty, however, were somewhat confused. On p. 84 he makes the Lord Orator say in an explanatory speech that under the proposed system sovereign powers were "distributed." It is difficult to avoid the conclusion either that the concept of sovereignty, like theoretical discussions of the origin of government, did not interest Harrington, or that he deliberately avoided it.

[27] P. 142.   [28] P. 143.   [29] P. 104.

that a commonwealth should be so constituted as to put the natural aristocracy in office,[30] that Athens "was plainly lost through the want of a good Aristocracy,"[31] and that the "superstructures" of a popular state require an aristocracy,[32] which was, indeed, "the very life and soul of it."[33] "There is," he declared, "something first in the making of a Commonwealth, then in the governing of her, and last of all in the leading of her Armies; which, though there be great Divines, great Lawyers, great men in all professions, seems to be peculiar unto the Genius of a Gentleman." All commonwealth institutors, he found, had been gentlemen, and all who had got a name in civil or military affairs had belonged to this rank.[34] Other statements might be cited to the same effect; for example, his remark that "where there is not a Nobility to bolt out the people, they are slothfull, regardlesse of the world and the public interest of liberty."[35] Many of Harrington's observations about the people would seem to suggest a man with aristocratic predilections. "Your mechanicks," he declared, "till they have first feather'd their nests, like the Fowles of the Ayr, whose whole imployment is to seek their food, are so busied in their private concernments, that they have neither leisure to study the publick, nor are safely to be trusted with it."[36]

The key to the apparent contradictions in Harrington's pronouncements on the nobility and the people is to be found in his conception of the nature of true nobility and its rôle in mixed government. For a nobility which was a "distinct order," and which possessed hereditary titles and the right to a seat in an upper chamber— for a peerage, in short, and for a nobility which held most of the power of a state, he had no use in spite of the fact that he came from a family connected with "eight Dukes, three Marquisses, seventy Earls,

---

[30] P. 123.   [31] P. 118.   [32] P. 117.   [33] P. 18.

[34] Pp. 34–35. Harrington was emphatic on the point that the aristocratic element in the government could be supplied only by a nobility and that the place of the nobility could not be taken by clerics or lawyers, both of whom he proposed to exclude from various offices in the government (pp. 173–74). He had a curious disdain for professional men, lumping lawyers, physicians, and clerics together as "tradesmen" (p. 118). It would be a "Solecisme in Prudence," he declared, for "a person engaged by his Profit unto the Lawes as they stand" to be taken "into the Power which is Legislative" (p. 174). What Harrington's objection to lawyers amounted to was the contention that the administration of government must be in the hands of gentlemen and that it cannot safely be left to a class of legally-trained civil servants of the sort which was establishing itself in several Continental countries at the time when Harrington wrote and which in France produced the *noblesse de la robe*.   [35] Pp. 34–35.

[36] P. 119. Cf. his remark that the art of government cannot be mastered without study and that it is a "vain imagination" to suppose that the people can have leisure to study.

twenty-seven Viscounts, and thirty-six Barons."[37] These were the
nobilities which he condemned as the "utter bane and destruction"
of a state.[38] Essentially he equated nobility with the gentry, explaining that he used the term in the sense of the French *noblesse*.[39] Adopting a remark of Machiavelli's, he defined the nobility in this sense as
"such as live upon their own revenues in plenty, without engage-
ment either unto the tilling of their lands, or other work for their
livelihood." The first basis of nobility, then, was "ancient riches."
Men whose minds and energies were not occupied with their own
affairs had leisure to reflect on the good of the whole state. When to
reflection they added the performance of services for the commonwealth, they acquired the second basis of nobility—virtue. When
certain families became distinguished for such services, "ancient
virtue" became the accompaniment of "ancient riches," and nobility
in the fullest sense was acquired. This was the nobility, not possessed
of hereditary privileges or powers beyond the inheritance of property,
which he saw as "the very life and soul" of a successful mixed state.
One gathers from his illustration of the twenty men that Harrington
thought of the nobility thus defined as constituting perhaps a third
of the population.

On the relation between this nobility and the people in a proper
sort of state Harrington was clear enough. "When the people,"
he declared, "have the election of the Senate, not bound unto a
distinct order, and the result [i.e. the power to make law] which is
the Soveraign power, I hold them to have that share in the Government (the Senate not being for life) whereof, with the Safety of
the Common-wealth, they are capable in nature, and such a Government for that cause to be a Democracy."[40] When it is recalled that
Bodin had made the power to make law of the very essence of
sovereignty,[41] and that the constitutional issue between parliamen-
tarian and royalist was in no small measure ultimately fought out on
the question of where the power to make law lay, it is obvious that
Harrington's statement is not as restrictive as it may sound and
that he intended a state in which at least the greater share of power
ultimately resided in the people. Other statements confirm this conclusion. "Power," we find him saying, "should be in the people,"[42]
and the sort of nobility which is not only safe but necessary in a well
constituted state he specifically declared to be one holding an "under-

[37] The computation is Toland's in the "Life" prefixed to his edition of the *Oceana and
other works* (London, 1700), p. xiii.   [38] P. 119.   [39] P. 118.   [40] P. 123.
[41] *Op. cit.*, I, viii, pp. 84 ff.; x, pp. 153 ff.   [42] P. 119. See also p. 108.

balance unto the people."[43] From the point of view of where ultimate power was to be placed, then, there can be no question that Harrington was an exponent of a mixed state in which the popular element was dominant. He justified this position by arguing that all experience proved aristocracies when unchecked to be ravenous, but not the people,[44] and by the contention that the people, of whom individually he was so critical, possessed collectively a high degree of political competence.[45] For a professed disciple of Machiavelli, these conclusions are in no way strange. In the matter of the placing of the ultimate power, Harrington stood with Machiavelli and against many other advocates of mixed polities in holding that in mixed states the predominance of power should reside in the people.

Yet there remain his flat assertion that a commonwealth should be so devised as to put the natural aristocracy in office, and his contention that there was something in the governing of a commonwealth and the leading of its armies which was peculiar unto the genius of a gentleman. There can be no question that he believed that the actual business of national administration should be in the hands of men chosen for their worth and ability from the nobility or aristocracy, and from this point of view he can be described only as an advocate of an aristocratic mixed polity.[46]

At this point in defining the respective shares of the democratic and aristocratic elements in a mixed government, it is well to recall his illustration of the two girls and the cake, and the fact that he spoke of the cake as divided into two equal portions. It would seem clear that with the democratic element over-balancing in the matter of ultimate power and the aristocratic element in actual administration, he sought to achieve that "equalness" in a commonwealth on which he placed the greatest importance, and without which he did not believe could be established that equilibrium on which the success of mixed polities depended.

Another interesting aspect of Harrington's theory of mixed government is the moralistic elements in his thinking. The reason that monarchy, aristocracy, and democracy degenerate into tyranny, oligarchy, and anarchy, he tells us, is that they contain no counter-

---

[43] P. 119.   [44] P. 155.

[45] "The people taken apart, are but so many private interests, but if you take them together, they are the publick interest; the publick interest of a Common-wealth (as hath been shewn) is nearest that of mankind, and that of mankind is right reason" (pp. 141–42). Cf. Machiavelli, *Discourses*, I, lvii–lviii.

[46] This conclusion is inescapable from the actual provisions of his proposed constitution. See below, pp. 73 ff.

balance to the natural tendency in man for passion to usurp the rule of reason. Indeed, he goes so far as to say that when the one, the few, or the many rule by reason, we have the three simple pure forms of government, and that when passion creeps in we have their corruptions.[47] From this position, it followed that the whole art of constitution making was so to contrive the state that the institutions of government would compensate for and overcome the natural evil in man.[48] Harrington thought that this could be done by mixed government. Significant of this attitude was his contention that the excellence of the Venetian government was due, not to the fact that the Venetians excelled in virtue, but to the fact that their constitution was so contrived as to overcome the natural evil which they shared with other men. The citizen may be sinful, he wrote, "and yet the common-wealth bee perfect," and "the Citizen, where the common Wealth is perfect can never commit any such crime, as can render it imperfect or bring it unto a natural dissolution."[49] Harrington did not believe, as did Richard Baxter,[50] that governments stood or fell because they were in the hands of good or evil men. He had no faith in the adequacy of the rectitude of even good men for the task of government. Hence we have his insistence on the Machiavellian principle that government is by law and not by men. "Give us good men and they will make us good Lawes," he declared, "is the Maxime of a Demogogue. . . . But give us good orders, and they will make us good men, is the Maxime of a Legislator, and the most infallible in the Politickes."[51] Indeed, he went so far in this matter as to make it a cardinal point of distinction between ancient and modern prudence. Government according to ancient prudence, he tells us, was "the Empire of Lawes and not of Men." But modern prudence makes government "an Art whereby some man, or some few men, subject a City or Nation, and rule it according unto his or their private interest."[52] Law being the very basis of government, two consequences followed. The first of these was the importance of the state resting upon a fundamental law or constitution which could not be changed.[53] The whole *Oceana* is in essence little more

[47] Pp. 13–14.

[48] Cf. Machiavelli's statement that "whoever desires to found a state and give it laws, must start with assuming that all men are bad and ever ready to display their vicious nature" (*Discourses*, I, iii). For an early English expression of a similar idea in a writer who shows evidences of Machiavellian influence see Ponet, *op. cit.*, sig. A2r.

[49] P. 185. See also p. 126, and cf. Kiffen's sonnet prefixed to Lewkenor's *Contarini*, in which Venice is described as a place where "all corrupt means to aspire are curbed."

[50] *The holy commonwealth* (London, 1659), p. 224. Swift makes the same point in *The sentiments of a Church of England man*, sec. ii.   [51] P. 56.   [52] P. 12.   [53] P. 85.

than such a fundamental law. The second consequence was Harrington's complete repudiation of the contemporary enthusiasm for government by "saints." He had no more faith in the chosen than in other men. He declared that "they of all the rest are most dangerous, who holding that the Saints must govern, go about to reduce the Common-wealth unto a party." But more than this, he observed that "men pretending under the notion of Saints or Religion, unto Civil Power, have hitherto never failed to dishonour that profession: the World is full of Examples."[54]

Closely related to the conception of the constitution as compensating for the natural evil in man, and in fact following from it, is the idea which gives the *Oceana*, for all that it was intended as an actual model for England, its most interesting utopian aspect. Harrington apparently believed that it was possible to construct a perfect "equal" state, that a state could be made which would last forever. To construct an "immortal commonwealth" was indeed the grandiose idea which underlay and motivated the whole *Oceana*.[55] The following passage in an address by the Archon, or law-giver, to the "dear Lords and excellent Patriots" makes the matter clear enough:

To come unto experience, Venice, notwithstanding we have found some flaws in it, is the only Commonwealth in the make wherof, no man can find a cause of dissolution; for which reason wee behold her (albeit she consist of men that are not without sin) at this day with one thousand years upon her back, for any internal cause, as young, as fresh, and free from decay, or any appearance of it, as shee was born, but whatever in nature, is not sensible of decay by the course of a thousand years, is capable of the whole age of nature: by which calculation for any check that I am able to give myself; a Commonwealth rightly ordered, may for any internal causes be as immortal, or long-lived as the World.[56]

The prominence of the example of Venice in this passage should be noted. Earlier exponents of mixed government like Machiavelli had not thought that mixed states were everlasting; all that he had claimed for them, as we have seen, was that they postponed for a long time the processes of decay. Later Venetian enthusiasts,

[54] Pp. 55–56.
[55] For other occurrences of this notion among the classical republicans see below, pp. 120–121.
[56] Pp. 185–86. Farther down on p. 186 Harrington says: "A Commonwealth that is rightly instituted can never swarve." See also p. 61, the statement on p. 124 that the Venetian Senate was "for ever uncapable of corruption," and the declaration of the Orator on p. 84: "Neither by Reason nor by her [Venice's] experience is it impossible that a Common-wealth should be immortall."

however, under the influence of Contarini had suggested that the republic would endure forever.[57] It seems obvious that in Harrington's case the myth of the longevity and changelessness of the Venetian constitution and its prospective immortality united with the concept of compensating for the natural evil in man to make him reject cyclic conceptions of government altogether and arrive at the utopian project of the ageless state.[58]

Harrington's preoccupation with the perpetual state serves to call attention to another striking aspect of his thought—his contention that a commonwealth should not only be equal in its institution but should have certain devices to keep it in balance once the equilibrium was established. He was not one of those who believed that the mere division of power between the three elements of a state was sufficient to provide stability, for "an equall Commonwealth is such an one as is equall both in the balance or foundation, and in the superstructures."[59] Like the Venetians, he would supplement the basic division of power with other devices and an elaborate system of checks and balances. Of these the most important, suggested to him by Roman precedents, was an agrarian law, or what he called an "equal Agrarian," established as a part of the fundamental law of the state. It is only when we see his agrarian proposals as a device for the maintenance of the balance of a mixed government that we are able to see their proper place in his thought. The necessity for an agrarian law he found, as he found most other fundamentals, in nature. Emerging as an exponent of the importance of economic factors in determining the course of history, he declared it to be a law of nature that wealth in the form of riches in a commercial state or of land in all extensive states is the source of power. Whoever holds the land will in the end hold the power.[60] Hence, in the creation of a state the land must be so divided that the

[57] See *Maxims of the government of Venice*, p. 2. Cf. Thuanus's couplet quoted above, p. 28, and Nevill, *op. cit.*, pp. 56–57 and 138. See also the prediction in the *Calendar of state papers, Venetian*, X, 312–13, that Venice would last "until the final dissolution of the elements themselves."

[58] For a classical counterpart to the idea of the everlasting state see Plato's *Laws*, the influence of which on Harrington is indeterminable. With Harrington's views should be compared those of Howell, that other admirer of Venice and mixed polities. In his *Survay*, he predicted that the republic would shine among the kingdoms of the earth "to the World's end, if she be still true to her self" (p. 3; cf. pp. 1, 5, 8), but his thinking was muddled in comparison with Harrington's even if it was more practical. He was conscious of the inconsistency between his frequent predictions that Venice would last forever and cyclic notions of political institutions, but he had difficulty in freeing himself from the cyclic theory (see *Dodona's grove*, pp. 59–63).

[59] P. 32.   [60] Pp. 14–16.

distribution will accord with the division of power. An "equal Agrarian" he defined as "a perpetuall Law establishing and preserving the ballance of dominion, by such a distribution, that no one man or number of men within the compasse of the Few or Aristocracy, can come to over-power the whole people by their possessions in Lands."[61] The Roman commonwealth fell through a neglect of its agrarian laws, as a result of which the nobility by stealth got into their own hands the conquered lands that should have been divided among the people. Power followed land, with the result that the Gracchi were unable to restore the situation, and the nobility overthrew both the people and the commonwealth.[62] It is, in short, fatal to a commonwealth for the ownership of land to shift predominantly into the hands of an aristocracy, or to any state for such ownership to pass into the hands of a class different from that which holds political power.

The second of the devices by which Harrington sought to maintain mixed government was the secret ballot. There were numerous examples of such voting to which he might have turned, but the one to which he did turn was the Venetian ballot box, which, he declared, "is of all others the most perfect."[63] The necessity for secret voting he saw to arise from the fact that "the election or suffrage of the people, is freest, where it is made or given in such a manner, that it can neither oblige (*qui beneficium accepit libertatem vendidit*) nor disoblige another; or through fear of an enemy, or bashfulnesse towards a friend, impair a mans liberty."[64] Secret voting, then, was essential in the interest of a free suffrage. Harrington's statement, however, is not to be construed as supporting an absolutely unrestricted suffrage, for he adopted from his Venetian model, not only the ballot box, but the complicated set of devices by which he sought to insure that the election of officers would be indirect, involving several different steps, and that the principles of both lot and election would be employed.[65] It should be noted also that Harrington contemplated the use of the secret ballot, not only in the choice of members of the legislative councils, but also, after the Venetian custom,

---

[61] P. 32. Cf. p. 15: "If the whole people be Landlords, or hold the Lands so divided among them, that no one man, or number of men, within the compasse of the Few or Aristocracy, overballance them, the Empire . . . is a Common-wealth."

[62] P. 40. See also p. 139. Harrington's views on the cause of the fall of the Roman republic were in flat contradiction to those of many other advocates of mixed governments who ascribed the failure to the excessive power of the people (see above, p. 20 and below, p. 118). His theory was, however, consistent with his contention that the over-balance of power in a mixed state should be committed to the people.

[63] Pp. 33, 99. Note also his remarks on the secret voting of the Romans.

[64] Pp. 33.   [65] Pp. 76–77.

in the decisions of the law-making bodies themselves.[66] In this he was actuated by the same desire as motivated the use of the practice in his model—to avoid the organized action of parties in government. He saw the members of legislative councils as individuals chosen for their intelligence and integrity, who voted, like Venetian senators, as individuals and not as members of those organized parties which he agreed with Machiavelli in seeing as the bane of government.[67]

Closely connected with Harrington's views on the ballot and indirect election was his insistence on the use of the principle of rotation. The opposite of rotation, he wrote, is "Prolongation of Magistracy, which trashing the wheel of Rotation, destroyes the life or natural motion of a Common-wealth." Mere rotation, however, was not enough for a mixed state. It was essential, he declared, that there should be an equal rotation, which he defined as "equall vicissitude in Government, or Succession unto Magistracy conferred for such convenient terms, enjoying equal vacations, as take in the whole body by parts, succeeding others through the free election or suffrage of the People."[68] The implications of this statement appear in his discussion of rotation as practiced in the Roman and Athenian commonwealths. Rotation in the latter was unequal "in regard that the Senate chosen at once by lot, not by suffrage, and changed every year not in part, but the whole, consisted not of the naturall Aristocracy, nor sitting long enough to understand, or be perfect in their office." The result was that it lacked the authority to withhold the people from that perpetual turbulence which in the end ruined the state.[69] An equal rotation, in short, was one so devised as to result in the choice of the natural aristocracy.[70] It was, moreover, one which was partial in character and did not result in the changing of an entire governmental body at any one time. On these points, as on so many others, Harrington was drawing theory from Venetian practice.[71]

[66] Pp. 116, 148.
[67] P. 55. See also p. 107. Harrington's warnings were directed mainly against a one-party government—"a Commonwealth consisting of a party will be in perpetuall labour of her own destruction," he declared—but it is clear that his objection extended to all parties, whether single or multiple, and that he contemplated a partyless state.
[68] P. 32.   [69] P. 36.   [70] See also p. 123.
[71] This is clear, not only from his statement that "the senate of Oceana like that of Venice being alwaies changing is for ever the same" (p. 124), but from his notions as to the other conditions involved in a satisfactory rotation—for example, his theory of ineligibility after holding an office for a period equal to its term, and his notion of taking in "the whole body by parts." The system of partial rotation which he admired in the Venetian senate was achieved by having it composed, in addition to the senators elected annually, of the Procurators of St. Mark, who were life senators, and various *ex officio* members who held office for all sorts of terms.

The other side of Harrington's conception of an equal rotation appears in his criticism of rotation as practiced in ancient Rome. This was unequal because it excluded all except a nobility of hereditary privilege and senatorial right from the Senate and most of the magistracies. The unhappy consequence of this was that the Senate prevented the operation of that "equal Agrarian" which would have "rendred that Common-wealth immovable."[72] An equal rotation, therefore, would be one which would make it possible to choose the natural aristocracy for governmental offices without regard to whether or not they belonged by hereditary right to an order privileged to occupy those offices.

The last of the devices by which Harrington sought to insure the maintenance of the balance of mixed states was that of a constitutionally-provided dictator to act in emergencies. In imperfectly-contrived states he thought that the employment of this instrument would be extremely common, and that the frequency of its use would diminish in proportion to the extent to which a commonwealth was made equal, but he did not believe that it could be entirely dispensed with. Let the state be as perfect as possible, there would still arise some occasions when the regular processes of government were not enough.[73] Hence we find him agreeing with Machiavelli that a commonwealth unprovided with a constitutional dictator could not survive. We find him repeating also the Italian theorist's contention that the necessity for such an institution arose from the fact that, the action of republics being slow, a crisis presented them with a dilemma of which both alternatives were ruinous. If the state proceeded in the customary manner, disaster would result before action could be taken to prevent it; if, on the other hand, it violated constitutional procedure in order to act with dispatch, it overthrew the very rock on which the whole state was founded, the supremacy and inviolability of law.[74] Harrington had, however, a keener sense of the dangers involved in even constitutional dictatorship than Machiavelli had. He was distrustful of committing dictatorial power to single persons and pointed out the ease with which such individuals could transform themselves into kings by the device of prolonging their magistracy under one pretext or another until it became too strong to be overthrown. Consequently, he preferred a councilar dictator like the Venetian Council of Ten to the Roman example. However, he borrowed from the Roman model to impose on dictators greater restrictions than those which prevailed at Venice, for though

[72] P. 36. See also pp. 120–22.   [73] Pp. 113–14.   [74] Pp. 114, 111–12.

the *Dieci* were always in existence and acted on their own initiative, he would have dictatorial bodies created by the action of the senate to meet specific situations.[75]

As Machiavelli influenced Harrington's views on the necessity for a constitutional dictator, so also he exerted an important influence on another striking aspect of Harrington's thought and one which had, from the beginning of the history of mixed government, been closely associated with it—the idea of the state, not as something which evolves out of the nature of a people, but as a work of art, as something made all at once by a single great legislator. Quoting Machiavelli, Harrington declared that "a Common-wealth is seldome or never well turned or constituted, except it have been the work of one man." Hence, "the greatest advantages of a Common-wealth are, first that the Legislator should be one man; and secondly that the Government should be made altogether, or at once."[76] The bases of these notions in classical theory and practice we have already examined. Harrington himself added an additional reason for the second of them by making explicit the implications involved in his conception of the life of the state as governed by a fundamental law and of the importance of the rule of law. A commonwealth made at one time, he asserted, had the great advantage that from the beginning it avoided the pitfall of trusting in the rule of men and depended instead on the true basis of political society, the rule of law. Sparta and Rome, he found, illustrated the point. The former, being made all at once and under the rule of law from the start, brought its citizens to an exemplary virtue. Rome, on the other hand, not having been created all at once, began imperfectly and moved toward perfection. But before this process could be carried out, the scope given by the initial imperfections to the corrupt manners of men so rent the edifice of the state that all the perpetual repairs of the consuls and the tribunes were unavailing and it ended in ruin.[77]

There is one additional and important point which must be noted in any review of Harrington's general political principles. He was clearly much impressed by Machiavelli's distinction between commonwealths for preservation like Venice and commonwealths for increase like Rome. The former consisted of polities with small populations and states in which the people were not entrusted with

---

[75] Pp. 111–12.   [76] P. 58.

[77] Pp. 58–59. Cf. p. 137: "As no man shall shew me a Common-wealth born streight, that ever became crooked; so, no man shall shew me a Common-wealth born crooked that ever became streight: Rome was crooked in her birth." See also p. 168.

arms. They had a high degree of internal tranquillity, but were subject to attack from without. Commonwealths for increase secured power by entrusting arms to a numerous people, but paid the price of internal disturbances. It was to the latter, as we have seen, that Machiavelli gave his preference, and Harrington agreed with him. He rejected, however, the idea that internal dissonance was the inevitable accompaniment of giving arms to the people. A people possessed of arms and holding therefore great military power grow rebellious, he declared, only when they are the victims of injustice. But if a state is perfectly equal, causes of injustice cannot arise, and a properly-constituted polity can therefore with perfect safety arm its people.[78]

Such essentially were the main aspects of Harrington's political thought. It is obvious that they formed an elaborate theoretical foundation for an attempt to construct an ideal mixed state. For their application to the field of practical politics, we must now turn to two things, his analysis of the government of Oceana down to the time of Cromwell, which largely occupies the part of his preliminary essay which he devoted to tracing "the Rise, Progresse, and Declination of Moderne Prudence," and the model constitution which he proposed.

II

Harrington's rather lengthy survey of the constitutional history of Oceana is notable for his complete rejection of those old English precedents to which so many political writers of the time appealed, and his repudiation of the idea, advanced earlier by Hunton[79] and Milton,[80] that the constitution of Oceana, in its original form as a mixed monarchy, was an ideal example of mixed government. Instead, he saw the monarchy down to the deposition of Charles I as defective at every stage in its history. No understanding of Harrington is possible without grasping this fact. He did not aim to reform traditional institutions.[81] He considered that they had collapsed and perished in the Puritan Revolution.[82] He would supplant them with new institutions based on classical models and their supposed modern counterparts. This position was only the inevitable consequence of his division of prudence into ancient and modern and his rejection of the latter. The government of Oceana he saw as defective in the first place because it was a monarchy. All monarchies

---

[78] Pp. 133–35.   [79] See above, p. 25.   [80] See below, p. 95.

[81] It is significant of this fact that he describes Megaletor at the end of the *Oceana* as 'not the Restorer, but the Founder of a Common-wealth" (p. 225).   [82] Pp. 54–55.

had the defect that they had to be maintained by an army or by a nobility. When the former expedient was employed, the armed forces had it in their power to cause constant turmoil and sedition, as the Janizaries in Turkey and the Praetorian Guards of Rome amply demonstrated. If a nobility was used to maintain the monarchy, this power was transferred to their hands, and the result was wars, like the feud of the Red and the White in Oceana, in which the people had no interest and were only victims.[83]

In its origin Harrington saw the monarchy of Oceana as a creation of the Teutons or Saxons, who followed in its institution that defective "Gothick ballance" on which the inferior political wisdom of modern times and most modern states rested.[84] Oceana had, indeed, the three orders of a state, for Harrington contended that the people had participated in the Saxon Witenagemotes,[85] but as a result of the feudal system of land tenure, it had that over-balancing of the aristocratic element which he considered to be a fatal defect in government.[86] After the Conquest the lands were divided in such a way that most of them were in 60,000 knights' fees, which were possessed by two hundred fifty lords and the lords spiritual. Therefore, Oceana continued as a government of the few or the nobility, "wherein the people might also assemble, but could have no more than a meer name."[87] The Norman kings aspired to be absolute, but having divided the land among the nobility, they discovered that they had also given the nobility power.[88] Hence wars arose which made the history of Oceana "no other than a wrestling match between King and Nobles."[89] Panurgus (Henry VII) seeking to abate the power of the nobles, carried through three statutes which in the end ruined not only the nobility, but the monarchy as well. The first of these, the Statute of Population, provided for the maintenance of all houses of husbandry having more than twenty acres of land. This confirmed a great part of the land to the prosperous "Yeomanry or middle people," and so freed them from dependence on the lords that the nobility lost control of their military services. The Statute of Retainers aided the process of depriving the lords of their military power by taking from them the retainers from whom they drew their cavalry and commanders. Finally, the Statute for Alienations made it possible for the nobles to sell their lands. The result of these meas-

[83] Pp. 30–31, 41, 50. [84] P. 43. [85] P. 45.
[86] Pp. 44, 47, 31. Cf. pp. 18, 119. [87] Pp. 46–47. [88] P. 47.
[89] P. 48. Cf. p. 124: "Your Gothick Polititians seem unto me rather to have invented some new ammunition, or Gunpowder, in their King and Parliament (*duo fulmina belli*) then Government."

ures was that the greater part of the land passed into the hands of
the people, power, as always with Harrington, accompanying it.
The destruction of the power of the temporal nobility by Panurgus
had its counterpart in the destruction of that of the lords spiritual
in the next reign through the medium of the dissolution of the monas-
teries. Queen Parthenia, observing these facts, wisely converted
"her reign through the perpetuall Love-tricks that passed between
her and her people into a kind of Romanze" and neglected the nobility. A monarchy, however, which is not supported by a nobility,
must be supported by an army, that "beast that hath a great belly
and must be fed." But the ability to maintain an army rests with whoever possesses the land, a truth which the last king of Oceana found
out to his cost when, abandoning "love-tricks," he attempted to rule
arbitrarily.[90] The result was the dissolution of the monarchy,[91] this
dissolution being the natural consequence of the fact that the balance
in lands and hence in power had passed into the hands of the people,[92]
and that monarchy and a dominant popular element were incompatible and could not exist together.[93]

But if Harrington found the monarchy of Oceana wanting, the
republic set up in 1649 pleased him no better. The Rump, he declared,
not only had no precedent in earlier English practice, but had no
parallel in either ancient or modern prudence. A government with a
single council both debating and resolving was not equal. It was not
even a commonwealth. It was an oligarchy, doomed to an early dissolution as all oligarchies were. He found the closest historical
parallels to the Rump in the Thirty Tyrants of Athens and the
Roman Decemvirs.[94]

Fortunately, there remained the army, loyal to Olphaus Megaletor,
in whom Harrington gave a concrete portrayal of the role he would
have Cromwell play. Megaletor, he tells us, was widely read in
masters of politics and was expert in the political philosophy which
Harrington claimed only to have sketched roughly. Reading in
Machiavelli that states were well made only when they were made all
at once by a law-giver, Megaletor pondered the matter and became
convinced of "the necessity of some other course than would be
thought upon by the Parliament." Hence, he laid the matter before
the army, with the result that the Parliament was deposed and he was

90 Pp. 48–50.   91 P. 50.
92 Cf. pp. 54–55: "The dissolution of the late Monarchy was as natural as the death
of a man."
93 Pp. 55, 30–31. This idea was, of course, the corollary of his contention that a
monarchy had to be supported either by an army or a nobility.   94 Pp. 57–58.

created "Lord Archon, or Sole Legislator of Oceana" with a council
of fifty to assist him "by labouring in the Mines of ancient Prudence," and a council of twelve "Prytans," who reported to the
people and listened to proposals from them in order that "the people
(who were neither safely to be admitted unto, nor conveniently to be
excluded from the framing of their Commonwealth" could believe
when it came forth that they had made it themselves.[95] The preliminary essay on the principles of government in the *Oceana* ended,
in short, with an invitation to Cromwell to become the Lycurgus of
Oceana, to use supreme authority, not to make himself absolute,
but to set up the perfect mixed state. Not the least extraordinary thing
about this offer is the fact that Harrington represents Megaletor at
the conclusion of the instituting of the state resigning his authority
and retiring to the country.[96] This, of course, was strictly consistent with the theory of the commonwealth institutor as the theorists of mixed government had developed it. Harrington apparently
thought, however, that Cromwell could not be induced to play out the
rôle to this perfection, for he tells us that Megaletor was called
back and made Archon or Protector of the state for life[97] and that
after fifty years in this position he left Oceana on his death a perfect state. To assure Cromwell of the fame which would come to
him, Harrington added a description of the equestrian statue erected
to his memory complete with the fantastic inscriptions for all four
sides with which the whole book closes. Cromwell, in short, was to
retain power for life but so to remake the government that on his
passing he would leave a smoothly-functioning mixed state. The
situation prevailing in England was, of course, sufficient in itself to
account for the proposal, but in view of Harrington's great indebtedness to Machiavelli, it is significant to note that the rôle he would
have Cromwell play had a close parallel in that which the Italian
theorist proposed to the Medici in his tract on the reform of the
government of Florence.[98]

III

We turn now to the constitution which Harrington proposed for
Oceana. Underlying the whole state would be two fundamental
laws, one providing for the control of wealth in land and the other
establishing the "Ballot of Venice" as basic in the state.[99] The

[95] Pp. 58–61.   [96] P. 208.   [97] P. 213.   [98] See above, p. 15.
[99] The "Fourteenth Order" constitutes the "Ballot of Venice, as it is fitted by several
alterations . . . to be the constant and only way of giving suffrage in this Commonwealth" (p. 98). The alterations referred to are mainly a matter of the degree of com-

end of the Agrarian Law would be to insure that ultimately no one would be permitted to possess lands yielding more than £2000 a year in England, or £500 in Scotland, the greater limitation being necessary in the latter country because existing conditions there made greater the danger of an over-balancing aristocracy.[100] To achieve this object, Harrington struck directly at the prevailing principle of primogeniture, providing that an estate had to be equally divided among a decedent's sons if the divided portions equalled in value more than £2000 each. Thus in a few generations, without any violent seizure or confiscation of great estates, all holdings of land ·would be reduced to the required maximum.[101] If a man's estate was such that the divided portions were less than that amount, they could be unequally divided among his sons, except that the eldest could not receive a portion worth more than the maximum. It was a further provision that no one not possessing at the institution of the law an estate worth more than £2000 could hold such an estate unless it was acquired by lawful inheritance. If a man had a daughter, or daughters, unless they were heirs, he was forbidden to leave or give them in marriage lands valued at more than £1500 a year. Harrington calculated that under this system the maximum size of estates would be between two and three thousand acres,[102] and that the number of landowners could never fall below five thousand;[103] in actual practice, no doubt, it would be much larger than that number inasmuch as many holdings would not come up to the maximum. "Five thousand Proprietors so seased," declared Harrington, "will not agree to break the Agrarian; for that were to agree to rob one another; Nor to bring in a King, because they must maintain him, and can have no benefit by him; Nor to exclude the People, because they can have as little by that, and must spoyl their Militia. So that the Common-wealth continuing upon the ballance proposed, though it should come into Five thousand hands can never alter; And that it should ever come into Five thousand hands, is as improbable as anything in the World that is not altogether impossible."[104] An incidental benefit, Harrington thought, would be

plexity in the mixing of lot and election in the use of the ballot in the various governing bodies of the state. I say degree of complexity because Harrington's ballot, even in its simplest forms, is hardly less involved than that used in the choosing of the Venetian Doge (see above, p. 30 and cf. *Oceana*, pp. 76–77).   [100] Pp. 86, 98.

[101] Harrington estimated that existing estates which exceeded the maximum numbered about three hundred (p. 93).

[102] P. 95.   [103] P. 92.   [104] Pp. 92–93.

that the Agrarian would lessen marrying for money and promote marrying for love as it ought to be.[105]

With his state firmly established on the ballot and agrarian legislation, Harrington laid down elaborate provisions for both local and national government. We are concerned here mainly with the latter. The national government would consist of a strategus and six commissioners forming the signory; a senate; and a prerogative tribe or house of deputies. In setting up these organs, Harrington drew heavily from the Venetian model, a fact which is amply demonstrated by his statements that his signory was "almost purely Venetian";[106] that in his senate there was "scarce any feature that is not Roman or Venetian";[107] and that his provisions for the choice of judges and military officers could "be easily perceived to be Venetian."[108] It may also be noted that the system which he provided for the choice of ambassadors virtually duplicated Venetian practices;[109] that the pre-considering committees of his senate have their closest parallel, as he himself pointed out, in the Venetian Sages or College of Preconsultors;[110] that he justified by Venetian precedents there being no appeal from the decisions of the Council of War in emergencies;[111] and that to support his exclusion of divines from the magistracies of the state he cited the Venetian rule barring those who had relationship with the Pope or with cardinals from participating in the election of magistrates.[112] Venice, of course, was not the sole model for the proposed constitution of Oceana, but it is beyond dispute that in many ways it was the main one.[113]

Harrington would begin by dividing the people into servants and freemen or citizens, the latter being further divided into the horse, those who had £100 in lands, goods, or money, and the foot. Citizens between eighteen and thirty would constitute the youth and form the marching armies; those over thirty would be considered elders and would supply the standing garrisons. Only citizens would be able to vote and they only upon attaining the status of elders.[114] The classical inspiration of these provisions is suggested by their recognition of thirty as the age of political competence.

[105] Pp. 96–97. [106] P. 106. [107] P. 104. See also p. 124. [108] P. 108.
[109] P. 107. Cf. Lassels's description of the Venetian system, Pt. II, p. 370.
[110] P. 113. [111] P. 148. [112] P. 173.
[113] This indebtedness was clearly recognized by Harrington's contemporaries as is shown by the quotation from Wren at the beginning of this chapter. I quote from *Considerations on Mr. Harrington's commonwealth of Oceana* (London, 1657), sig. A4v. I regard as not in accord with the facts Smith's contention that Harrington owed more to Athens, Sparta, and Rome than to Venice (*op. cit.*, pp. 72–73). [114] Pp. 64–65.

Once a year the elders in each parish would choose from the horse and the foot one-fifth of their number to be deputies, no citizen being eligible to serve for two successive years. Adjacent parishes having a total of about one hundred deputies would combine to form a hundred,[115] of which divisions Harrington estimated that there would be one thousand in England. Twenty hundreds would form a tribe. There would, therefore, be fifty major political divisions in the country, each with an "annual place of rendezvous" with a pavilion equipped with three urns for the elaborate system of voting and open on one side and looking into a field capable of the muster of four thousand men.[116] Annually the whole body of the deputies of the tribe, about two thousand in number,[117] the horse divided into troops and the foot into corresponding companies, would assemble and hold elections, choosing on the first day the tribal officers and on the second, the representatives of the tribe in the Senate and House of Deputies.[118] In each case choices would be made by a system beginning with a double lot by which four sets of six electors each would be chosen, horse and foot being alike eligible. For each office, each set of electors would then nominate one to the deputies, four being thus placed in nomination, from whom the deputies would proceed to choose one by majority vote.[119] The administrative officials of the tribe so chosen would consist of six magistrates of the prime magnitude, who, together with the overseers of the parishes, the justices of the peace, and the jurymen of the hundreds, sixty-six in all, would constitute the Phylarch or Council of the Tribe.[120]

On the second day of the annual balloting, the deputies would proceed to choose, for terms of three years, the nine magistrates of the gallaxy, for which positions only married men would be eligible, and of which two would be knights chosen from the horse, three deputies likewise chosen from the horse, and four deputies chosen from the foot. Two knights and seven deputies chosen annually in each tribe would result in the election of one hundred senators and three hundred fifty deputies. On the first Monday after March, the knights would go to the Pantheon or Palace of Justice in the metropolis, where they would take their places as members of the Senate. Likewise, the deputies would become members of the Pre-

[115] P. 70.
[116] P. 73. The architecture of the pavilions would be classical. They would stand with one open side "upon fair Columnes like the porch of some ancient Temple."
[117] The illustrative tribe of Nubia is represented as having twenty-two hundred deputies, of whom seven hundred were of the horse and fifteen hundred of the foot (p. 77).
[118] Pp. 74–81.   [119] Pp. 76–78.   [120] P. 79.

rogative Tribe or Equal Representative of the people.[121] Under this system of annual election for triennial terms, which Harrington called an "Annual Triennial and Perpetuall Revolution,"[122] the total membership of the Senate and the Prerogative Tribe would be three hundred and one thousand fifty respectively, with one-third of the membership retiring each year. Harrington was at pains to make clear that the bodies thus chosen would be perpetual, not, to use his own term, "alternate." "Alternate life in Government," he declared, "is the alternate death of it." It was part of the Gothic system of which he so strongly disapproved. The Senate of Oceana, on the other hand, "like that of Venice, being alwaies changing" would also be "forever the same."[123] At the same time, however, in conformity with his rotative principle, Harrington provided that neither knight nor deputy would be eligible to serve for a second term until he had skipped a term.[124]

The Senate would sit every Monday and at other times when necessary, its sessions being attended by two tribunes of the horse and two of the foot, who were free to observe but had no vote. The same privilege would be extended also to the "Judges of the Land." The admission of the tribunes to the Senate, Harrington tells us, he drew from Roman practice; the inclusion of the judges, he asserted, was based on ancient English precedent.[125] The functions of the Senate would be two, "election" and "instruction," the former being of three sorts, annual, biennial, and extraordinary. By the first of these elections would be chosen for annual terms the Lord Strategus, the Lord Orator, and the First and Second Censors, for which magistracies all members of the Senate would be eligible; and for terms of three years the Third Commissioner of the Seal and the Third Commissioner of the Treasury, who would have to be chosen from the newest one-third of the Senate. The Lord Strategus, for whom Harrington cited Greek precedents,[126] would be the First President of the Senate and the General of the Army when in the field. In the event of his being in the field, a second Strategus would be chosen to be First President of the Senate and General of the Second Army. If he, too, was called into the field, a third Strategus would be elected. The Lord Orator, the one magistrate in the national administration for whom Harrington cited English antecedents, comparing him to the Speaker of the House of Commons,[127] would be "second and more peculiar President of the Senate, to whom

---

[121] Pp. 80–81.   [122] P. 82.   [123] P. 124.   [124] P. 81.
[125] P. 104. See further on the tribunes, p. 128.   [126] P. 106.
[127] P. 106. The Orator and Strategus are also compared to the Roman consuls.

it appertaineth to keep the House unto Orders."[128] The two Censors would be chancellors of the two universities and presidents of the Councils for Religion and Magistrates. They would also preside over the ballot in the Senate and would have the power, subject to an appeal to the whole body, to remove erring members and magistrates. The first of these powers Harrington derived from Venice, the second from Rome.[129] The three Commissioners of the Seal would be judges in chancery and the three Commissioners of the Treasury would have charge of financial matters.

At the annual elections of the Senate would be chosen also members of the four councils or committees of that body, those of State, War, Religion, and Trade. The first of these would consist of fifteen members, of whom five would be elected annually from the newest one-third of the Senate for terms of three years. This council would receive all foreign negotiations and ambassadors and instruct the ambassadors of Oceana; it would consider also all laws to be enacted, amended, or repealed and levies of men or money so far as to repare them for presentation to the Senate. The Council of War would be composed of nine senators, of whom three would be elected each year out of the newest one-third of the Council of State, and the four tribunes. It would have charge of all military matters and carry on such affairs as required secrecy for the defense of the state without communication to the Senate until such time as safety permitted. It would have power also without appeal to try and execute any person attempting to introduce debate into any popular assembly of the commonwealth. The third council, that of Religion, would have care of the national religion and of liberty of conscience. In any matter concerning the national religion, it would consult with the divines of the universities above forty years of age and report to the Senate. Liberty of conscience as well as a national religion being a part of Harrington's scheme, the Council of Religion would also have the duty of preventing any coercive power being used in religious matters and would be charged with seeing that religious congregations were neither molested nor interrupted but "vigilantly, and vigorously protected and defended."[130] This council would examine every petition addressed to the Senate except that of a tribe. The Coun-

---

[128] P. 105.   [129] P. 106.

[130] P. 110. This page contains an excellent summary of Harrington's religious views. The relation of his national religion to other religions is defined by his remark that the teachers of the national faith would be "no other then such as voluntarily undertake that calling; and their Auditors or Hearers, no other then are also voluntary." He did not, however, extend toleration to Catholics, Jews, or idolaters.

cil of Trade would consist of twelve senators elected four each year from the newest one-third of the Senate and would advise and report to the Senate on all matters of trade. Harrington completed the committees of his Senate by providing that each third of each council would weekly elect a provost to serve on a Council of Provosts, no member being eligible for reëlection until each member of the third had served. This council, "being the affability of the Common-wealth," would assemble daily towards evening to hear and discuss any proposal made by anyone for the good of the state.[131]

The biennial elections of the Senate would result in the choice of ambassadors in ordinary, one ambassador being chosen at each election. In successive two-year terms, he would represent the state at Paris, Madrid, Venice, and Constantinople. Thus every two years the state would be benefited by the return of "a Statesman enriched with eight years of experience, from the prime Martes of Negotiation in Europe." For the coveted position of ambassador, neither senators nor members of the Prerogative Tribe would be eligible, nor would anyone who had passed the age of thirty-five.[132]

In addition to holding annual and biennial elections, the Senate would participate also in the process, which Harrington described as partly Venetian and partly Roman in inspiration and which he called "election by the Scruteny," by which ambassadors extraordinary, vice admirals, polemarches or field officers, judges, and sergeants of the law would be chosen. Under this system, if the officer to be elected was an ambassador, the Council of State would nominate one and the Senate four, the Senate then choosing among the five nominees; if a military officer was to be chosen, the Council of War would function in place of the Council of State. Any military officer, however, if he was not a member of the Senate or the Prerogative Tribe, would have to have his selection confirmed by the latter body.[133]

The instructive functions of the Senate cannot be considered without first looking at the Signory of Oceana, which in number, organization, and function forms a very close counterpart of the body which stood at the apex of the Venetian system.[134] The Signory would consist of the Lord Strategus, adorned in a scarlet robe after the fashion of a duke, and the six commissioners, who would wear

---

[131] On the organization and functions of the councils, see pp. 106, 109–11.
[132] P. 107.   [133] P. 108.
[134] The only essential difference was the life magistracy of the Venetian doge as opposed to the annual one of the Lord Strategus.

robes similiar to those of earls. These officials would likewise during their term of office be entitled to the "title, place, and honour" of dukes and earls. Anyone bearing the same magistracy three times would have "his respective place, and Title during the terme of his Life, which is all the honour conferr'd by this Commonwealth, except upon the Master of Ceremonies, the Master of the Horse, and the King of the Heraulds, who are Knights by their Places."[135] The Signory would consider all matters of government, and any one of them, as well as the whole body, would be able to propose measures to the appropriate council for consideration. They would also have the right to sit and vote in every council of the Senate.[136] When a matter had been discussed in council, any member of the Signory would be able to assemble the Senate, where freedom of debate would prevail subject only to a complicated system of determining the order of speakers. The Senate would debate only the proposals made by the councils; in the event of several measures being brought in and none securing a majority, all would be thrown out.[137] They could, however, be re-presented by a council; if the Senate again failed to give a majority to one of them, they would be considered dead. Measures presented to the Senate in this manner were divided by Harrington into matters of state or government "according to Law enacted already," and matters of "Law to be enacted, repealed, or amended." Matters of state would be settled by the vote of the Senate; matters of law, however, would be invalid until they had been passed by the Prerogative Tribe.[138]

The Prerogative Tribe, or Representative of the People, drawn three-sevenths from the horse and four-sevenths from the foot,[139] would have two powers, those of result and judicature. When the Senate had a measure to propose to the Tribe, it would appoint as its proposers any two of the Commissioners or the two Censors, and the Tribunes would thereupon assemble the Tribe, to which the proposers would present the measure and explain its provisions. It would then be published for six weeks, and if at the end of that time it was passed by the Tribe it became a law, the vote being taken in the presence of the proposers and counted by the Tribunes, who reported the result to the Senate. If the measure was not approved, it could either be rejected finally or returned to the Senate for further

---

[135] Pp. 103–04.   [136] Pp. 106, 115–16.   [137] Pp. 115–16.   [138] P. 117.

[139] By this arrangement, Harrington thought that he would secure "the support of a true and natural Aristocracy, the deepest root of a Democracy" (p. 145).

debate. All matters involving the declaration of war and the levying of men or money, as well as all "matters of law," would have to be approved by this procedure.[140] In exercising its legislative function, the Prerogative Tribe would at no time debate a matter under consideration, the members being under oath not to debate or to suffer debate to be introduced into the body. It was Harrington's settled conviction that popular assemblies were ruined the moment debate was permitted in them and that one secret of the success of Venice and Sparta was the exclusion of debate from such bodies.[141] During the six weeks' period between the proposing and the voting on a measure, the Tribunes and the Censors would be charged with seeing that there was "no laying of heads together or canvassing" lest the Tribe should be split into parties and factions.[142] In its judicial capacity, the Prerogative Tribe would be the court of final appeal in all matters but two: neither it nor any other body in the commonwealth would be able to review the measures taken by the Council of War for the defense of the land or the martial law of the Strategus when in the field. When the Tribe sat as a court, the Tribunes would be presidents of it.[143] It would fix penalties, including that of death, and determine guilt and innocence by ballot, the placing of last resort in the Tribe being a recognition of the principle that magistracy "should be accountable unto the people from whom it receives its powers."[144]

Such would be the bodies which would normally operate in the perfect state of Harrington's dreams. We must now look at the institution by which he sought to realize concretely his conviction that in order to survive a state must have a constitutionally provided body to act in emergencies. We have seen that if a matter was twice presented to the Senate by one of the councils and failed of securing a majority, it was to be considered dead. But to this there was to be one exception. If the situation was one which admitted no delay, the Senate upon failing to agree on a measure would proceed to the creation of the Dictator. This would be effected by choosing nine "Knights extraordinary" to be added to the Council of War for the term of three months. The body thus created would have power to make war and peace, levy men and money, enact laws which would be valid for one year unless they were sooner repealed by the Senate and the Prerogative Tribe, and administer the affairs of the common-

[140] Pp. 142–43.   [141] Pp. 127–28; cf. p. 129.
[142] P. 142.   [143] P. 143.   [144] P. 146.

wealth for the three months period subject only to the restriction that "the Dictator shall have no power to do anything that tendeth not unto his proper end and institution."[145]

Harrington's Dictator owed as much to the Venetian precedent as most of his other institutions did, as he himself pointed out,[146] but there were two closely related aspects of his thought in which he departed wholly from the Venetian model to follow that of Rome —the military system of Oceana and the imperial destiny which he foresaw for his ideal state. His views on both of these matters were the natural consequence of his conclusion that Oceana should be— to use his own distinction following Machiavelli—a commonwealth for increase rather than one for preservation, and that only states so constituted could be safe.

It was, Harrington believed, one of the grand errors of modern prudence that it armed the poor and largely excused the rich from military service, a system which he declared could have only the consequence that men would become the vassals of their servants.[147] The Romans discovered the secret of success in a militia by arming only those who were rich enough to be freemen and excusing the indigent. In Oceana, in accordance with ancient prudence, servants would be excluded and the militia formed entirely of those who were citizens, the horse being equally liable with the foot. The youth of the land, those between eighteen and thirty, would be subject to three military "essays."[148] By the first of these one hundred thousand men would be chosen by lot annually in the parishes, one man in five being taken, who would meet at their respective hundreds and choose their own captains of companies and ensigns or cornets. Games and military exercises would then be held on a competitive basis with choice arms as the prizes in each hundred, a system which Harringon estimated would in ten years result in the creation of a group of thirty thousand men armed with the finest equipment. The second "essay" would result in the choice by lot of a standing army of thirty thousand foot and ten thousand horse, who, upon war being declared, would be delivered to the Strategus and become the third "essay."[149] In the event of an invasion, the elders would be subject to a similar muster.[150] The relation of this system to that of ancient

---

[145] P. 112.   [146] Pp. 113–14.   [147] Pp. 176–77.

[148] Those who entered the professions of law, medicine, and theology would be exempt (pp. 163–64). He exempted also only sons and provided that not more than half of the sons of any one family would be liable to service. The penalty for refusal to serve would be to be "deemed an Helot or publique Servant" (p. 167).

[149] Pp. 163 ff.   [150] P. 181.

Rome, Harrington himself defined. The military system of Oceana, he declared, was "but a Repetition or Copy of that Originall . . . from whence the Commonwealth of Rome . . . derived the Empire of the World."[151] Still following Rome, Harrington would double the size of the standing army by auxiliaries so that the commonwealth would go forth to battle with an immediately available force of eighty thousand men. To those to whom such a force seemed unnecessarily large and expensive, he replied that it was the error of modern princes to make wars with small forces and that the Romans by having adequate armies made their wars both short and successful.[152]

We have now to look at the last and in some ways the most interesting aspect of Harrington's classical republicanism—his imperialism. The notion that republics are not or should not be imperialistic was no idea of the classical republicans. Indeed, the implications of their thinking were all in the contrary direction, for in the great dispute among advocates of rival political systems in this period, whether Rome had attained its height under the emperors or under the republic, it was a favorite contention of the republicans that Rome ceased to expand when it gave up senators for monarchs.[153] Those who saw in the Roman republic an ideal which they would establish in the modern world were fired with the vision of an English commonwealth which would spread its rule, like ancient Rome, over the whole world.[154] Of this group Harrington must be accounted the chief. The concluding pages of the *Oceana* were a call to his countrymen to embark on a career of world dominion. His words are unequivocal, their import many times repeated.[155] Rome inspired the vision and supplied not only the military system but, as we shall see, the colonial system, by which he hoped to secure its realization. At this point, however, we must notice a coalescing of the spirit of antique republicanism with that of Puritanism. The

[151] P. 176. Cf. his remark on p. 177 that the levy of an army in time of war "proceedeth according to Polybius." It is significant of the extent to which his views were influenced by the Roman model that he saw the armies of Oceana going forth to battle against "horses and chariots" (p. 184).   [152] P. 180.
[153] For the documents in this controversy see above, p. 47.
[154] See R. H.'s *A discourse on the national excellencies of England* (London, 1658). Had the republic established in 1649 lasted, the author wrote, it would have excelled "Sparta, Athens, Carthage, and Venice," and he "could not assign it less than the whole globe at last for its portion." In the brief time it had lasted it had made a more glorious beginning than Rome. I quote from the large extracts from this tract printed in the "Memoirs" prefixed to the 1772 edition of the *Works* of Algernon Sydney, p. 20.
[155] Pp. 188, 193 and the citations in following footnotes.

Puritan conscience was dominated by the sense of election and by a feeling that it was incumbent upon God's chosen to be zealously about doing God's work in this world. Transfer this feeling from the individual to the national plane, and one has provided the basis for the feeling that God had chosen England to lead the world to truth and righteousness. That such a transference was not only possible but actually did occur may be illustrated by Milton, who, for all his Arminianism, had plenty of the sense of election, the two conceptions not being necessarily contradictory, as *Paradise lost*, III, 173 ff., shows clearly enough. Milton's early tracts were a trumpet-call to an elected nation to show the world the way to truth and true religion. God, he asserted in the *Areopagitica*, revealed himself first to His Englishmen; they had great argument to think that His favor was "in a peculiar manner propitious and propending" toward them, and that they would be the leaders "in some new and great period in his church, even to the reforming of reformation itself."[156] Now of this sense of England as a divinely-favored nation with an obligation to lead the world, there was very definitely an element in Harrington, for all his scorn of "saints." Add to it a strong sense of patriotism of a particular quality and a great admiration for the world-domination of ancient Rome, as these things were added in the case of Harrington, and one has laid the basis, not merely of a world leadership in thought, but of world dominion. Some such coalescing of the Puritan spirit with the imperialism of antique republicanism accounts for the presence in Harrington of such statements as that Oceana would be "a minister of God upon earth, to the end that the world may be governed with righteousness," and that it would spread its arms "like a holy Asylum unto the distressed world, and give the Earth her Sabbath of years, or rest from her labours."[157] It explains, too, his declaring that Oceana was "not made for herself only, but given as a Magistrate of God unto mankinde, for the vindication of common Right, and the law of Nature."[158] "Do not think," he wrote, "that the late appearances of God unto you, have been altogether for yourselves; he hath surely seen the affliction of your Brethren, and heard their cry, by reason of their taskmasters."[159]

It would be a mistake, however, to over-emphasize the rôle of what I have referred to as the Puritan spirit in Harrington's imperialism. That element was present, but it was only one of several.

[156] *P.w.*, II, 91.   [157] P. 188.   [158] P. 187. Cf. p. 184.   [159] P. 194.

Purely moral and practical considerations also actuated him. An imperial policy, he contended, was feasible, necessary, and morally obligatory. It was feasible because England would have two hundred men to do with for every hundred that Rome had, and because sea-power made it possible for her to send armies quickly to any part of the world, and to hold what she took.[160] That it was necessary was a consequence of the state of the world as Harrington saw it existing in his own time. All the nations of the modern world, Venice only excepted, were languishing in the dregs of modern or Gothic prudence. They had been ill-contrived states to begin with, and were now collapsing. If Oceana did not take the divinely-presented opportunity to secure the empire of the world, some other nation would assuredly have it. It was Harrington's conviction that the first modern state which recovered the health of ancient prudence would "assuredly govern the world."[161] It was his guess that if it was not England, it would be France.[162] It could never, of course, be Venice, which was a commonwealth for preservation, not expansion. The moral obligation Harrington saw as arising from the perfection with which he proposed to endow the government of Oceana. The common brotherhood of man imposed on a nation which had arrived at the felicity of government the obligation to further the cause of truth and justice in the world. "To ask," he asserted, "whether it bee lawfull for a Commonwealth to aspire unto the Empire of the World, is to ask whether it bee lawfull for her to do her duty; or to put the World into a better condition than it was before."[163]

Such statements make clear the quality of Harrington's imperialism. We must now examine its relation to the imperial policy of ancient Rome. The colonial policy which Harrington would have Oceana follow was to be as close a copy of what he conceived to be Roman practice as was his military system. Following Machiavelli, he found that states could expand in any one of three ways. The first was by imposing the yoke, the method used in ancient times by the Athenians and Spartans and by the modern monarchies. This was a contravention of the principles of the ancient commonwealths which used it, and Harrington called on his countrymen to avoid it. If they took this way to dominion, they would rain snares, but catch or hold nothing. "Lying lips," he declared, "are an abomination unto the Lord, if setting up for liberty you impose yoaks, hee will assuredly destroy you."[164] The second method of expansion

160 P. 196.   161 P. 197.   162 P. 197.   163 P. 193.   164 P. 195.

was by means of equal leagues, the method exemplified by the Swiss
and Dutch republics. But this method, he thought, was both useless
to the world and dangerous to the state employing it because the lack
of central authority made it impossible to marshal its resources ef-
fectively.[165] The third method of increase was by "unequal leagues,"
a system which Harrington thought had never been used in the
world, to its shame, except by republican Rome. The initial growth
of Rome, he declared, was by colonies; its later expansion by unequal
leagues, that is, relationships with other states which gave them varying degrees of local rights and government and other privileges, but
which still did not put them on a footing of equality with Rome itself. Roman leagues, Harrington found, were of two kinds, social
and provincial, the former being divided into those involving the extension of Latin right and those based on the granting of Italian
right. Citizens of a state to which Latin right had been granted had
their own laws and magistrates, but paid certain sums to Rome and
yielded to her in the conduct of all matters relating to the common
welfare. They also were adopted citizens of Rome with limited
privileges of suffrage unless they had borne magistracy of the rank
of *Aedile* or *Quaestor*, in which case they received full privileges.
Citizens of a state to which Italian right was extended also had
their own laws and magistrates in local government and some of the
privileges of Roman citizens but not the right to participate in
the Roman suffrage. Provincial leagues granted to a conquered people
varying privileges in accordance with their merits and capacities,
provinces being governed by a Roman magistrate, either a *Praetor*
or *Consul* in accordance with the rank of a province, and a *Quaestor*
who collected the revenue, from both of whom the province could
appeal to Rome.[166] Harrington illustrated the working of the Roman
system by an account of the three conquests of the Macedonians by
the Romans. When the first occurred, the Romans gave Philip of
Macedon's kingdom back to him on no other condition than that
he should set free the cities in Greece and Asia which he held in
subjection. Thus was effected a donation of Italian right to the
Greeks, some families and citizens for special merit being admitted to
Latin right. The second conquest resulted in a similarly liberal settlement, but on the second rebellion of the Macedonians, they were
considered to be incapable of liberty and were reduced to a province.[167]

[165] P. 189.   [166] Pp. 189–90.   [167] Pp. 190–92.

Such was the system which Harrington called on his countrymen to adopt. "If you have subdued a Nation that is capable of
liberty," he declared, "you shall make them a present of it, as
Flaminius unto Greece, and Aemilius unto Macedon; reserving unto
your selves some part of that revenue, which was legally paid unto
the former government, together with the right of being head of
the League, which includeth such Levyes of men and mony as shall
bee necessary for the carrying on of the publick work, for if a
people have by your means attained unto freedom, they owe both
unto the cause and you, such aid as may propagate the like fruit
unto the rest of the world."[168] But since all nations were not fit
for liberty, Harrington would have his countrymen diligently observe the degree of liberty which might be granted them and make
their arrangements accordingly. Oceana would then possess what
Cicero saw ancient Rome as having had, not so much the empire,
as the patronage of the world. Its rôle would be to lead the world
to civil liberty and liberty of conscience. The Lord of Hosts would
be its captain, and it would be a praise unto the earth.[169]

IV

Harrington did not get *Oceana* before the public without difficulty. It was seized while in the press by Thurloe's secret service,
and the material was not recovered until the author had secured
the intercession of Lady Claypool, Cromwell's daughter.[170] It came
out finally in the autumn of 1656 and caused a stir. "No sooner did
this Treatise appear," wrote Toland, "but it was greedily bought
up, and becom the subject of all men's discourse."[171] Cromwell
read it but was not impressed; he did not intend, he is reported to
have said, to give up his power for "a little paper shot."[172] A lively
interest in the book continued in the following year. Marchamont
Nedham, that turncoat of pamphleteers, attempted to ridicule it in
Mercurius politicus,[173] and Matthew Wren produced a serious attack
in his *Considerations on Mr. Harrington's commonwealth of Oceana*,
to which Harrington replied shortly with his *Prerogative of popular
government*. He published also in 1657 the correspondence with
Henry Ferne in a controversy in which he had become involved.[174]

---

[168] P. 195.   [169] P. 194.   [170] Toland, *op. cit.*, p. xix.
[171] P. xxiv.   [172] *Ibid.*, p. xx.   [173] No. 352.
[174] *Pian piano, or an intercourse between H. Ferne, Doctor in Divinity, and James Harrington, Esq.*

When the death of Cromwell in September, 1658, seemed to open new opportunities, Harrington again advanced his ideas in *Divers models of government.* The period which began with the summoning of Richard Cromwell's Parliament for January 27, 1659, and ended with Monk's dismissal of the Rump on February 21, 1660, was to be Harrington's great year, a year which saw in succession the Protectorate of Richard Cromwell, the reassembling of the Long Parliament, Lambert's coup of October 13, which sent the Parliament home and led to the Committee of Safety, and the recall of the Rump on December 26 and its final inglorious sitting. The instability of the government and the necessity of settling it upon some firm foundation if a restoration of the monarchy was to be avoided, invited the activities of constitution-makers. Plans of all sorts were in the air.[175] It was Harrington's great chance, and both he and his followers made full use of it. With indefatigable zeal he poured forth a steady stream of pamphlets explaining his ideas or showing how they could be put into effect.[176] An anonymous follower produced *A modest plea for an equal commonwealth against monarchy*, and other tracts appeared reflecting one aspect or another of Harrington's views.[177] He also had his champions in the Commons. The Parliament which assembled on January 27, 1659, contained several professed Harringtonians who made repeated speeches advocating his proposals.[178] Among these speakers was Henry Nevill, a republican so closely identified with Harrington that he was rumored to have had a hand in the *Oceana* itself.[179] Nevill in conjunction with Henry Marten and John Wildman, both well-known republicans, presently published a letter to Fleetwood advocating Harringtonian ideas. The

[175] Edmund Ludlow, *Memoirs* (Vevey, 1698–99, 3 vols.), II, 98–99.

[176] These included in 1659 *Pour enclouer le canon*, written to show how the Long Parliament could institute Oceana; *A discourse upon this saying: the spirit of the nation is not yet to be trusted with liberty; A discourse shewing that the spirit of parliaments, with a council in the intervals is not to be trusted for a settlement; Politicaster*, an answer to Wren; *Aphorisms political; A parallel of the spirit of the people*, in reply to an attack by John Rogers; and *Valerius and Publicola, a dialogue.* In the first months of 1660 came *The rota; The ways and means whereby an equal and lasting commonwealth may be suddenly introduced; The art of law-giving;* and *A word concerning the house of peers.* He had worked his scheme out once and for all in the *Oceana* and none of these later tracts made any essential modification in it.

[177] *Speculum libertatis Angliae re restitutae; Chaos; The leveller.*

[178] These are well treated by Smith, *op. cit.*, pp. 82–84, who quotes Burton's *Diary*, III, 31, 132–33, 147, 321, 331, 335. Smith's account of the activity of the Harringtonians is excellent and I wish to acknowledge my indebtedness to it in this section.

[179] This seems to me to be extremely unlikely. The *Oceana* has such a strongly marked character of its own and is so much of a piece in both conception and style that it is improbable that more than one hand could have produced it.

Long Parliament, which assembled in May, was cold to the advocates of *Oceana*, as a body so tenacious of existence well might be. *The humble petition of divers well-affected persons* which Nevill presented to this group on July 6 was received with thanks, but elicited nothing more. The period of Harrington's greatest activity came with the dismissal of this body as a result of Lambert's coup on October 13. But at this point Harrington's story becomes inseparable from that of the famous Rota Club which he founded to expound his ideas, and which was in full swing by the middle or first part of the month. Milton's friend, Cyriack Skinner, sometimes presided, as did also William Poulteney, who was later, after the Restoration, to commit Harrington to the Tower. Nevill, of course, was one of the principal participants. Others included Wildman, Sir William Petty, Roger Coke, all well-known figures, and John Aubrey, who left in his *Brief lives* the interesting description which is one of our chief sources of information about the club.[180] Pepys attended a meeting on January 17, 1660, and it was visited also by Harrington's friend Andrew Marvell. Other visitors included a great variety of personages, among whom military men were not uncommon. "The room," Aubrey tells us, "was every evening full as it could be cramm'd." The meeting place was "at the (then) Turke's head, in the New Palaceyard, where they take water, the next house to the staires, at one Miles's, where was made purposely a large ovall-table, with a passage in the middle for Miles to deliver his Coffee." On occasions when the crowd became too large, the club "adjourned to the Rhenish-wine howse." In the same writer's opinion, the debates were incomparably superior to those to be heard in Parliament. It seemed to him that the discourses of the "disciples, and the virtuosi" were "the most ingeniose and smart" that ever he had heard. Harrington published the rules of the club in his tract *The Rota* early in 1660. From these, it appears that the procedure followed a fixed pattern. A proposer⋅brought in a model of a free state, after having it printed, and presented it to the group. At least one day had to elapse before it could be considered. It was then discussed clause by

---

[180] Ed. Andrew Clark (Oxford, 1898, 2 vols.), II, 288–91. With Aubrey's account should be compared Anthony à Wood, *Athenae Oxonienses*, III, 115 f. A good deal can be gleaned also from *The censure of the Rota upon Mr. Miltons book entituled, The ready and easie way to establish a free commonwealth* (London, 1660). This clever tract, a royalist burlesque at the expense of both Harrington and Milton, purports to record an evening at the club at which Milton's views were discussed and voted down. A facsimile reproduction of this pamphlet may be found in Professor W. R. Parker's *Milton's contemporary reputation* (Columbus, O., 1940).

clause, and the question was put to the ballot-box. "This gang," wrote Wood, "had a balloting box, and balloted how things should be carried, by way of *tentamens*." He adds, rather maliciously, that the circumstance of this "being not used or known in England before" was the reason for the crowds which attended the meetings. Sometimes the orderliness of the proceedings was disturbed by unfriendly invaders. "One Stafford, a gent. of Northamptonshire, who used to be an auditor," says Wood, "did with his gang come among them one evening very mellow from the tavern, and did much affront the junto, and tore in pieces their orders and minutes. The soldiers who commonly were there, as auditors and spectators, would have kicked them down stairs; but Harrington's moderation and persuasion hindered them."

The immense activity of Harrington and his friends provoked another type of attack, that of the pamphleteers. In addition to *The censure of the Rota*, which argued that commonwealths were founded in "Faction, Sedition, Rebellion, Rapine, and Murther,"[181] and that the republicans drew all their ideas from lying declaimers among the ancients,[182] the chief were Richard Baxter's *Holy commonwealth*, which assailed Harrington for following the model of Venice, "where Popery ruleth and whoredom abounds,"[183] and condemned *Oceana* as an example of that democracy which he considered the worst of all governments;[184] and Matthew Wren's *Monarchy asserted, or the state of monarchicall and popular government*, which attacked Harrington's division of prudence into ancient and modern,[185] and condemned the notion of an immortal government, devoting an entire chapter to proving that Sparta, Venice, and Oceana were all imperfect.[186] This idea was criticized also in a royalist tract of 1660 attributed to Sir Roger L'Estrange and described as "an efficacious antidote against republicans," which came out under the title of *A plea for limited monarchy, as it was established in this nation before the late war*.[187] Masson records a royalist squib of November 12, 1659, in which the Rota-men were represented as indulging in the project of surveying the government of the moon and as recommending Harrington's *Aphorisms* to Jamaica.[188]

Such attacks had no influence whatever on the activities of the Harringtonians. The Rota Club flourished during November, December, and January, and meetings continued through most of

[181] Pp. 6–7.   [182] P. 8.   [183] Pp. 225–26.   [184] Pp. 67, 69.
[185] (Oxford, 1659), pp. 2–3.   [186] Pp. 65–90.
[187] P. 14.   [188] *The life of John Milton*, V, 509.

February. It was flying, however, in a direction counter to the course of history, and presently it met obstacles too formidable to be overcome. About February 20 or 21, says Aubrey, "upon the unexpected turne upon generall Monke's comeing-in, all these airie modells vanished."[189]

---

[189] Harrington's subsequent fate was a melancholy one. After the Restoration, he busied himself in writing a new version of his theories in *A system of politics*, a work which was left in manuscript and first published by Toland in his edition of 1700. Late in 1661, he was arrested for treason and charged with being implicated in a republican plot against the government and the king (Toland, pp. xxx–xxxi). There is little or no reason to suppose the charges against him well founded. His plea that Aristotle, Livy, and Machiavelli had been permitted to utter republican sentiments while living under other forms of government went unheard. He was first imprisoned in the Tower, then on St. Nicholas Island off Plymouth to thwart a habeas corpus, and finally in Plymouth. He was badly treated during his imprisonment, a circumstance which affected both his health and his mind (*ibid.*, pp. xxxv–xxxvi). It is hard to know whether the treatment administered by his physician was the result of malice or the medical ignorance of the age (*ibid.*, p. xxxvii). He was never brought to trial and was finally released, spending the remainder of his years in retirement. He died in 1677.

CHAPTER FOUR

IMMORTAL GOVERNMENT: THE FREE COMMONWEALTH

I refuse not the pains to be so much historical, as will serve to show what hath been done by ancient and famous commonwealths.—Areopagitica
Did you not remember that the commonwealth of the people of Rome flourished and became glorious when they had banished their kings?—First defense of the English people

THE SPIRIT of antique republicanism hovered over John Milton from the very beginning of the Puritan Revolution, long before he himself realized that he was a republican. Aubrey's statement that it was the poet's "being so conversant in Livy and the Roman authors, and the greatness he saw done by the Roman Commonwealth" that induced him to write against monarchy[1] doubtless does not represent the whole truth, for the course of contemporary events and other factors were also largely involved, but it certainly represents an important part of it. In the *Areopagitica*, he justified by classical precedent his giving advice to Parliament, and like an orator of old undertook to instruct an assembly which he saw in terms of the Areopagus of ancient Athens and which he advised to imitate the "old and elegant humanity of Greece" and "those ages, to whose polite wisdom and letters we owe that we are not yet Goths and Jutlanders" rather than the "barbaric pride of a Hunnish and Norwegian stateliness."[2] In the middle decade of the century, the classical republics were ever in his mind. He saw the great figures of his own time as Catos and Brutuses. He compared Vane to a Roman senator,[3] Fairfax to Scipio and "the heroes of antiquity,"[4] Cromwell to "Cyrus . . . Epaminondas, or any of the great generals of antiquity."[5] In the *Second defense*, even in the very moment of denying that an extravagant emulation of the ancients had produced the events of the time, he made explicit the parallel between himself, defending the people of England, and the "illustrious orators of antiquity."[6] In *The ready and easy way to establish a free commonwealth* he chided

---

[1] *Op. cit.*, II, 69.   [2] *P.w.*, II, 52–53.   [3] Sonnet XVII.
[4] *P.w.*, I, 287. Cf. p. 23.   [5] *P.w.*, I, 286.   [6] *P.w.*, I, 218–19.

his countrymen for the delay in building Rome anew in the West.[7]

But it was not merely that Milton's view of the contemporary situation was colored by a vision of the splendors of antique republicanism. Two theories of the age which he connected specifically with his political hopes gave to classical models an added significance. One of these was the notion, widely prevalent in the seventeenth century, of the decay of the universe— the idea that the world was running down and nearing its end.[8] This theory carried with it clear implications for modern man. It led easily to the conclusion that the later ages were the lesser ages; that the moderns did not and, worse yet, could not equal the ancients; that, as Sir Thomas Browne put it, it was too late in time to be ambitious;[9] and that there was nothing left for modern men but to imitate the more perfect ages. As a young man, Milton had looked at this view of things insofar as it related to the physical universe, and denied it in his *Naturam non pati senium*. But it is clear that it was a notion that troubled him. In the *Areopagitica*, he welcomed the intellectual ferment of the time as a sign that "betokens us not degenerated, nor drooping to a fatal decay."[10] Elsewhere he considered the possibility that "the fate of this age" might be against him.[11] As if it were the expression of an ill-suppressed fear, the word "degenerate" sprang easily to his lips when things did not go as he wished.[12] In *The tenure of kings and magistrates* he alluded to the possibility that future ages might prove to be degenerate,[13] and in Book IX of *Paradise lost* he considered gravely the possibility that an age "too late" might damp his hopes to produce the great poem that after ages would not willingly let die.[14]

The other widespread belief of the time which was not without its influence on Milton's political thinking was the idea that climate profoundly influenced the physical and mental characteristics of peoples as a result of its effect on the humors of the body. This idea, which rested ultimately on a famous passage in Aristotle's *Politics*,[15] had been elaborated by the beginning of the seventeenth

---

[7] *P.w.*, II, 114.

[8] This theory has been much studied in recent years, notably by R. F. Jones in *Ancients and moderns: a study of the background of the "Battle of the books,"* (Washington university studies in language and literature, New series, St. Louis, 1936), pp. 23–42.

[9] *Works*, ed. G. L. Keynes (London, 1928–31, 6 vols.), IV, 45.   [10] *P.w.*, II, 94.

[11] *P.w.*, II, 478–79.   [12] *P.w.*, II, 114.   [13] *P.w.*, II, 34.   [14] Ll. 41–47.

[15] In VII, vii, Aristotle contrasted the Greeks with dwellers in cold climates like the Northern Europeans, who were full of courage but wanting in understanding and the arts and deficient in political capacities, and with the Asiatics, who had quick understandings but were wanting in courage. The Greeks, being situated between the two, were described as both courageous and intelligent and as being governed in the best possible manner.

century, at the hands of such writers as Bodin and Botero, into a
complex set of notions, prominent among which was the idea that
cold northern climates such as that of England made men dull-witted
and lacking in subtlety.[16] This curious idea, which was much noticed
in England[17] and of which traces long survived in English thought,[18]
bothered Milton even more than the notion of the degeneracy of the
modern world.[19] In his most optimistic moments, by which I mean
the period before his disillusionment in the Presbyterians, he could
at times shake it off,[20] but the fear that it was true was a recurrent

[16] Bodin, op. cit., V, i, pp. 547, 548, 550, 554, 561, 563, 567; Botero, Relations, pp.
1–19; A discovery of the great subtiltie and wonderful wisedome of the Italians (London,
1591), sig. A2v. The theory varied somewhat from writer to writer. I cite these three
as representative of characteristic forms of it, not as exhaustive of the subject. For a discussion of their views see Appendix A.

[17] Nashe, Works, ed. R. B. McKerrow (London, 1904, 6 vols.), III, 322; Cowley,
Preface to Poems, 1656 in Critical essays of the seventeenth century, ed. J. E. Spingarn
(Oxford, 1908, 3 vols.), II, 80–81; Thomas Wright, The passions of the minde (London,
1630, 2nd ed.), sig. A7v; John Barclay, The mirrour of mindes: or Barclays Icon animorum,
trans. Thomas May (London, 1631), ch. x. It is symptomatic of the seriousness with
which the theory was viewed that one finds English writers attempting by various shifts
to dodge the implications of its full acceptance. Thus Barclay asserted that though the
climatic theory was generally true, there were in every climate exceptions to it, and
Thomas Wright centered his attention upon correcting by education and knowledge the
defects caused in his countrymen by their climate. The theory, however, did not by any
means pass unchallenged in England. See my reference to Nashe above and also Wright,
sig. A5r. Cf. Samuel Daniel, Works, ed. A. B. Grosart (London, 1885–96, 5 vols.),
III, 26.

[18] In the Prologue to Aureng-Zebe Dryden wrote: "And wit in northern climates will
not blow." Pope alluded to the idea in the Essay on criticism as one held by a certain type
of false critic (II, 398–401). See also Sterne, Tristram Shandy, ed. James A. Work (New
York, 1940), pp. 151–52 and cf. p. 64; The guardian, No. 144 (August 26, 1713); and The
mirror, No. 18 (March 27, 1779).

[19] It bothered him, of course, not only because of his political plans, but also because
of its relation to his poetical hopes and ambitions, a matter of which he was very much
aware. One of his earliest references to the influence of climate, that in the Mansus,
ll. 24 ff., involves the question of whether climate and poetical genius are related. The
question appears again in the passage in The reason of church government in which he
discusses his poetical plans (P.w., II, 478–79). In the Second defense he welcomed the
example of Queen Christina of Sweden as evidence that in some, at least, genius could
flourish even in the frozen north (P.w., I, 250). The most interesting passage, however,
is that near the beginning of Book IX of Paradise lost in which he includes "cold climat"
among the things which might damp his intended wing (ll. 41–47). For a fuller treatment
of this matter together with the suggestion that the effect of the climatic theory was
ultimately to force Milton back upon greater dependence on the idea of divine inspiration as a means of overcoming the defects caused in Englishmen by climate, see my
article "Milton and the theory of climatic influence," in The modern language quarterly,
II (1941), 67–80.

[20] In the Mansus passage Milton describes himself as a "youthful traveler from Hyper-
borean realms" and says that Manso in his kindness "will not disdain so distant a Muse,
who reared under hard conditions in the frozen North, recently dared in her rashness to
fly through the cities of Italy." The tone sounds apologetic, as if he were conceding

one[21] and in his most pessimistic hours he was sure it was. How he felt at such moments and how it influenced his political thinking is vividly brought out by the following passage in that *Character of the Long Parliament* which he wrote sometime between 1647 and 1649 as part of the Third book of his *History of Britain* and later suppressed when that work was published:

For Britain, to speak a truth not often spoken, as it is a land fruitful enough of men stout and courageous in war, so it is naturally not over-fertile of men able to govern justly and prudently in peace, trusting only in their mother-wit; who consider not justly, that civility, prudence, love of the public good, more than of money or vain honour, are to this soil in a manner outlandish; grow not here, but in minds well implanted with solid and elaborate breeding, too impolitic else and rude, if not headstrong and intractable to the industry and virtue either of executing or understanding true civil government. Valiant indeed, and prosperous to win a field; but to know the end and success of winning, unjudicious and unwise: in good or bad success, alike unteachable. For the sun, which we want, ripens wits as well as fruits; and as wine and oil are imported to us from abroad, so must ripe understanding, and many civil virtues, be imported into our minds from foreign writings, and examples of best ages: we shall else miscarry still, and come short in the attempts of any great enterprise."[22]

Milton's subsequent references to the climatic theory are not all in a tone as dismal as this one, but they suggest that at no time after the late 1640's was he able wholly to put the idea aside. Contemplating the effect of events on his attitude toward the theory at the time when he wrote the *Character*, one is led to suspect that a

that the North had a harmful effect on poetical genius, but in the lines immediately following he very definitely undertakes to vindicate his countrymen from the charge of being "useless to Phoebus" and in effect denies the whole climatic theory. Also symptomatic of his earlier attitude is the "Lords and commons of England" passage in the *Areopagitica* (*P.w.*, II, 90). It is true that this passage says nothing about climate directly, but no one familiar with the climatic theory can read it without seeing that the virtues which it claims for Englishmen are precisely those which that theory would deny them. This circumstance when coupled with the fact that a reference elsewhere in the tract shows that the climatic theory was in Milton's mind at the time (p. 53) leaves little room for question as to what he was thinking of.

[21] The fact is suggested by the frequency with which he alluded to the notion. There are at least eight direct references. In addition to those referred to in the two preceding notes, see *In quintum Novembris* and the so-called "Digression" in the *History of Britain* (*P.w.*, V, 240). Cf. also *Ad Salsillum*, ll. 9–16; the remarks on the "fluxible fault" in *The ready and easy way* (*P.w.*, II, 124); *Of education* (*P.w.*, III, 468); and *The reason of church government* (*P.w.*, II, 470). T. B. Stroup calls attention to several oblique allusions in "Implications of the theory of climatic influence in Milton," in *Modern language quarterly*, IV (1943), 186.

[22] *P.w.*, V, 240. For a discussion of the date and other questions connected with the *Character* see Appendix B.

similar result was produced by the events of the late 1650's, alike disappointing to him, a conjecture which the reference to the effect of cold climates in the Ninth book of *Paradise lost* tends to confirm. It would seem a reasonable inference that the long-time effect of both the theories which troubled Milton, that of climatic influence and that of the decay of the world, was to bolster his feeling that his countrymen would do well to imitate the "best ages"—which always meant to him the classical ages.

But if Milton looked to classical precedents in political theory, his attitude was not an uncomplicated one, nor was it wholly of a piece with Harrington's. In the thought of the two men, indeed, there were important differences. Harrington examined the English constitution only to show that it had been defective at every stage in its history; he dismissed it in one summary designation of it as having the characteristic defects of Gothic or modern prudence. He did this with no violence to his feelings of patriotism, for all his patriotism was concentrated on his glowing vision of a future in which an England reformed by ancient prudence would lead the world. But with Milton the situation was not so simple. His mind had dwelt lovingly on the heroic legends of his race, which, when the Civil War opened, he was still planning to celebrate in a great epic poem. Patriotic feeling in Milton was not without its glance at the future,[23] its roseate vision of the present, but it was haunted in the earlier years with memories of an heroic past. The man who declared that God revealed truth first to His Englishmen[24] had his moments when he could declare that his countrymen were acting without precedents,[25] that they stood in no need of foreign examples, either ancient or modern,[26] that their ancestors had provided them with examples as noble as any in the world and that they had fashioned the English state "with no less prudence, and in as much liberty as the most worthy of the ancient Romans or Grecians ever founded any of theirs."[27] Even so

[23] The military aspects of Harrington's imperialism find little counterpart in Milton, but of what may be called intellectual imperialism, as I have pointed out in the preceding chapter, there was plenty. A passage in the *Second defense* in which he saw his countrymen as destined to lead the world in the recovery of liberty is so remarkable that I quote it in full: "Surrounded by congregated multitudes, I now imagine that, from the columns of Hercules to the Indian Ocean, I behold the nations of the earth recovering that liberty which they so long had lost; and that the people of this island are transporting to other countries a plant of more beneficial qualities, and more noble growth, than that which Triptolemus is reported to have carried from region to region; that they are disseminating the blessings of civilization and freedom among cities, kingdoms, and nations" (*P.w.*, I, 220). See also Milton's statement in *The doctrine and discipline of divorce:* "Let not England forget her precedence of teaching nations how to live" (*P.w.*, III, 178).
[24] *P.w.*, II, 91. [25] *P.w.*, II, 34. [26] *P.w.*, I, 210.
[27] *P.w.*, I, 177. See also p. 210.

late as *The ready and easy way* he could take a fling at those who would follow "exotic models" in reforming the state.[28] The existence of this attitude in Milton's political thinking was to be a complicating factor from the start; it accounts for the direction which his ideas took on certain matters, and it made imperative an attempt on his part to reconcile it with his regard for classical political thought. Feeling as he did in the early years of the 1640's, he could not have begun his career as a tractarian as he did begin it, supplied with a political theory borrowed from classical sources, without finding an essential harmony between that theory and traditional English practice. In fact, it was precisely with such a harmony established that he started.

II

Milton's relation to the theory of the mixed state is clear and definite at the beginning of his career as a political thinker. He knew Polybius; he accepted the theory of the superiority of mixed government; he saw in Rome and Sparta models of political organization; he thought of England as having a mixed constitution, of the English monarchy as being, indeed, in its proper constitution a supreme example of the balanced state; and, with approval, he conceived of the English government as representing that type of mixed state in which the noblest and worthiest men, the aristocratic element, held through the Parliament the preponderance of power. These are not matters for conjecture; two passages in *Of reformation in England* present us with indisputable evidence of his position:

The best-founded commonwealths and least barbarous have aimed at a certain mixture and temperament, partaking the several virtues of each other state, that each part drawing to itself may keep up a steady and even up-uprightness in common. . . . There is no civil government that hath been known, no not the Spartan, not the Roman, though both for this respect so much praised by the wise Polybius, more divinely and harmoniously tuned, more equally balanced as it were by the hand and scale of justice, than is the commonwealth of England; where under a free and untutored monarch, the noblest, worthiest, and most prudent men, with full approbation and suffrage of the people, have in their power the supreme and final determination of highest affairs.[29]

This passage, it is clear, describes England in its proper constitution before its perversion by the corruptions of the time. In the second key passage, Milton is speaking of the benefits which would result from the abolition of those corruptions:

Then shall the nobles possess all the dignities and offices of temporal

[28] *P.w.*, II, 127.   [29] *P.w.*, II, 408.

honor to themselves, sole lords without the improper mixture of scholastic and pusillanimous upstarts; the parliament should void her upper house of the same annoyances; the common and civil laws shall be set free.[30] It is clear from the first of these passages that Milton saw the monarchial or magisterial element as represented in England by the king, and the democratic element as consisting of the "full approbation and suffrage of the people." What he saw the aristocratic element as being is to be deduced from both statements. On the carrying out of the reforms he proposed, he tells us that the nobility would then have "all the dignities and offices of temporal honor." He meant exactly what he said. But I hasten to add that, as is true of all of the classical republicans, it is important to notice what he meant by nobility. Of the nobility of title he was scornful.[31] Fundamentally he saw in virtue, goodness, godliness, and patriotic and disinterested service to one's country the essence of nobility. Those were noble who labored virtuously and learnedly for God and the happiness and glory of England.[32] In this sense Milton himself—he who sought to teach the truth to his countrymen—was a nobleman.[33] Whatever may have been Francini's intentions in addressing his complimentary ode to "Signor Gio. Miltoni Nobile Inglese," Milton himself would not have repudiated this description. The source of true nobility, then, was personal worth, godliness, and goodness in the service of the state. With this conception went two other ideas: that nobility derives in some cases, at least, from the inspiration of God,[34] and that the "middle sort" of people are the great fountain head of that virtue from which true nobility proceeds.[35] Yet Milton did not by any means repudiate wholly the conception that nobility is conferred by distinguished descent. Though stoutly maintaining that

[30] *P.w.*, II, 409. The remark about scholastic upstarts is not, of course, to be construed as an attack on learned men in government, which would indeed be a most un-Miltonic thing. "Scholastic" refers to scholastic learning, and has in this passage all the connotations of ignorance and illiteracy which scholasticism suggested to Milton. The charge is that the bishops should have no part in the government because among other things they were ignorant. A few paragraphs below, Milton asserts that for twelve centuries the bishops had been ignorant and illiterate (p. 411). Cf. III, 87.

[31] *P.w.*, I, 154, 170; II, 23. Milton repeatedly pointed out that anciently the commons were comprehended in the terms "peers" and "barons" (*P.w.*, I, 167, 175).

[32] *P.w.*. I, 16; II, 266–67; *Works*, Columbia ed., XVIII, 195, 340.

[33] See Milton's description of himself as one who had zealously prepared to serve God and his country (*P.w.*, III, 112–13). [34] *Works*, XVIII, 195.

[35] *P.w.*, I, 155. Cf. I, 291. Among the "middle sort," says Milton, "the most prudent men, and most skilful in affairs, are generally found; others are most commonly diverted either by luxury and plenty, or by want and poverty, from virtue, and the study of laws and government." Cf. Sir Walter Raleigh on "the middle sort of people" in *Remains*, p. 16.

the nobility of personal worth was as high as any in the land, he would have agreed with the idea later advanced by Algernon Sydney that the descendants of those whose virtue had ennobled them should be considered noble until their actions proved them otherwise.[36] From the nobility thus defined Milton saw the members of Parliament, particularly the House of Commons, as being selected. In the Commons he saw an assembly of the "noblest, worthiest, and most prudent men," chosen from the true aristocracy of the state and representing therefore not merely the whole people by the manner of their selection, but the true aristocracy by the class from which they were selected. Parliament, particularly the House of Commons, was therefore the aristocratic element in the mixed state which Milton conceived England to be. Moreover, he believed that it was the element which should have predominant power. The "noblest, worthiest, and most prudent men," he says specifically, "have in their power the supreme and final determination of highest affairs." Thus there emerge from *Of reformation in England* two great political ideas: that mixed states are superior to all others, and that in a mixed state the nobility, the wise and the good, the aristocratic element, should dominate. These, we shall find, are the constant elements in Milton's political thought. They will not change, though much else will.

Our first problem is that of the relation of the principle of mixed government to Milton's arguments against episcopacy. In the *Commonplace book* is the following significant entry: "The clergie commonly the corrupters of kingly authority turning it to tyrannie by thire wicked flatteries even in the pulpit."[37] The argument to which this leads when coupled with the idea of the superiority of mixed government is obvious. In *Of reformation in England* it is pre-

---

[36] In the *First defense* Milton declares that some of the Puritan leaders came from noble ancestry equal to any in the land, and that others had "taken a course to attain to true nobility by their own industry and virtue, and are not inferior to men of the noblest descent" (*P.w.*, I, 16). He was at great pains to vindicate the essential nobility and even gentle descent of the Puritan leaders. He tells us in one place that most of the members of Parliament were "either of ancient and high nobility, or at least of known and well-reputed ancestry" (*P.w.*, III, 145). See further his description of Cromwell's ancestry (*P.w.*, I, 285). One basis of Milton's attack on episcopacy was that it raised to positions of influence in the state men of mean and ignoble birth (*P.w.*, III, 166; cf. II, 409). What was Milton's attitude toward his own ancestry? In the *Second defense* he remarks that he came of honest stock ("*genere honesto*") (*P.w.*, I, 254). The anonymous *Life of Milton* tells us that he was said to be descended from "an ancient knightly family of Buckinghamshire" (*The student's Milton*, ed. F. A. Patterson [New York, 1933, rev. ed.], p. xvi). Edward Phillips says that Milton was said to be descended from the "ancient family of the Miltons of Milton" (*ibid.*, p. xxxii).   [37] *Works*, XVIII, 175.

cisely this coupling which is made, together with the parallel idea
that just as episcopacy seeks to undermine the liberty of the people,[38]
so does it seek to get into its own hands the powers of the king.[39]
England, the argument runs, is a supreme example of the mixed state
in which the king, the aristocracy, and the people all have their due
shares. Episcopacy is a foreign element in the state[40] composed of men
whose aim is the aggrandizement of civil power and ultimately
the establishment of their own supremacy,[41] and who in the pursuit
of this object seek at once to undermine the liberties of the subject
and to seize the prerogatives of the king.[42] Episcopacy, in short, is
incompatible with, and ultimately destructive of, such a mixed
government as Milton conceived England to have. It is, indeed, incompatible with any mixed or balanced state because its aim is the
overturn of all balance and the establishment of its own theocratical
tyranny. The damage which had been done by the bishops in England
was great. A state which was in its own proper form and constitution the most perfect pattern of government in the world had been
turned into the "floating carcase of a crazy and diseased monarchy
or state."[43] But it was not too late and the damage was not irreparable.
On the twin beliefs that England in its proper constitution was a perfect example of the mixed state and that episcopacy, the corrupting
element, the wen, needed but to be removed to bring about the perfectly functioning state, Milton's utopian fervor in 1641 took wing
and soared to the extraordinary apostrophe with which *Of reformation in England* ends.

One more observation on the anti-episcopal tracts. We have seen
Milton taking over the theory of the mixed state from classical,
specifically Polybian sources,[44] and discovering that England in its

[38] Cf. Milton's assertion in the *Apology for Smectymnuus* that the clergy seek the dissolution of law and the erection of an arbitrary sway (*P.w.*, III, 163).

[39] *P.w.*, II, 393 f.

[40] Significant is Milton's comparison of episcopacy to a wen which should be cut off
(*P.w.*, II, 398).

[41] Milton advances as a perfect example of his argument the way in which the bishops
of Rome seized more and more power until eventually they made themselves supreme
temporal rulers (*P.w.*, II, 394–95). See also p. 396. On p. 397 he tells us that men have
as good reason to fear civil usurpation by the Anglican episcopacy as in former times
they had of the papal.

[42] Milton rather confusingly uses the term "supremacy of the king," but by the very
theory of mixed government which he explicitly sets forth in the tract (*P.w.*, II, 403,
408), "supremacy" can mean nothing more than the just powers of the monarch under
the law.   [43] *P.w.*, II, 391.

[44] That he got it also from Machiavelli is clear. There are repeated references to the
Discourses in the *Commonplace book*. See *Works*, XVIII, 160, 183, 197, 199, 200, 210, 211,
212, 215, 217.

proper constitution exemplified the theory. What he was really asserting was that the original institutions of the country involved the
principles of mixed government, and this, in fact, is precisely what
his argument later turned into in the *Eikonoklastes*[45] and the *First
defense*.[46] The point is an important one because it was by this conception that he attempted to harmonize the idea of the mixed state
and following the "best ages" and best examples—Rome, Sparta,
Athens,[47] and later Venice—with his patriotic pride in England and
his proposal to reform the country by the pattern of its ancient institutions. The attempt succeeded well enough at first, but after
the early 1640's it was never too successful. It came closest to success, perhaps, in the *First defense*, in which the specific adherence
to the theory of the mixed state, the citations of old English practice,
and the constant references to classical authorities and examples
presuppose that all three led to common conclusions.[48] Yet even in
this work we find Milton on one page exalting clear classical precedents over medieval obscurities and on another declaring that the
English had the best laws in the world and stood in no need of outside examples.[49] In the end, as we shall see, the attempt to harmonize
the notion of a return to old English principles with imitation of the
great classical mixed states was destined to break down.

III

We have seen Milton in 1641 an adherent of the theory of mixed
government. The tracts of 1649 and the early 1650's show him holding fast to the idea. Three specific statements, one in the *Eikonoklastes*[50] and two in the *First defense*,[51] make the matter clear. These
tracts involve us, therefore, in three great problems: the relation of
kingship and of the doctrines of popular sovereignty and parliamentary supremacy to the theory of mixed government.

As we have seen, the doctrine of sovereignty did not play an important role in discussions of the mixed state before and even during

[45] *P.w.*, I, 351.   [46] *P.w.*, I, 172, 210.
[47] On the way in which Athens had been assimilated into the theory of the mixed
state see above, p. 57. There was, therefore, no inconsistency between Milton's acceptance of the theory of mixed government and the admiration for Athens which he
expressed (*P.w.*, II, 136).   [48] *P.w.*, I, 15, 88, 160, 167, 172–77, 183, 188.
[49] *P.w.*, I, 168, 210, 177. Cf. 205.   [50] *P.w.*, I, 363. Cf. 360–61.
[51] *P.w.*, I, 88, 160. The first of these is particularly significant because in it we find him
citing Lycurgus as the introducer of mixed government in Sparta and remarking that he
had "left a good example" to modern times. In the second passage Sir Thomas Smith
is quoted as authority for the statement that a government would not last long unless it
was mixed.

the greater part of the sixteenth century. Polybius, like Sir Thomas Smith, was content to say that in such a state power was divided.[52] Once the idea of mixed government was complicated, however, by the concept of sovereignty, a development which was made inevitable by Bodin's great exposition of "*puissance souveraine*"[53] and his use of the concept to attack the theory of mixed government, three positions were possible. One could hold in defiance of Bodin, as Sir Thomas Smith quite probably would have held, had the problem occurred to him, that in a mixed state sovereignty was divided; or one could hold that sovereignty is indivisible and that therefore a mixed state was an impossibility;[54] or one could maintain that though sovereignty itself is indivisible, power could be delegated in varying proportions to different bodies in the state representing the magisterial, aristocratic, and democratic elements, and that therefore there was no inconsistency between the doctrine of indivisible sovereignty and the concept of mixed government. The first of these positions was sometimes adopted by exponents of mixed polities, but it was highly vulnerable to attack by absolutists like Filmer who had read Bodin and learned how easy it was to prove sovereignty indivisible.[55] The second idea afforded absolutists who found sovereignty to reside in the monarch one of their leading arguments, as we shall shortly see. The third position, or some modification of it, was that toward which many advocates of mixed government gravitated.[56] Moreover, by the idea of the delegation of power, it was possible to believe at once in indivisible sovereignty, mixed government, and popular sovereignty, for if one conceived of sovereignty as residing in the people, one could then think of power as partly retained and partly delegated to the aristocratic and magisterial elements of the state. This was precisely the position at which Milton arrived. The result of his preoccupation in *The tenure of kings and magistrates* with the idea of an indivisible popular sovereignty[57]

---

[52] See the comments of J. W. Allen, *A history of political thought in the sixteenth century* (New York, 1928), p. 262.   [53] *Op. cit.*, I, viii, pp. 84 ff.; x, pp. 153 ff.

[54] That sovereignty is indivisible was asserted by both Bodin (II, i) and Hobbes (*Leviathan*, II, xix, xxix). That a mixed state was therefore an impossibility was Hobbes's contention (*op. cit.*, II, xix).

[55] See, for example, the high sport which Filmer has with Hunton's remark in the *Treatise of monarchy* that in a mixed monarchy the sovereign power must be originally in all three estates (*The anarchy of a limited or mixed monarchy*, pp. 242–43). See further Hobbes, *op. cit.*, I, xxix.

[56] See, for example, Algernon Sydney, *Discourses concerning government*, I, xx.

[57] That Milton did not believe in the theory of divided sovereignty is clear from the fact that he repeatedly points out that the whole power of a king is delegated power,

was not to lessen in any way the hold of the idea of mixed government on him, but to develop that theory by harmonizing with it the concept of the sovereignty of the people.[58] What resulted from the amalgamation of the two ideas was a theory the cardinal points of which were precisely that sovereignty is indivisible, that it resides in the people,[59] and that it is partly retained by them[60] and partly delegated to bodies in the state representing the monarchic and aristocratic elements, namely, the magistracy and the Parliament. The fundamental Polybian theory of the mixed state, the idea that permanency and stability are secured by a division of power among the three elements of the state, remained.

I say that Milton arrived at a harmony of the concept of the mixed state and popular sovereignty, but before he could fully vindicate his position, he had to meet Salmasius. There were many points at issue between these two controversialists, but not the least of them was whether England was in its proper constitution a mixed state or an absolute monarchy with the indivisible sovereign power residing in the king. This was, indeed, a central issue of the whole controversy. Salmasius, as Milton understood him, based his case on two main points: that sovereignty is indivisible,[61] and that it resides in the king.[62] To prove that it resides in the monarch, Milton saw him resorting to the law of God,[63] the law of nature,[64] the theory of divine investiture,[65] and an analogy between the state and the family, if not indeed to the theory that the king is absolute as the inheritor of those divinely instituted, absolute parental rights out of which, by way of the expansion of the family into the state, government was supposed by some to have originated.[66] That sovereignty

that no share of power inheres in a king by divine or any other right simply because he is a king (*P.w.*, II, 11, 14). Likewise, the power of Parliament was delegated power (*P.w.*, I, 11; II, 121). I consider myself fully justified, therefore, in seeing in Milton an exponent of indivisible sovereignty. Anyone investigating Milton's views of the matter must look for the thing, not the word. His use of the word is somewhat ambiguous. That he was acquainted with it, however, in the sense which Bodin gave it is clear from the fact that it is used in that sense and that its meaning is expounded in Sir Walter Raleigh's *The cabinet council*, which Milton published in 1658 (see pp. 2–3).

[58] *P.w.*, II, 8–17; I, 88, 160.   [59] *P.w.*, II, 9 ff.; I, 33, 76; II, 121.
[60] *P.w.*, II, 14, 121; I, 33.   [61] *P.w.*, I, 160.
[62] *P.w.*, I, 30.   [63] *P.w.*, I, 60.   [64] *P.w.*, I, 32.   [65] *P.w.*, I, 94.
[66] *P.w.*, I, 20–21, 114, 156. Cf. Bodin, *op. cit.*, I, ii, and Sir Walter Raleigh, *Three discourses* (London, 1702), p. 105. For the views of Filmer, the great expounder of the doctrine in relation to the theory of divine right, see above, p. 27. For other treatments of the relation of the family to the state see *The bounds and bonds of publique obedience* (London, 1649), p. 17; and *Jus populi, or a discourse wherein clear satisfaction is given, as well concerning the rights of subjects, as the right of princes* (London, 1644), pp. 32–33. Consult also the answers to Filmer by Sydney, Locke, and Tyrrell noted above, p. 27.

was indivisible Milton did not dispute, but to the contention that it resided in the monarch by divine and natural law, he replied with the doctrine of popular sovereignty and the social compact[67] and with his own interpretations of the law of God[68] and the law of nature.[69] Salmasius's argument implied that a mixed state was the negation of all law and government.[70] Milton replied with the flat assertion that a pure tyranny or unmixed state such as Salmasius talked about neither ever had existed nor ever could exist.[71] He was, indeed, so far from abandoning the theory of mixed government as to assert, not merely that the best governments are mixed, but that all actual governments can never be anything else.[72] The central issues in the Milton-Salmasius controversy were well chosen. However absurd his argument may appear to us today, Salmasius knew what he was about, and Milton leaped to meet him on the issues which he had set. The result in the poet's mind was a triumphant vindication of the theory of mixed government and popular sovereignty.

As the controversy with Salmasius turned on whether England was a pure monarchy or a mixed state, so Milton's preoccupation with kingship in 1649 and the early 1650's resolved itself, philosophically considered, essentially into the question of how in a mixed state the monarchic or magisterial element could best be represented. It is clear that in 1641 he saw it as represented by the king. That it might be represented by a king he was still willing to admit in the *First defense*.[73] But that it was best when not so represented, many things conspired to convince him. Polybius had shown clearly that

Figgis is correct in saying that though the patriarchal theory is no essential part of the theory of divine right, it affords the best justification of it (*The divine right of kings*, p. 148). I am inclined to think, however, that he underestimates the importance of the idea in political thought before Filmer. The notion itself is, of course, as old at least as Aristotle (see *Politics*, I, ii) insofar as it relates simply to the origin of government, a fact which Filmer himself was careful to point out (*Observations upon Aristotle's Politiques*, ed. 1684, p. 91, and Preface, sig. G7r). The theory was, of course, not the only one about the origin of government which was held by advocates of royal supremacy. By the fiction that power once delegated could not be resumed, Hobbes contrived to make the idea of a social contract into an argument for the supremacy of the ruler, however the ruler was conceived (*Leviathan*, I, xiv; II, xviii). Filmer himself on occasion was capable of finding the social compact compatible with absolutism (*The anarchy of a limited or mixed monarchy*, pp. 245–54).

[67] *P.w.*, I, 42, 43, 46, 47, 76.   [68] *P.w.*, I, 35 ff.   [69] *P.w.*, I, 108–16.

[70] Cf. Filmer's *Anarchy of a limited or mixed monarchy* (1648).

[71] To prove the point he quotes Aristotle (*P.w.*, I, 37–38, 160) and Sir Thomas Smith (I, 160; cf. *Works*, XVIII, 176) and denies that even the kings in Oriental despotisms had absolute power (*P.w.*, I, 37).

[72] *P.w.*, I, 88, 160.   [73] *P.w.*, I, 33, 79, 88. Cf. I, 223, 249; II, 130.

the monarchic element might be present without there being any king. Rome not only proved the possibility but suggested that kings were best dispensed with. Such an exponent of the mixed state as Machiavelli told Milton that a republic was superior to a monarchy.[74] Plato and Aristotle taught him that monarchy was prone to degenerate into tyranny. The course of Charles I seemed to him to offer concrete proof of the assertion. Presently we find him saying that of all forms of government, monarchy was the one which turned most easily into tyranny.[75] But tyranny was by very definition inconsistent with, and destructive of, mixed government. Holding this principle, Milton was led inevitably to reject monarchy, that is, to reject kingship as a satisfactory representative of the monarchial or magisterial element in the state. It is doubtless futile to attempt to discover the precise point at which he arrived at this conclusion. Fundamental changes in men's views are frequently of long maturation, and the point at which one opinion is given up and another adopted is hard to define even if such a "point" exists to begin with.[76] But we can say that by the *First defense* Milton had arrived very definitely at the conclusion that a republic is superior to a monarchy as a means of realizing the ideal of a mixed state.[77]

We can go further. Not only had Milton definitely rejected monarchy. One can already see in the germ in the *First defense* the idea out of which developed his ultimate conception of what the monarchial or magisterial element in a mixed state ought to be. The significant passage runs as follows:

And there is nothing more common than for our parliaments to appoint committees of their own members; who, when so appointed, have power to meet where they please, and hold a kind of little parliament amongst themselves. And the most weighty affairs are often referred to them, for expedition and secrecy—the care of the navy, the army, the treasury; in short, all things whatsoever relating either to war or peace.[78]

The "committees" of this passage are identical in conception with the committee of the Grand Council which, as the "Council of State," constituted a few years later the monarchial or magisterial element of Milton's free commonwealth.[79] He came, in short, to see the magisterial element in a mixed state as ideally consisting of a small

---

[74] *Works*, XVIII, 199.   [75] *P.w.*, I, 114. Cf. 38–39.

[76] Gooch's remarks on Milton's transition to republicanism are interesting (*The history of English democratic ideas*, pp. 180–83). He sees the *Eikonoklastes* as the key document, and such it undoubtedly is as far as overt expressions of republicanism are concerned (*P.w.*, I, 482, 485).   [77] *P.w.*, I, 33.   [78] *P.w.*, I, 15.

[79] *P.w.*, II, 121. Note the similarities in phrasing between the two passages.

council of wise and able men created by, and responsible to, Parliament. He was traveling toward this view, if he had not actually adopted it, in 1651; in 1660 he expressed it as a settled conviction in *The ready and easy way*. One may conclude, I believe, that Milton's experiences with Charles I did more than make him reject kingship, that they made him reject all single-person magistracies whatsoever in a functioning mixed state.[80]

If this interpretation is correct, it will doubtless be inquired how Milton's support of Cromwell and his faith in great leaders are to be explained. The explanation, I think, is both clear and simple and lies essentially in two facts. The first of these is that Milton never at any time throughout the Puritan Revolution thought that his ultimate ideal had been attained. From 1641 on, except for those periods when he saw one obstacle or another holding up the progress of things,[81] he saw his countrymen in a state of transition from corruption and tyranny to a new and well-nigh perfect order in both church and state. In the earlier anti-episcopal tracts, one gets the impression that Milton came close to thinking that episcopacy was the great source of evil in the state, as well as in the church, and that once it was removed all would be well.[82] But shortly he discovered that other things were necessary. It was always thus. Most important for our purposes is that it was thus when Milton wrote the *Second defense* and when his faith in Cromwell was at its height.[83] He says specifically that the government of the country was such as the storms of faction and the convulsions which disturbed the state admitted of, not such as was to be wholly desired.[84] The second cardinal point has to do with Milton's conception of the rôle of great leaders in times of transition from one government to another. Until the later 1640's, he saw in Parliament the agency which was carrying out the great reform and guiding the country in the transition from tyranny and corruption to a new and better order. But already in 1641 he had

[80] *The ready and easy way* is clear on this point. So great was Milton's distrust of all single-person magistracies that he would tolerate not even a powerless "duke of Venice." See Clark's remarks in his edition of this tract (*Yale studies in English*, LI, New Haven, 1915), p. xxxv and Gooch's acute observations in his *History of English democratic ideas*, p. 244. G. S., the author of *The dignity of kingship asserted* (1660), quite properly singles out Milton's objections to a single person as an essential point in his argument.

[81] Such a period was 1647–48, when he accused the Presbyterians of having brought the great reformation to "ridiculous frustration" (*P.w.*, v, 236 ff.).   [82] *P.w.*, II, 408–09.

[83] I say at its height because there is no other tract in which he puts his hopes as completely in Cromwell as in the *Second defense*. Cf. *P.w.*, I, 288–89, with the views expressed in the *First defense* (I, 15). That his faith even at its height involved fears and reservations is, of course, clear from the warnings to Cromwell (I, 290 f.).

[84] *P.w.*, I, 294–95. The statement occurs near the end of the tract and clearly was written after the establishment of the Protectorate.

entertained the opinion that in periods of transition it was sometimes necessary for a great individual to exercise vast temporary powers. "Brutus, that expelled the kings out of Rome," he tells us, "was for the time forced to be as it were a king himself, till matters were set in order, as in a free commonwealth." Pericles, too, he finds, exercised such great powers that he was like a prince, yet he had no more than a temporary sway.[85] Moreover, the example of Lycurgus and the rôle assigned to him by political writers as the creator of the ideal mixed constitution of Sparta encouraged Milton, as it encouraged Harrington, in the belief that it was possible through the agency of a single great law-giver or leader to establish an ideal state.[86] Milton believed in heaven-sent, divinely-appointed great leaders, but it is significant that he saw them as deliverers from bondage and tyranny like Samson, as institutors of liberty like Brutus, or as great teachers like himself,[87] not as all-powerful executives in a settled and smoothly functioning mixed state. In Milton's scheme of things, great leaders make their appearance on the stage of history and play their proper rôles in times of transition from bondage to freedom. He accepted, then, the fact that sometimes it was necessary in periods of transition to set up a virtual dictator. But it is important to note that although he accepted the idea of the transitional dictator, in the end he utterly repudiated the notion that in an established and properly contrived mixed government it was ever necessary, even in times of crisis, to confer dictatorial power on either any council or single person in the government. In *The ready and easy way*, as we shall see, he put his whole faith in a perfectly contrived state which would run as smoothly in times of crisis as in periods of calm. There is no provision whatever for a constitutionally recognized dictator to act in emergencies—such a dictator as Machiavelli, Harrington, and those prime examples of the mixed state, Rome and Venice, cannot have but suggested to him. In *Paradise regained* there is evidence that he went further and implied that when regularly-constituted authorities fail in times of crisis, dictatorship is a vain and futile refuge.[88]

It is only in the light of these facts that one can draw any true

[85] *P.w.*, II, 429.

[86] That Lycurgus made a strong impression on Milton is attested by his numerous references to him. See especially *P.w.*, II, 57, and I, 88, where Lycurgus is held up as having set a pattern for others to follow. In *Of education* Milton mentions Lycurgus first in the list of Grecian law-givers whose "extolled remains" he recommended to students (*P.w.*, III, 472). In view of the care with which he went through the *Discourses* of Machiavelli (see above, p. 98), we may suspect that, like Harrington, he was also influenced by Machiavelli's views on the desirability of an institutor.

[87] *P.w.*, II, 98.   [88] See Appendix C, below.

conclusions regarding Milton's attitude toward Cromwell. That from viewing Parliament as the institutor of the new order in the 1640's, he had been reduced to putting his hopes in Cromwell when he wrote the *Second defense*, no one will dispute,[89] but it was of the essence of Milton's view of the Protector that he saw him essentially as a transitional dictator, as an institutor or law-giver. The *Letter to a gentleman in the country* which Thomason and Masson attributed to the poet[90] probably is not a genuine Miltonic document, but when the writer saw Cromwell as a divinely appointed great leader who was to finish the great reform begun but not yet completed,[91] he expressed sentiments which were Milton's own. But more important, the conception colors the whole eulogy of Cromwell in the *Second defense*. The anxious warnings to the Protector in this work center around the apprehension that he might make himself permanently supreme, that he might seize the sovereignty which all had yielded to him to achieve the instituting of the ideal state.[92] Moreover, and most significantly, we find Cromwell compared to that Brutus who had driven the kings out of Rome and of whom Milton had earlier written that he was forced for a time to be, as it were, a king himself.[93] Milton, then, saw Cromwell as an institutor of the ideal mixed state of his dreams.[94] The new government of the Protector had "begun to shed its splendor on the world,"[95] and in it Cromwell was supreme and might do much, but it was only a transition to something better; it was, be it remembered, such a government as the distractions of the time admitted of, not such as was to be wished.[96]

There is additional evidence that Milton was under the influence of the idea of the great institutor. When he wrote his *Letter to Monk* early in 1660, he invited the General to assume essentially the rôle which he had seen Cromwell playing earlier. This may be dismissed as simply a last desperate gamble on Milton's part, of course, and such no doubt in a very considerable measure it was, but that he was still under the influence of the idea of the Lycurgus-like institutor is suggested, not only by the phraseology of the letter itself,

[89] *P.w.*, I, 288, 289. [90] *Life*, IV, 520 ff.
[91] See the *Letter* in Masson, IV, 521. [92] *P.w.*, I, 290 ff. [93] *P.w.*, I, 297.
[94] What I am suggesting, of course, is that in this respect Harrington and Milton, both under the influence of the theory of the mixed state and with the Lycurgean example before them, saw Cromwell in much the same way.
[95] *P.w.*, I, 289.
[96] It is indicative, I think, of the hold of the idea of a concilar magistracy in a normally functioning state on Milton that he would have even Cromwell in his rôle of transitional dictator associate with himself the great leaders on the Puritan side (*P.w.*, I, 290).

but also by the letter which on December 20, 1659, he addressed to Henry Oldenburgh, in which he remarked that the great need of the time was someone to settle the government on a firm foundation.[97] The *Letter to Monk* was not an invitation to assume permanent power, but to institute a mixed state, the outlines of which Milton was careful to set forth.[98] If it was, therefore, a product of the moment, it was nevertheless strictly consistent with views which he had expressed elsewhere, even to the justifying of the use of armed force by the institutor.[99] I think it is not unreasonable to infer that in 1654 and again early in 1660, Milton saw the contemporary situation in terms of the notion of transitional dictatorship and placed his hopes for the mixed state in a great institutor.[100] Both Cromwell and Monk were products of the times and of events; Milton called on each in turn to become a Lucurgean legislator.[101] In Cromwell he was doubtless convinced, at first, that God and the age had produced such a leader; in the case of Monk, it was the brave hope that the General might be induced to play the rôle that prompted Milton to address him.

We have now surveyed Milton's developed conception of the magistracy in a mixed state and his conception of the relation of dictatorship to the institution of such a state and to the state when instituted. We have next to look at the development of his views on the relation of Parliament to mixed government. We have seen that in 1641 he believed that preponderant power in such a government should reside in the nobility, the good and the wise. He never believed anything else.[102] The principle of the dominance of the virtuous, the truly noble, those who were "more than vulgar bred up,"[103] is as unchanging an element in his thought as the ideal of the mixed

---

[97] *P.w.*, III, 520.   [98] *P.w.*, II, 106 ff.

[99] *P.w.*, II, 108. The evidence is clear that Milton was not averse to using armed force to attain the free commonwealth. He had earlier specifically defended it in the *First defense* (*P.w.*, I, 25). The notion was not uncommon with other commonwealth planners. Compare Harrington's representation of Olphaus Megaletor as using the army to get himself appointed Archon (above, p. 70).

[100] Milton would have seen no inconsistency between his doctrine of popular sovereignty and the notion of a great leader's instituting the ideal state by force inasmuch as he obviously thought of the better part of the people, whom, as we shall see, he saw standing for the whole people, as consenting to the acts of the institutor (*P.w.*, II, 108).

[101] It is characteristic of Milton as a political reformer that he did not distinguish early enough and clearly enough the differences between his own aims and those of the persons whom he supported. When this was not the case, he harbored the illusion that they could be brought to see the truth his way. Hence the *Areopagitica*. The result was a series of disappointments. This fact is echoed in the *Second defense* in the stridency of his remark about continually cherishing "illusory expectations" (*P.w.*, I, 291).

[102] *P.w.*, I, 88, 111, 265, 288; II, 125; V, 240.   [103] *P.w.*, V, 240.

state itself. It rested, as he proclaimed in the two *Defenses*, on the highest authority he recognized—conformity to the law of God and the law of nature.[104] It is clear also that in 1641 he saw in Parliament a well-nigh perfect organ for the representation and functioning of the aristocratic element in the ideal mixed state which he considered England in its proper constitution to be.[105] He saw his native country, in short, as having a mixed government in which the people, the monarch, and Parliament all shared in the power, but in which, as it should be, Parliament, the aristocratic element, held such a preponderance of power as to have "supreme and final determination" in all matters. Hence his allusions to Parliament in the early tracts as the "supreme senate" or the "supreme court" of the nation.[106] In Milton's political thought to begin with, then, there was the clear implication that the acts of the monarchial element were subject to review by the aristocratic element, the Parliament, the principle which he repeatedly asserted in 1649 and thereafter and which he then developed at length in terms of the amalgamation of the idea of the mixed state with the doctrine of sovereignty which we have seen that he made. In accordance with these views, he wrote *The tenure of kings and magistrates*, in which he tells us that parliaments were set up as a check on the monarch after the establishment of kingship, and that they had the power at all times, with or without the monarch, to take all measures for the public safety when danger or crisis threatened.[107] The theory afforded him a means of justifying the use of virtually unlimited power by Parliament in times of crisis, and it is repeated essentially in the *Eikonoklastes*, in which we find him asserting that "in all wise nations the legislative power, and the judicial [i.e. the executive or magisterial] execution of that power, have been most commonly distinct and in several hands; but yet the former supreme, the other subordinate," and asserting that when the need arose Parliament could unmake the king.[108] But by the time he wrote the *Eikonoklastes* he had gone a step further in the development of his theory of the rôle of Parliament in a mixed government. The theory at which he ultimately arrived was, not merely that parliaments had the right to pass on the acts of the monarchial element and were supreme over it in the

---

[104] *P.w.*, I, 111, 265, 288.   [105] *P.w.*, II, 408.
[106] *P.w.*, III, 176, 278. Cf. 144, 319.   [107] *P.w.*, II, 11.
[108] *P.w.*, I, 363, 398. See also the statement on p. 401 that "the parliament, therefore, without any usurpation, hath had it always in their power to limit and confine the exorbitancy of kings, whether they call it their will, their reason, or their conscience."

last instance, but that the magisterial element was itself a creation
of the aristocratic, that is, the parliamentary element, and from it,
acting for the sovereign people, derived all the power it had.[109]
Symptomatic of this development is the change in the theory of the
origin of the state between *The tenure of kings and magistrates* and the
Observations on the articles of peace, written a few months later.
Whereas in the former he saw parliaments as set up after kings as a
check on them, in the latter he declares that parliaments or general
assemblies are the most ancient organs of government and that they
existed before ever kings were heard of.[110] The *First defense* repeats
the idea with the additional statement that kings were created to put
the laws of Parliament into execution.[111] These changes may be taken
as representing an attempt to bring his views on the origin of government into harmony with his developing conception of a magistracy
created by, and dependent upon, the aristocratic element of the
state. At any rate, that conception is repeated in the *First defense*[112]
and it is the basic principle in the magistracy which he proposed in
The ready and easy way.[113]

At this point, the reader will doubtless be tempted to feel that
Milton so exalted Parliament in 1649 and the early 1650's and again
in 1660 as quite to lose sight of the ideal of the mixed state. Nothing
could be further from the truth. Although it is perhaps an open
question whether the position at which he arrived did not really involve a unitary conception of government, nothing is more clear
than that *he* did not see it that way, a fact which is proved by his reit-
erated adherences to the idea of mixed government throughout the
whole period from 1640 to 1660 and even in the very moments
when he was most highly exalting Parliament.[114] Milton saw no
contradiction between the two ideals because in terms of contemporary theory there was none. Such a magistracy as he arrived at,
and such a predominant parliament or aristocratic element as he
conceived were, in fact, of the very essence of the theory of mixed
government in seventeenth-century thought. That theorists did not

---

[109] *P.w.,* I, 398. Cf. II, 121.   [110] *P.w.,* II, 187.

[111] *P.w.,* I, 180. For an anticipation of this view in the *Tetrachordon* see *P.w.,* III, 315,
where Milton asserts that it was Parliament that first put the sceptre into the hands of an
English king. In the *Second defense,* on the other hand, he seems to revert momentarily
to the notion of Parliament having been created as a check on the monarch (*P.w.,* I,
264). Doubtless he had no profound conviction of the historical truth of either theory
and to some extent used whichever one served his purpose better.

[112] *P.w.,* I, 180. Cf. 15.   [113] *P.w.,* II, 121.

[114] *P.w.,* I, 88, 160, 363; II, 115, 125.

view the giving of preponderant power to some one of the three elements of the state as inconsistent with the idea of mixed government, we have seen. That the preponderant element should be the aristocratic one was, as we have likewise seen, the opinion of various writers. That the preponderance of power in the aristocratic element should be so great as to involve the creation of the magistracy, and that the magistracy should be subject to the control of the aristocratic element—these were precisely the theories which were illustrated in the government of Venice, the importance of which as a great example of mixed government was as definitely in Milton's mind by the 1650's as it was in that of other champions of mixed polities.[115]

Unfortunately, no sooner had Milton developed his theory of what the rôle of Parliament in a mixed state should be than he discovered that Parliament as it was did not measure up to his ideal, that it would have to be remodeled before it would be a fit repository of the great power which he proposed to give it. There is no need to trace here the earlier steps by which Milton's vast confidence in Parliament expressed in the anti-episcopal and other early tracts[116] was dissipated. It is sufficient to point out that by the time he wrote the *Character of the Long Parliament*,[117] his criticism was sweeping and unequivocal.[118] It is important, however, to notice in this passage that he places the blame for the great reform's having come to "ridiculous frustration" squarely on the members of Parliament, even on the cold climate of the country,[119] but not on the institution itself. Had this not been the case, he could hardly have written as he

---

[115] *P.w.*, II, 103, 104, 124; *Works*, XVIII, 1 ff. The reference to a "duke of Venice" in *P.w.*, II, 128, is not uncomplimentary of the Venetian doge but of the persons whom Milton accuses of using the idea of a magistrate like the Venetian doge to cloak a design for the restoration of monarchy. It is, however, true that one thing that Milton would not borrow from Venice was the doge, for his abjuration of "single persons," even mere figureheads, was complete. In other respects his conciliar magistracy, although lacking the detailed resemblance of Harrington's, has a striking general likeness to the Venetian council which was the real magistracy of the state.

[116] *P.w.*, III, 105, 145–50, 179, 281, 287, 315, 316, 321.

[117] See Appendix B, below.

[118] Most of the parliamentarians, he tells us, had got their places by wealth or ambition rather than by merit. They had pursued private profit, delayed and denied justice, determined matters by spite and favoritism, and been guilty of treachery, oppression, and unjust taxation. "Some who had been called from shops and warehouses, without other merit, to be set in supreme councils and committees, (as their breeding was,) fell to huckster the commonwealth." The crowning charge, and an ironical one indeed in view of the position at which Milton arrived a few years later, is that they had deliberately fomented "troubles and combustions" in order to perpetuate themselves in power (*P.w.*, V, 236–38).   [119] *P.w.*, V, 240.

did of the Rump or purged Parliament in the *Eikonoklastes*[120] and the *First defense*.[121] Already in 1649, however, he was beginning to see that Parliament itself needed remodeling. The first step in making the reality conform to the ideal was the rejection of a house of lords. This was an implication of his very conception of the nature of true nobility and of Parliament as the supreme council of the good and wise of the nation. When, therefore, in February-March, 1649, the upper house was actually abolished, he was already prepared to accept the move. We find him declaring in *The tenure of kings and magistrates* that the word *baron* or *peer* imported only "every worthy man in parliament," and that hereditary titles were vain and empty.[122] In the *Eikonoklastes* there was further criticism of the Lords.[123] In the *First defense* he argued flatly that a house of lords was no essential part of an English parliament and never had been, and that the Lords had been properly abolished.[124] This was another opinion which, once arrived at, he did not change. In *The ready and easy way* he wanted in his Grand Council no more men addicted to a house of lords than those addicted to a single-person magistracy.[125] Abolition of the Lords, then, was the first step in Milton's remodeling of the traditional English Parliament.

It was not long before he began to think that other changes were necessary. In the *Second defense* we find him highly critical of Parliament. The Rump had "artfully procrastinated" its business, its members were intent on their own selfish interests, they had deluded the country with fallacious promises. Cromwell had rightly put an end to their sitting. The succeeding Barebones Parliament had met, had done nothing but weary itself with dissensions, and had fully exposed its incapacity to the nation.[126] Milton had discovered, in short, that Parliament was far from being the ideal aristocratic element which he had once thought it to be. The solution of the problem thus presented was not to turn the country over permanently to a single great leader or to such a leader and his immediate associates, although that would do temporarily and seemed, indeed, at the time the only expedient, but to discover how Parliament could be remodeled further in order to make it a fit organ to exercise preponderant power in the ideal mixed state of the poet's dreams. The solution to this problem, which Milton clearly thought that he had found when he wrote *The ready and easy way*, was not yet in 1654

---

[120] *P.w.*, I, 361, 363, 367, 401, 402.   [121] *P.w.*, I, 15.
[122] *P.w.*, II, 23. Cf. I, 175.   [123] *P.w.*, I, 365.
[124] *P.w.*, I, 176, 190.   [125] *P.w.*, II, 121. Cf. 120.   [126] *P.w.*, I, 288.

wholly clear to him. But two important passages in the *Second defense* indicate that the two principal reforms which he was to propose in the later tract were, if not actually taking form in his mind, being prepared for by the direction which his thought was taking. In the first of these, after asserting again that Parliament was the supreme council of the nation, he argues against its being compelled to refer its acts and decisions to the people who had set it up to act for them.[127] Here we can see developing that distrust of annually or frequently elected parliaments which culminated in *The ready and easy way* in the proposal of a perpetual Grand Council.[128] The other significant passage comes near the close. It is one in which he assails the misuse of the "right of unrestrained suffrage" for factional and selfish purposes, and asserts that parliaments elected by such a misuse of the voting power would lead his countrymen straight back to servitude and tyranny.[129] No one who reads this passage will be surprised at the restrictions which Milton places on the suffrage in *The ready and easy way* and the system of successive siftings which he proposes for the election of members of the Grand Council.[130] In the end, then, he proposed to remodel Parliament in the interest of making it truly the noble or aristocratic element, by two fundamental changes: the transforming of it into a perpetual senate and the placing of severe restrictions on the suffrage.

The first of these objects would be achieved by having a senate or grand council the members of which would hold office for life, a body which is described in the following significant passage:

The ground and basis of every just and free government (since men have smarted so often for committing all to one person,) is a general council of ablest men chosen by the people to consult of public affairs from time to time for the common good. In this grand council must the sovereignty, not transferred, but delegated only, and as it were deposited, reside; with this caution, they must have the forces by sea and land committed to them for preservation of the common peace and liberty; must raise and manage the public revenue, at least with some inspectors deputed for satisfaction of the people, how it is employed; must make or propose, as more expressly shall be said anon, civil laws, treat of commerce, peace or war with foreign nations. . . .

[127] *P.w.*, I, 264–65.
[128] *P.w.*, II, 122. In the *Eikonoklastes* Milton had supported the Triennial Bill and even had sought to show that not triennial, but annual, parliaments represented the true old English custom (*P.w.*, I, 351 ff.). That he still retained something of this older view and did not see clearly in 1654 the direction in which his thought was developing may be surmised from the charge of "artful procrastination" which he hurled at the Rump in the *Second defense* (*P.w.*, I, 288). [129] *P.w.*, I, 297–98. [130] *P.w.*, II, 126.

And, although it may seem strange at first hearing, by reason that men's minds are prepossessed with the notion of successive parliaments, I affirm, that the grand or general council, being well chosen, should be perpetual: for so their business is or may be, and ofttimes urgent; the opportunity of affairs gained or lost in a moment. The day or council cannot be set as the day of a festival; but must be ready always to prevent or answer all occasions.[131]

To demonstrate the necessity of such a body, he filled the tract with arguments against successive or frequently elected parliaments. He could not see how his countrymen could "be advantaged by successive and transitory parliaments," and found that they were "much likelier continually to unsettle rather than to settle a free government, to breed commotions, changes, novelties, and uncertainties, to bring neglect upon present affairs and opportunities, while all minds are in suspense with expectation of a new assembly, and the assembly, for a good space, taken up with the new settling of itself."[132] In such a body as he proposed, on the contrary, "the death now and then of a senator is not felt, the main body of them still continuing permanent in greatest and noblest commonwealths and as it were eternal."[133] But if ambition could not be satisfied by such a system, or it was thought that long continuance in power would corrupt even the best men, a system of rotation could be employed which would not result in the whole body being changed at any one time. Clearly alluding to Harrington's Venetian rotative principles, and indeed reproducing Harrington's system with the suggestion that the interval between elections might be made more than one year, he wrote: "The known expedient is, and by some lately propounded, that annually (or if the space be longer, so much perhaps the better) the third part of senators may go out according to the precedence of their election, and the like number be chosen in their places, to prevent their settling of too absolute a power, if it should be perpetual: and this they call 'partial rotation.' "[134] Milton made it clear, however, that he hoped that it would not be necessary to adopt this alternative proposal. Partial rotation had to a certain extent the same defect as successive parliaments—it turned out experienced men and put novices in their place. He was sure, moreover, that in the nicely-balanced state which he was proposing there

---

[131] *P.w.*, II, 121–22. The remark about sovereignty in this passage is not to be construed as indicating that Milton would give all final authority in the actual operation of the government to the Grand Council, for he specifically says that the council would have "certain limitations" in the performance of its duties (p. 127).

[132] *P.w.*, II, 122; cf. 124.   [133] *P.w.*, II, 123–24.   [134] *P.w.*, II, 122.

would be no danger of the Grand Council attempting to secure too much power.[135]

The second fundamental change to be made in the remodeling of Parliament, that of instituting a system of successive winnowings in the choice of members, would be achieved by a procedure which he was careful to describe. "The way will be," he wrote, "to well qualify and refine elections: not committing all to the noise and shouting of a rude multitude, but permitting only those of them who are rightly qualified, to nominate as many as they will; and out of that number others of a better breeding, to choose a less number more judiciously, till after a third or fourth sifting and refining of exactest choice, they only be left chosen who are the due number, and seem by most voices the worthiest."[136]

There was one other, less fundamental, change which he proposed. Salmasius had annoyed Milton by asserting that no record of parliaments could be found before William the Conqueror. Milton replied in the *First defense* by accusing his opponent of quibbling over a word and asserting that the thing was always in existence whether the word was or not. "It is not worth while," he declared, "to jangle about a French word."[137] The attitude here expressed developed in the following years into outright dissatisfaction with the name *parliament*. The word came to have for him unfortunate connotations, and he ended by proposing to abolish it and substitute for it *grand* or *great council*.[138]

The changes which Milton proposed in Parliament to insure a body which would be worthy of preponderant power in a mixed state were doubtless, in part, the product of his own experiences with government, but that he was also encouraged in them by Rome, the Greek states, and Venice, the great acknowledged examples of mixed government, and that these examples determined to a very real extent the actual form which his proposed changes took is equally clear. For his perpetual senate or grand council in which members held office for life, he cited, with references to "greatest and noblest commonwealths," the Roman and Spartan Senates and the Areopagus

---

[135] *P.w.*, II, 123. Milton, who doubtless heard much about Harrington's proposals from Cyriack Skinner, who sometimes presided at the Rota Club, was critical of several aspects of them, especially the ballot and the two-chambered legislature. See pp. 125–26, 127–28.   [136] *P.w.*, II, 126.   [137] *P.w.*, I, 167.

[138] The change is proposed no fewer than three times: in the *Proposalls for a firme government* (*Works*, XVIII, 4); in *The ready and easy way* (*P.w.*, II, 127); and in the *Letter to Monk* (*P.w.*, II, 107).

of Athens.[139] The parallels between his magisterial element, councilar in character and created by, and responsible to, the aristocratic element, and the Venetian councilar magistracy we have already noticed. Further parallels are to be found between his proposals and Venetian practices in the conception of his Grand Council, a fact which might be surmised, had we not the parallels themselves, from the circumstance that he includes Venice as one of the "greatest and noblest commonwealths" in his list of examples in both *The ready and easy way*[140] and the *Proposalls for a firme government*,[141] that shorter version of a commonwealth which he composed between October 20 and December 26, 1659.[142] His Grand Council has striking similarities with both the Grand Council and the Senate of the Venetian system. It is like the former in being a perpetual body not subject, ideally at least, to recurrent elections or, indeed, to any form of rotation. It is like the latter in the peculiar combination of functions, partly executive and partly legislative, which Milton assigns it, a fact which can be seen in a moment by comparing the passage in which he describes its functions[143] with Howell's and Contarini's accounts of the Venetian Senate.[144] What makes these parallels the more striking is the fact that Milton, when referring to Venetian practices, makes just such an amalgamation of the Senate and Grand Council as his own Grand Council represents.[145] We may notice further that Milton's second-best plan, that which would involve partial rotation, was obviously drawn through Harrington from Venice.[146] It is clear

[139] *P.w.*, II, 123–24; *Works*, XVIII, 1 ff. He cited also the example of the Sanhedrim, which exponents of mixed government, as we have seen, saw as embodying the same principles as those of Greece and Rome. Cf. Harrington's statement that the Hebrews got the principles of mixed government from God and the Greeks and Romans from following the law of God as revealed in the law of nature (see above p. 52). Milton certainly believed that mixed government had its basis in the law of God, and the law of nature, and in the *First defense*, in replying to Salmasius, who had brought the matter up, he had cited the ancient Hebrew state to show that in it, no more than in other antique models was the magistracy supreme, but I do not find him making any such specific identification of the Hebrew state with Greek and Roman conceptions of mixed government as Harrington makes. That this was, however, an implication of his position is clear, and we need not, therefore, be surprised at seeing the Sanhedrim appear with other models in *The ready and easy way*. See *P.w.*, I, 33, 44–45.   [140] *P.w.*, II, 124.
[141] *Works*, XVIII, 3–4.   [142] See Appendix D for the dating of this tract.
[143] Quoted above, p. 112.   [144] Quoted above, pp. 29–30.   [145] *P.w.*, II, 124.
[146] The importance of the example of Venice in Milton's thought was clearly recognized by his contemporaries. G. S., in *The dignity of kingship asserted*, a work intended as a reply to *The ready and easy way*, devoted an extended passage to showing that the political reputation of Venice was ill-founded (pp. 101–02). See also the remarks on Venice in *The censure of the Rota*, which was, along with being a burlesque on the Rota Club, a reply to Milton's tract (pp. 7, 15).

that, by *The ready and easy way*, the attempt which we have seen him making earlier to square the ancient institutions of England with the demands of the theory of the mixed state had broken down; and as such old English precedents as annual parliaments, of which he had made so much in the *Eikonoklastes* and the *First defense*, failed him, he was driven back more and more on antique models and their supposed modern counterparts. He ended by proposing to his countrymen a perpetual senate which he named after the example of Venice and advanced on the authority of Rome, Sparta, Venice, and Athens.[147]

It remains to consider Milton's views regarding the rôle of the people in a mixed state. What Milton saw this as being in 1641 is clear from his remark that the "noblest, wisest, and most prudent men," that is, Parliament, carried on their work with the "full approbation and suffrage of the people."[148] It is obvious that in the early 1640's Milton's hopes for the people were high. In the controversy over episcopacy, he condemned one of his opponents for referring slightingly to the "mutinous rabble,"[149] and in the *Areopagitica* he was sure that all were fit to be trusted with an English pamphlet, and that the common people were not "giddy, vicious,and ungrounded."[150] Partly these estimates were due, no doubt, to the utopian fervor of the time; partly they were the result of the ease with which Milton, as a habit of thought, identified the better part of the people, whom he saw as the fountain-head of virtue and nobility, the middle sort, with the whole people. But even in the early 1640's he was beginning to make some unpleasant discoveries. In the *Apology for Smectymnuus* he noticed in "most men" a "carelessness of knowing what they and others ought to do,"[151] and in the *Doctrine and discipline of divorce* we hear of "the draff of men, to whom no liberty is pleasing."[152] By 1649 he had harsh things indeed to say about the people. In the *Tenure of kings and magistrates* he finds most men characterized by "sloth or inconstancy and weakness of spirit," and he tells us that the few labor "amidst the throng of vulgar and irrational men."[153] In the *Eikonoklastes* his condemnation is sweeping. The people are filled with envy and infinite prejudice; they are "exorbitant and excessive in all their motions" and prone to idolatry, and have a "besotted and degenerate baseness of spirit." The virtuous among them are few. A mad multitude, they are pos-

[147] *P.w.*, I, 121–24; *Works*, XVIII, 1 ff.   [148] *P.w.*, II, 408.
[149] *P.w.*, III, 154–55.   [150] *P.w.*, II, 81.   [151] *P.w.*, III, 94.
[152] *P.w.*, III, 173.   [153] *P.w.*, II, ·3; cf. 77.

sessed and hurried on by "boisterous folly and superstition."[154] The reader may wonder why, having arrived at these opinions, Milton did not wholly reject the idea of a mixed state, in which the people played a definite, even if subordinate, rôle, and propose to deprive them of all participation whatsoever in the government. That he did nothing of the sort, of course, is clear. Not only do we find him reaffirming in these very tracts, as we have seen, his belief in the superiority of a mixed state, but it is in these same places that we have seen him developing the doctrine of popular sovereignty. Moreover, the rôle which he assigns to the people in 1649 is essentially the same as that which he had given them in 1641: the people, we are told, having delegated the preponderance of their power to the Parliament, retained the power of choosing its members[155] in what Milton thinks would ideally be annual elections.[156]

What is the explanation of the apparent contradiction in the poet's thought? It lies in an important passage in the *Eikonoklastes*. In the midst of his castigation of the people, he pauses to say that the degeneracy among them which he blames is due, not to their natural disposition, but to their long corruption by the prelates and— he now adds—the Presbyterian clergy.[157] If they were for the most part "imbastardized from the ancient nobleness of their ancestors," the fault was not theirs. The idea served Milton well in 1649, but it did not long remain wholly adequate. The conviction grew upon him that the people had graver deficiencies than the prelates could be made responsible for. But as this view emerged, he made another discovery—that not all the people were either virtuous or wicked, that they consisted, in short, of a better part and a worse part. In the *First defense* we find him speaking of the "better" part in both the quantitative and qualitative senses of the term, his contention being that the most virtuous part of the people was also the larger part."[158] By the time he wrote *The ready and easy way*, if not, indeed, by the *Second defense*, it was clear to him that this was not the case.[159] But majority or minority, the better part came to constitute in his thought the whole people. He tells us specifically in the *First defense* that the better part might be considered as standing for the whole,[160] and it is clear that this notion henceforth dominated his thinking. The identi-

[154] *P.w.*, I, 309, 313, 314, 317.   [155] *P.w.*, I, 322, 361.
[156] *P.w.*, I, 351.   [157] *P.w.*, I, 313.   [158] *P.w.*, I, 154; cf. 155.
[159] Hence the various justifications of decisions by a virtuous minority of the people until or unless a majority could be brought to virtue by a proper government and a proper educational system (*P.w.*, II, 112, 132). Cf. the *Second defense* (*P.w.*, I, 265).
[160] *P.w.*, I, 154.

fication which it had always been easy for him to make unconsciously he came, in short, to make consciously and deliberately. The *Second defense* shows him moving toward the restriction of the suffrage to the better part,[161] and in *The ready and easy way* he not only flatly limited the voting power to the "rightly qualified,"[162] but proposed the elaborate system of election by successive winnowings which we have noticed and by which he sought to insure that the better part would control.[163] The people, thus defined and limited, he by no means proposed to exclude from the government. They were to choose the members of the Grand Council,[164] they were to have inspectors who would examine the disposition of the public revenues by it,[165] and through their local assemblies in every county they were to have, by a majority vote of all the assemblies, a kind of veto power over its acts.[166] Local government would remain almost wholly in their hands,[167] and he refers to still other limitations.[168] Nor had Milton departed from the doctrine of popular sovereignty.[169]

The people, then, as was proper in a mixed state, were to play their part in the government. But it was to be a subordinate part. All his experience had only confirmed the belief he had started with, that a mixed state was properly balanced and stable only when the part played in its actual operation by the people was restricted. Moreover, the example of Rome seemed to him to enforce the lesson of his own experience. We find him arguing that it was the exercise of excessive power by the popular element that upset the balance and brought about the fall of the Roman republic.[170] Venice, with just such a pre-

---

[161] *P.w.*, I, 297.   [162] *P.w.*, II, 126. See also the *Letter to Monk* (*P.w.*, II, 107).
[163] *P.w.*, II, 126.   [164] *P.w.*, II, 118, 121, 123.   [165] *P.w.*, II, 121.
[166] *P.w.*, II, 126, 135.   [167] *P.w.*, II, 107, 135. Cf. 126.

[168] Milton seems to have envisioned a standing militia of the "well affected" as a guaranty against the seizure of tyrannical power by the Grand Council (*P.w.*, II, 123), and he refers to other limitations on p. 127. In the *Letter to Monk* he says that though the supreme council would be perpetual, its power would be so limited and the people would have so much authority remaining in their hands that there would be no possibility of the Grand Council establishing a tyranny (*P.w.*, II, 107).   [169] *P.w.*, II, 121.

[170] "The main reason urged why popular assemblies are to be trusted with the people's liberty, rather than a senate of principal men, because great men will be still endeavouring to enlarge their power, but the common sort will be contented to maintain their own liberty, is by experience found false; none being more immoderate and ambitious to amplify their power, than such popularities, which were seen in the people of Rome; who, at first contented to have their tribunes, at length contended with the senate that one consul, then both; soon after, that the censors and praetors also should be created plebeian, and then the whole empire put into their hands; adoring lastly those, who were most adverse to the senate, till Marius, by fulfilling their inordinate desires, quite lost them all the power for which they had so long been striving, and left them under the tyranny of Sylla" (*P.w.*, II, 125). The idea that Rome fell because the people secured too much power and upset the balance was a favorite one, as we have seen, with advocates of mixed polities. For Paruta's expression of the same idea see above, p. 19 f.

dominant senate as he wished and its supposed record of centuries of unchanging government, doubtless gave him additional confirmation of the correctness of his views, for its example led positively to the same conclusion to which Rome led negatively.[171] The result of these considerations was that we find him arguing against giving the people any greater checks on the Grand Council than he had himself proposed.[172]

The reader will doubtless feel that Milton's discovery that the better part of the people could be taken as standing for the whole even when they were a numerical minority removed whatever genuinely popular elements there may once have been in his political theory. The fact, however, that there would appear to be nothing truly democratic about Milton's conception of the people in 1660 must not be permitted to obscure the fact that he saw the better part of the people as constituting the democratic element in his ideal commonwealth. Nor in doing so was he in any sense departing from contemporary notions of mixed government, for his better part of the people formed just such a minority of the whole population as did the citizens of Venice who were eligible to sit in the Grand Council and whom Contarini saw as constituting the democratic element in that republic.[173] The situation which prevailed in ancient Athens and Sparta would afford further parallels. In this respect, indeed, it can be said that Milton's thought was in 1660 closer than it had been in 1641 to the practice of what the age saw as the great historical examples of mixed government. It is by no means certain, however, that Milton saw as permanent the situation that would prevail with regard to the people upon the instituting of a mixed state. He had always had extraordinary faith in what could be accomplished by proper governmental institutions and a proper system of education, and something of this earlier faith, it is clear, still survived when he wrote *The ready and easy way*. He would reform the "corrupt and faulty education" which prevailed and institute in its place a system which would "teach the people faith, not without virtue, temperance, modesty, sobriety, parsimony, justice," and which would instill into them the subordination of selfish interests to "the public peace, liberty, and safety."[174] By such a system and by

---

[171] In this fact, I think, is to be found one explanation of the emergence of Venice as a model in Milton's mind and the real significance it came to have for him in 1659–60.

[172] *P.w.*, II, 124–25.

[173] See above, pp. 54, 59–60. It is doubtless to be assumed that Milton thought of the virtuous in England as being proportionately far more numerous than the Venetian citizens, but that of course does not alter my point that in each case the democratic element was a minority.   [174] *P.w.*, II, 126.

"the orderly, the decent, the civil, the safe, the noble effects" of the perfectly functioning governmental institutions which would be set up, he cherished the idea of winning some, at least, of those who in the beginning would either have to be suppressed by force or excluded from the government.[175] Clearly there remained something of the old idea that if the people were for the most part evil, it was due in part to corrupting institutions and faulty education. To what extent he thought in 1660 that they could be reclaimed by correcting these things can only be conjectured. Doubtless he had come to feel that a certain portion of the people would always be the worse part. One can surmise as much from the institutions which he devised to exclude them from the government. Whether he had hopes of winning enough of them to make the better part a numerical majority, no one can say. As a matter of fact, there is no reason to suppose that this aspect of the matter bothered him. He may have hoped that the better part might become an actual majority. But unless or until such a condition could be attained, he was ready to justify the performance of the people's share in the government by a virtuous minority.

IV

We have now arrived at the point at which it is possible, with some understanding of their background, significance, place, and development in Milton's thought, to assemble the principal ideas which found expression in *The ready and easy way*. The guiding principle, one to which he had stated his allegiance in 1641, which he had reaffirmed in 1649 and the early 1650's, which he had never abandoned, was that of a state which would possess stability because it was mixed, because it had a perfect balance among the three orders of which a state was composed, the popular, the aristocratic, and the magisterial.[176] So far indeed was Milton from abandoning this idea in the early months of 1660 that he now expected to achieve more by it than ever before. He proposed by a perfect balancing of the three elements to set up, like Harrington, nothing less than a perpetually healthy state which would work perfectly and last unchanged even to the very end of the world. To make this statement involves no

---

[175] See the *Letter to Monk* (*P.w.*, II, 108).

[176] *P.w.*, II, 115, 125. The second of these passages, with its insistence on balance as the grand secret in government, is especially significant. The term Milton uses to describe his free commonwealth is "equal," a favorite expression of proponents of mixed government to express the balance or stability which such a state was supposed to have. See Milton's own earlier use of the term in discussing the mixed government of England (*P.w.*, II, 408), and cf. Harrington's use of it in *Oceana* (p. 33).

strained inferences from the text. The ageless state is the four times specifically avowed purpose of his proposals.[177]

For a Milton who believed that external liberty rested on internal liberty, that when peoples become corrupt, states decay, and who had asserted that when God had "decreed servitude on a sinful nation, fitted by their own vices for no condition but servile, all estates of government are alike unable to avoid it,"[178] the project of a perpetual state may seem at first glance a strange one indeed. On examination, however, whatever contradiction there may seem to be disappears. In Milton's state, with perfectly working institutions, true religion, and a proper educational system, the better part of the people who would stand in the political life of the state for the whole would not become corrupt and sinful. Not only would the state and education serve to promote moral and civil virtue in them, but, as we have seen, even some of the worse part might be won over. With such conditions prevailing, it did not seem to Milton unreasonable to suppose that a state might last as long as the world itself.

The aim, then, was clear. To achieve it, he proposed a state in which sovereignty resided in the people, but in which they delegated preponderant power to the aristocratic element, the Senate or Grand Council,[179] and consented to numerous restrictions on their participation in the actual operation of the state. To make the Senate worthy of the power he proposed to give it, to insure that it would be truly made up of the good and the wise, he suggested an elaborate system of election. To insure that it would have sufficient freedom from the demands of faction to formulate wise laws and foster truth and justice, he proposed to make it perpetual, with the members holding office for life. To aid in executing its commands, he proposed that it set up, and delegate some of its authority to, a magistracy. To prevent this magistracy from exerting too much power, he repudiated

---

[177] *P.w.*, II, 113, 121, 124, 127. In a sense, Milton's thought was bolder even than Harrington's. He conceived the grand problem in government to be, not providing a constitutional dictator to take over authority when institutions perfectly adequate to performing the tasks of peace broke down in times of crisis, but the creation of absolutely perfect institutions as sufficient unto themselves in times of emergency as in ordinary periods. In such a state as he proposed, a constitutional dictator would be wholly supererogatory.   [178] *P.w.*, V, 308.

[179] Milton retained in 1660 exactly the notion of 1641: that members of the Grand Council should be chosen from those among the "nobility and chief gentry" who had proved their wisdom and virtue and who constituted, therefore, the true aristocracy of the land (*P.w.*, II, 135). Hence, as in 1641, the Grand Council would represent the whole people (the better part), but it would also in Milton's own peculiar way represent what was in effect an aristocracy within an aristocracy of virtue.

all single-person executives, insisted that it should be councilar, and made it definitely subordinate to the Senate. To insure against the seizure of unlimited power by the Senate, he provided the people with inspectors and other safeguards, such as a militia. Truly, the system was one of checks and balances with a perpetual equilibrium as its object.

Between 1641, when Milton first expressed his allegiance to the idea of a mixed state, and 1660, much changed in Milton's thinking on political matters. But the principle of the mixed state with a preponderant aristocratic element did not change. If *The ready and easy way* culminated in an utopian dream, the dream was implicit in his thought from the start. It is not claiming too much to say that every major change which events brought about in Milton's political thinking during the Puritan Revolution represents him modifying parts in one ideal whole in the light of his experience and the "best ages" and examples. The ideal remained the same; it was only the means by which he hoped to achieve it that changed.

CHAPTER FIVE

PLATO REDIVIVUS

IN THE rush to monarchy which accompanied the restoration of Charles II in 1660, Milton's brave hope for a Polybian free commonwealth with a dominant aristocracy of virtue was swept away, and the efforts of the Harringtonians, zealous to the end, seemed to have come to naught. It has sometimes been said that with the Restoration, republicanism in England was dead. In a practical sense, no doubt, this is true. But from another point of view, it is not true at all. When the honeymoon between the king and his subjects was over, much was again to be heard of the notions of classical republicanism, and they were once more to become an issue in English politics.

Several reasons may be advanced to explain why this should have been the case. For one thing, Charles was moderate in his demands for the punishment of his enemies; on his return there was nothing like any systematic attempt to exterminate those who held republican views.[1] Of those who were notorious commonwealth men, some, like Harrington and Wildman, were imprisoned; some, like Henry Nevill, sought safety in inconspicuous retirement; and some, like Algernon Sydney and Edmund Ludlow, found it prudent to live abroad. The republicans were scattered and they were silenced, but they remained alive, for the most part, and were ready to teach old doctrines should new opportunities occur.

Another circumstance which made it certain that classical republicanism would reappear if the right circumstances presented themselves was the failure of the Restoration to produce a really effective attack on the political reputation either of the classical states to which republicans looked or of their supposed modern counterpart. Attacks, of course, were made, but they were of a character which was not fundamentally destructive of the objects at which they were aimed. The assertion was made that the reputation of the antique states rested on lying historians and declaimers,[2] and royal-

---

[1] Royalist vengeance, however, did sporadically pursue republican exiles on the Continent. Both Sydney and Ludlow were objects of plots for their assassination.

[2] See the passage from *The censure of the Rota* (1660), p. 8, quoted above, p. 1.

ists were fond of repeating Filmer's old contention that the greatness of Rome under the emperors outshone that of the republic,[3] but such charges scarcely damaged in any basic way the reputation of either Rome or the Greek states. A more serious charge the royalists did indeed make when they asserted that Rome under the republic was torn by internal dissensions, but even of this argument they scarcely made effective use.[4] Partly this was due to the fact that republicans themselves had pointed out the fact often enough, as we have seen, and had explained it as being due, not to republicanism, but to defects in the balance of the state.[5] The comparative ineffectiveness of the royalist attack is illustrated also by what happened in the case of Venice. The political reputation of the Most Serene Republic was hardly demolished by anything said against it in *The censure of the Rota*[6] or by Baxter's exclamations over Venice being a place where popery and whoredom held sway.[7] A few writers did indeed bring forth the really damaging arguments that the idea of the age-old tranquillity of the city was a myth and that the government was in fact a tyrannical oligarchy.[8] Some undertook, too, to demonstrate that the greatness of Venice was due, not to its government, but to such accidental and external causes as its location.[9] But even these charges were not presented with the fullness of evidence which enforces conviction. Nothing was said that would have caused old republicans to repudiate one of their principal models. Moreover, circumstances conspired to keep Venice favorably before the public eye. The political reputation of the republic was, in fact, so firmly established, that royalists found that the simplest thing to do with it was to revert to the old pre-revolutionary view that the Venetian doge was really a king and Venice a limited monarchy something like England.[10] It is clear that interest in the city remained high. Books concerned with it continued to appear and sources of information were ample.

But in the case of Venice this is not all that we have to observe. It is clear that as the battle lines were drawn in the 1670's between Charles and his opponents, there was a heightening of interest in the

---

[3] G. S. declared in *The dignity of kingship asserted* (1660) that "as an Empire Rome flourished as long, and was incomparably more glorious, then in its own condition when a Common wealth" (pp. 99–100).   [4] *Ibid.*, p. 99.

[5] Milton, *P.w.*, II, 125; Harrington, *Oceana*, p. 36.   [6] Pp. 7, 15.

[7] *Holy commonwealth*, pp. 225–26.   [8] Wren, *Monarchy asserted*, pp. 72 ff.

[9] G. S., *op. cit.*, p. 101. Cf. Wren, pp. 69 ff., and the attack on the models of the republicans in *Vox vere Anglorum, or Englands loud cry for their king*.

[10] G. S., *op. cit.*, p. 101.

city. In a dozen years no fewer than ten titles appeared in which English readers found extended discussions and descriptions of one aspect or another of the government of the republic.[11] There is evidence that some of this interest centered around the Venetian balloting-box which Harrington had sought so strongly to recommend, and proposals for introducing it into England.[12] But it is clear that it was not only the ballot in which there was a renewal of interest. The scheme for the government of Carolina drawn up in 1669, a scheme variously attributed to Locke and to Shaftesbury,[13] and complete not only with the ballot, but a Grand Council, a nobility, and the prediction that it would last forever, shows that many features of the Venetian constitution were once more engaging attention. Further evidence leading to the same conclusion is afforded by the plan drawn up, probably by William Penn, in 1676 for the government of New Jersey. This has not only the ballot and a Grand Council with Harringtonian features, but an imitation of the Venetian Council of Ten in the provision that seven honest persons could accuse of treason anyone suspected of planning to alter the constitution.[14]

No one who keeps these facts in mind will be surprised at the reappearance of republican sentiment during the reign of Charles II. Sometime in the second half of the 1670's the powerful political poem known as *Britannia and Rawleigh* was composed. The authorship is perhaps uncertain, but a good case can be made for the traditional

[11] Jean Gailhard, *The present state of the princes and republicks of Italy, with observations on them* (London, 1668); the same author's *The present state of the republick of Venice, as to the government, laws, forces, etc. of that commonwealth* (London, 1669); Richard Lassels, *The voyage of Italy, or a complete journey through Italy* (Paris "to be sold at London," 1670); Battista Nani, *The history of the affairs of Europe in this present age, but more particularly of the republic of Venice,* trans. Sir Robert Honywood (London, 1673); John Ray, *Observations, topographical, moral, and physiological; made in a journey through part of the Low-Countries, Germany, Italy, and France* (London, 1673); Trajano Boccalini, *The politicke touchstone,* trans. Henry Earl of Monmouth (London, 1674); [César Vischard de Saint-Réal], *The conspiracy of the Spaniards against the state of Venice* (London, 1675); *The works of the famous Nicolas Machiavel,* trans. Henry Nevill (London, 1675; 2nd ed., 1680); [Abraham Nicolas Amelot de la Houssaye], *The history of the government of Venice, wherein the policies, councils, magistrates, and laws of that state are fully related, and the use of the balloting box, exactly described* (London, 1677); *Reliquiae Wottonianae* (London, 1672).

[12] The title-page of the 1677 translation of Houssaye's *History of the government of Venice* pointed out as one of the features of the work that it contained "the use of the balloting box, exactly described." Ray in his *Observations,* fol. 157, made a collection of descriptions of the ballot out of the Venetian historians. This is cited in the tract proposing the introduction of the ballot into England which is considered below, p. 138.

[13] These attributions are discussed by Russell Smith, *op. cit.,* pp. 159 ff., who favors Shaftesbury.   [14] Russell Smith, pp. 161 ff.

attribution to Andrew Marvell.[15] There is no uncertainty whatever about the author's program. A long and bitter attack on the corruptions of the court of Charles II and his tyrannical tendencies leads Britannia to give up the attempt,

> The Stuart from the Tyrant to devide,[16]

and to turn instead to a republic on the Venetian model:

> To the serene Venetian state I'le goe
> From her sage mouth fam'd Principles to know.[17]

Like Harrington, Britannia finds Venice the embodiment of antique political wisdom. She announces that in the Most Serene Republic she will,

> the Prudence of the Antients read
> To teach my People in their steps to tread.[18]

Moreover,

> By those great Patterns such a state I'le frame
> Shall darken story, Ingross loudmouthd fame.[19]

[15] The poem is attributed to Marvell in the 1689 *Poems on affairs of state* and in most editions of that poet before Margoliouth's (Oxford, 1927, 2 vols.). It is also given to Marvell by the hand which added ascriptions to some of the satires in Harleian Ms. 7315 in the British Museum. On the ground that the "tone and style are unlike Marvell's" and that the poem is not sensible, moderate, or witty, Margoliouth inclines to the view that it was not Marvell's and assigns it to the unknown author of *Oceana and Britannia*, a political satire formerly attributed to Marvell but now recognized from internal evidence to belong to 1681 (see *Complete works*, ed. A. B. Grosart [n. p., 1872–75, 4 vols.], I, lix–lxi). These arguments are not very convincing. One can grant that the poem is not sensible only if one is prepared to admit that the whole complex of ideas associated with classical republicanism was not sensible, a very large admission indeed and one which, considering not only the ideas themselves but the stature of the men who held them, I am very far from being willing to make. Moreover, inasmuch as hardly a single satire of those attributed to Marvell can be proved beyond question to have been among those written by him, it is difficult to see by what process an editor arrives at the conclusion that the tone and style are unlike those of Marvell's satirical poems. Certainly one can form no valid notions about Marvell's satirical style from his garden poetry, which dates from a much earlier period and was produced in a wholly different mood. Moreover, in content the poem has two characteristics which favor the traditional attribution. It was obviously written by a person who had been influenced by Harrington. We have to connect Marvell with Harrington the fact that the two men were close friends and that Marvell had attended meetings of the Rota club (see Smith's *Harrington*, p. 127). In the second place, the poem was written by an admirer of Venice. Marvell's admiration of, and interest in, Venice is explicit not only in poems of doubtful authenticity like *Nostradamus's Prophecy* (l. 48), but in *Last instructions to a painter* (l. 402), of which Margoliouth expresses the opinion that it is, of all the satires attributed to Marvell, the one about the authenticity of which there is the most certainty (I, 268). See further Grosart's note on Marvell's repeated citations of Venice, I, 336.

[16] L. 142.   [17] Ll. 155–56.   [18] Ll. 157–58.   [19] Ll. 159–60.

But until this ideal can be achieved, Britannia calls on Raleigh to teach England's noble youth,

> to scorn the Carwells, Pembrookes, Nells,
> The Cleavelands, Osbornes, Barties, Lauderdales.
> Poppea, Tegeline and Acte's name
> Yeild to all these in Lewdness, lust, and shame.
> Make 'em admire the Sidnies, Talbots, Veres,
> Blake, Candish, Drake, (men void of slavish fears)
> True sons of Glory, Pillars of the state,
> On whose fam'd Deeds all tongues, all writers wait.[20]

Clearly, what the author had in mind was a state on the Venetian model led by an able and active aristocracy. Moreover, like Harrington, he saw in "Greek arts and Roman armes" the key to the future of the land. The poem concludes with a truly Harringtonian vision of the imperial destiny of an England remade by ancient prudence:

> Greek arts and Roman armes in her conjoyned
> Shall England raise, releive opprest mankind.
> As Joves great sunn the infested globe did free
> From noxious Monsters, Hellborn tyranny,
> Soe shall my England by a Holy Warr
> In Triumph lead chaind tyrants from afarr.
> Her true Crusado shall at last pull down
> The Turkish Crescent and the Persian sun.
> Freed by thy labours, Fortunate blest Isle,
> The Earth shall rest, the Heavens shall on thee smile,
> And this kind secret for reward shall give:
> No Poisonous tyrant on thy ground shall live.

This poem was not published until 1689, when it appeared in *Poems on affairs of state*. To what extent it circulated in manuscript, it is impossible to say. Its mere existence is striking evidence of the revival of classical republicanism, at least as an ideal, in the 1670's.

The protracted struggle between Charles II and the various groups opposed to arbitrary monarchial power reached its crisis in the latter part of that decade and the early 1680's. It was a struggle intensified by bitter religious rivalries and one in which civil war was feared and often predicted.[21] In 1678, Titus Oates appeared with his tale of a great Popish plot aimed at killing Charles II, putting his brother, the Duke of York, on the throne, and reëstablishing the Roman

[20] Ll. 169–76.

[21] Sir John Dalrymple, *Memoirs of Great Britain and Ireland* (London, 1771–88, 3 vols., 2nd ed.), I, 54.

church. The details were fantastic. London was to be fired, Protestants were to be massacred, and a French and Irish army was to invade England. According to one story, the murder of Charles was to be accomplished by poison administered by the Queen's physician; another had it that he was to be shot by silver bullets; still another, that he was to be set upon by ruffians and stabbed with a consecrated knife.[22] Both the supporters of the king, presently to be known as Tories, and the country party, or Whigs, sought cynically to make use of the plot for their own purposes. It lent itself, however, most easily to the designs of the latter group, and it was among them that its most ardent suppressors, led by Shaftesbury, were to be found. Tory pamphleteers charged that the plot was largely an invention of the Whigs to cloak and at the same time further their own treasonable designs.[23] The Whigs, taking advantage of the popular clamor, took up the whole question of the succession, a matter rendered acute by the Duke of York's being a communicant of the Church of Rome. Various projects were advanced, among which were two principal schemes. One was to accept the succession of York but under limitations which would have rendered him powerless to overturn either political or religious liberty. The other and more popular plan, favored by those Whigs who accepted the leadership of Shaftesbury, was to exclude York entirely and provide for the succession of Charles II's illegitimate son, the Duke of Monmouth. In pursuance of this latter scheme, the Whigs passed through the Commons in 1679 the First Exclusion Bill, which Charles prevented from going to the Lords by proroguing Parliament in May, 1679. For more than a year, until the autumn of 1680, he refrained from calling that body. The period was one of intense agitation and excitement. Stories were circulated of a mysterious "Black Box" which was supposed to contain proof of the legitimacy of the Duke of Monmouth.[24] "Petitioners," who prayed the King to assemble Parliament, were answered by "Abhorrers," who denounced the idea. The air was thick with charges of plots and counterplots.[25] Charles maneuvered the opposition leaders into a reconstitution of the Privy Council, on a plan suggested by Sir William Temple, and then coolly maneuvered them out, having in the meantime paid no attention to them. Parliament met again in 1680. Once again the

---

[22] See below, p. 148.   [23] See below, p. 137.

[24] These were attacked in the Tory tract *The interest of the three kingdoms with respect to the business of the black box* (London, 1680).   [25] Dalrymple, I, 53 ff.

Exclusion Bill was presented and passed the lower house, only to be narrowly defeated in the Lords, and once again Parliament was prorogued and finally dissolved. Charles's last parliament met at Oxford on March 21, 1681.[26] The circumstances under which it assembled were extraordinary. The Whigs, greatly in the majority and in an angry mood, were determined to clip the royal prerogatives and exclude James from the succession. They went backed with bands of armed men. Charles likewise appeared in force, and the road to Oxford was lined with his supporters.[27] Civil war indeed seemed a likely outcome.

It was to influence the King and the Parliament "about to assemble" at Oxford that *Plato redivivus* was published. The Henry Nevill who was the author of this remarkable work was the same one whom we have met previously as an old friend of Harrington's and who had been extremely active in the affairs of the Rota Club just before the Restoration. Since that time he had lived in retirement, keeping up his association with the author of *Oceana* until the latter's death in 1677. *Plato redivivus* shows that he was as completely under the influence of the complex of ideas associated with classical republicanism as he had ever been. The Roman republic was "the best and most glorious Government that ever the sun saw";[28] Lycurgus, "the greatest Politician that ever Founded any Government";[29] Machiavelli, whom Nevill translated, was "the Divine Machiavil,"[30] the "best and most honest of all the modern Politicians."[31] Governments, if properly instituted, might last for centuries, even eternally.[32] We meet also, as we would expect, the theory of mixed government, though in a curious form which obviously represents a skillful adaptation of the idea to the purposes which he had in mind.[33]

The book is in the form of a dialogue, as its title suggests, be-

---

[26] On the Oxford Parliament see Dalrymple, I, 58–59.

[27] A somewhat biased but striking picture of the assembling of the Oxford Parliament is contained in *A caveat against the Whiggs* (London, 1714), pp. 82–83.

[28] (London, 1681), p. 24. [29] P. 52. [30] P. 21. [31] P. 217.

[32] Pp. 35, 66, 138–39, 229.

[33] Lest it should seem that he was arguing openly for classical republicanism, he suppresses both the classical origin of the theory of mixed government and its republican connotations, not only taking the theory over and applying it to the English monarchy as various writers had done ever since the sixteenth century, but making the bland assertion that mixed government was unknown to the ancients (pp. 92, 175). As an old Harringtonian and translator of Machiavelli, of course, he knew better. He chose to tell only part of the truth and that not unmixed with falsehood.

tween an English gentleman, who is Nevill's spokesman; a physician, who represents the exclusionist view of which Nevill disapproved;[34] and a noble Venetian visiting in England. The relation of the Venetian model to the proposals of the English gentleman, who carries the burden of the dialogue, is precisely indicated at the outset when he turns to the visitor with the remark that "your Government is this day the only School in the World that breeds such Physicians as are able to cure ailing Governments."[35] Nevill, moreover, approached his task with all the old notions about Venice in mind. We find him praising the "admirable Stability" of the republic and repeating the favorite notion of Venetian admirers that the state had lasted for twelve centuries without change.[36] It is clear that, like Harrington, he viewed the republic as being in many ways the modern counterpart of the antique commonwealths. Fundamentally, what he proposed was the remaking of the existing monarchy on the basis of two major proposals, both of them Venetian in character. The first of these was a revival of the old project of making the English king "somthing like a Duke of Venice," a project which Laurens had seen as the object of some of the Independent leaders back in the late 1640's.[37] When the English gentleman enumerates the constitutional restraints on the king, the Venetian observes that the King of England was much like a Venetian doge.[38] The English gentleman points out, however, that the similitude is not exact inasmuch as the English king exercised several powers not possessed by a Venetian duke. Specifically, these are enumerated as control over foreign affairs, the disposal of the public revenue, the appointing of civil and ecclesiastical officers, and the absolute disposal of the land and naval forces.[39] Inasmuch as these are exactly the powers in the exercise of which Nevill proposes to limit the king when, a hundred-odd pages later, he passes from the descriptive to the remedial part of his dialogue,[40] it is clear that the effect of his proposals was intended to be to make the king, insofar as his powers were concerned, very much like a Venetian doge indeed.[41]

Nevill's second proposal was likewise Venetian in character. He remarks that the four great powers of which he proposed to "abate" the crown could hardly be abolished, for that would mean an end to

---

[34] P. 183. It seems reasonable to suppose that the physician stands for Locke, who was closely associated with Shaftesbury.   [35] P. 24.   [36] P. 24.
[37] See above, p. 46.   [38] P. 120.   [39] Pp. 120–21.   [40] Pp. 256–59.
[41] Nevill remarks that he would abate the royal prerogative "in those matters only which concern our enjoyment of our All, that is, our Lives, Liberties, and Estates" (p. 254). Charles may well have wondered why he inserted the word "only."

government.[42] Nor did he think that they should be wholly given to
Parliament, for Parliament was a body "more fitted to make laws
than execute them." He would, therefore, set up four councils to
act with the king in the exercise of the "four great *Magnalia* of
Government." These councils would be appointed in Parliament for
terms of three years and would be subject to the principle of rotation,
one-third being newly chosen each year. At the conclusion of his
term no councillor would be permitted to serve on any of the councils
until a time equal to that during which he had served had elapsed.[43]
The members of the councils would be responsible to Parliament,[44]
and with the consent of a majority of the members of the appropriate
council, and only with their consent, the King would exercise, like a
Doge of Venice, the four great "*Magnalia.*"[45] In such a system, of
course, Nevill was faced with the problem of what to do with the
Privy Council, a problem rendered the more pressing by the recent
attempts of Sir William Temple to give it greater importance in
the government. Nevill met it by arguing that the Privy Council
was no essential part of the constitution, a contention which suggests that he would willingly have seen it abolished. His proposal,
however, was to relegate it to "meddling" with "the Affairs of
Merchants, Plantations, Charters, and other Matters," but with
the provision that it "act nothing in any of the Matters properly
within the Jurisdiction of these four councils."[46] The Venetian and
Harringtonian inspiration of these proposals is obvious. Not only
the rotative feature in them but several others owed much to the
Venetian model. In function, organization, and purpose, they have
points in common with the Councils of Sages or Preconsultors, committees of the Senate, who in the Venetian system sat with the Doge
and the Council of Six in considering all matters of importance,
though Nevill perhaps thought of them as having greater executive
authority than in the Venetian system. Not only do these parallels
exist, but in at least one respect their Venetian inspiration is specifically acknowledged. After outlining his councilar scheme, the
English gentleman says to the Venetian: "This I learnt from your
Quarantia's at Venice: and the Use is excellent; for being in such
a Circulation, and sure to have their intervals of Power, they will
neither grow so insolent as to brave their King, nor will the Prince
have any occasion to corrupt them, although he had the means to do
it, which in this new Model he cannot have."[47] The resemblance be-

[42] P. 255.   [43] P. 259.   [44] P. 260.
[45] P. 259.   [46] P. 251.   [47] P. 259.

tween Nevill's proposals in these matters and Venetian precedent is important, for it establishes the connection between that model and the proposals for councilar magistracies responsible to Parliament which were made by Milton, Harrington, and Nevill and the later development of cabinet government in England. In these men, under the influence of the ideas evolved by classical republicanism, the principle of cabinet government and Parliamentary responsibility was expressed long before it became an actual fact in English constitutional procedure.

Such were the two basic proposals by which Nevill undertook to remodel the monarchy. Two additional features of his discussion show the influence of Venetian precedents. We find him providing for the suspension by a judge of the right of *habeas corpus* on the return of a warrant of imprisonment issued by any one of the four councils when the public safety was threatened, a council issuing such a warrant being responsible to the next meeting of Parliament.[48] This proposal for a constitutional suspension of one of the prime guaranties of English liberty will surprise no one who remembers the characteristic notions of classical republicanism. Harrington had incorporated similar provisions in the constitution of Oceana in imitation of the Venetian Council of Ten, with the object of providing the state with a means of meeting conspiracies swiftly and with adequate power. With both theory and the atmosphere of plots in which *Plato redivivus* was composed suggesting it to him, it is not difficult to see why Nevill should have made his proposal.

The other respect in which the book shows Venetian influence is in the discussion of the upper house of Parliament. The Venetian suggests that it would be better to have in place of a house of lords a senate composed either of members elected annually or of life members.[49] The suggestion embodies, of course, the two principles involved in the constitution of the Venetian Senate. There can be little question that it represented Nevill's view of the ideal situation, for he uses in *Plato redivivus* conceptions regarding the nature of the balance in England which are very similar to those which he had advanced in his speeches of 1659 to argue against a peerage and a house of lords.[50] On the principle, however, of as little change at present as possible, the plan is rejected for the traditional House of Lords.[51]

To achieve the instituting of his system, Nevill proposed no resort to arms; instead he professed to hope that the King could be in-

48 P. 265. 49 P. 272.
50 Burton, *Diary*, III, 132–33, 321, 331. 51 P. 273.

duced to see the necessity of voluntarily surrendering part of his power, and that he would emulate Theopompus, King of Sparta, who freely consented to the creation of the Ephors, as a check on his power.[52] To persuade Charles of this necessity, Nevill developed an elaborate argument which turns out on examination to be thoroughly Harringtonian. The basic maxim in politics, we are told, "is that Empire is founded in Property."[53] The king and the peers had formerly controlled most of the land and hence possessed the basis of political power; but with the passage of time, various causes had operated to transfer the ownership of land predominantly to the people, by whom Nevill meant, of course, the land-owning classes. Inasmuch as these classes rather than the king now possessed the greater part of the basis of power, the foundations of the existing monarchy were unstable. The fundamental cause of the distractions of the realm was that the king possessed more power than the existing conditions of property permitted.[54] To give him more power would only aggravate an already impossible situation; he must, therefore, have less. Unless the disproportion was rectified by voluntary action on the king's part and that of a coöperating Parliament, Nevill saw in the future only civil war, the ruin of the state, and subservience to France. The argument is worth noting: we have Harringtonian agrarian theories presented to explain why a Venetian remodeling of the monarchy was a natural necessity. It was an argument that more than one group could make use of.

Nevill's book made a considerable stir. It was answered in 1684 by Thomas Goddard in *Plato's demon; or, the state physician unmaskt. Being a discourse in answer to a book called Plato redivivus*. It can be said of this author that he scarcely understood what Nevill was about. He repeats all the usual Tory notions, particularly those which had received their classic statement in Filmer,[55] without doing very much damage to Nevill. More effective answers had already appeared. The author of *Antidotum Britannicum* (1681) condemned Nevill for following foreign models. *A seasonable address to both houses of Parliament*, which appeared in the same year, flatly charged that the author of *Plato redivivus* was trying to make the king a "Doeg [sic!] of Venice."[56] A similar clarity about Nevill's proposals characterizes a tract of 1682, *The apostate protestant. A letter to a friend*. "I do not wonder," wrote the author, "that this Gentleman should indeavour, as he

[52] Pp. 237–40.   [53] P. 35.   [54] Pp. 232–33, 167–69.
[55] See especially his repetition of the patriarchal argument on p. 87.
[56] P. 9. See also p. 15.

doth, to persuade the King (as if he could Cully him out of his Rights) to share those four great Branches of his Prerogative among the people. . . . For if these things were done, the Ends of this Gentleman, and of his Party, would soon be served, and His Majesty would shrink into a Duke of Venice strait."[57]

One of these attacks alleges that Nevill's real aim was a republic.[58] We must now examine this charge. On the face of it, *Plato redivivus* was an attempt to realize at least some of the aims of classical republicanism within the frame of the monarchy. When the Venetian gentleman remarks that he begins to smell a republic, the Englishman replies that it is not necessary to overturn the monarchy in order to achieve the desired reform of the constitution, and that it would be wicked and impious to attempt a republic under the prevailing circumstances.[59] One would infer from such statements, as well as the general character of the proposals themselves, that nothing more than a reformed monarchy was Nevill's aim. No doubt as far as immediate aims were concerned, this was true. But the man himself and various considerations invite us to make a distinction between immediate and ultimate aims, and to ask whether the author of *A seasonable address* was not correct in his analysis. We may observe, for one thing, that Nevill finds the balance of property and hence of power to reside in his own time in the people, the land-owning classes in general. Although this class was in fact an aristocracy, it was the people in Nevill's scheme of things. The present state of England inclined, therefore, as he declared, to a "popularity."[60] Now there was no idea of which such classical republicans as Harrington were more convinced than that a monarchy had to be supported by an army or a powerful aristocracy, and that it was incompatible with the situation in which the people held preponderant power.[61] Nevill does not make this deduction, for to have done so would have been incompatible with his professed aims, declaring that the prevailing situation could be remedied by the king's giving up some of his power, but it is hard to believe that a man so full of Harringtonian notions as he obviously was did not also entertain this one. Moreover,

---

[57] P. 36. See further the passage on *Plato redivivus* in *Oceana and Britannia* (ll. 114 ff.), an exclusionist satire on both James and Nevill which predicts the institution of a Harringtonian state by Monmouth. This poem is printed by Grosart in his edition of Marvell in a section of "Unauthenticated pieces," I, 443 ff. It also appears in the first volume of *Poems on affairs of state: from the time of Oliver Cromwell to the abdication of K. James the Second* (n. p., 1703–07, 4 vols.).

[58] *A seasonable address to both houses of Parliament*, p. 9.

[59] Pp. 227, 229.   [60] P. 189.   [61] See above, p. 70.

various statements in *Plato redivivus* compel the raising of the question of his ultimate aims. A republic is declared to be very advantageous,[62] and the disclaimer of republican intentions is limited to the "circumstances we are now in." It is limited, moreover, to the period while "we are under Oaths to a Lawful King."[63] But most significant of all, perhaps, is his declaration that he could have made a better government and that the government proposed was only the best that the people were ready for and that could be achieved at the time.[64] It would seem proper to conclude that Nevill was still in principle a republican, that his ideal was a republic, that he sought to realize immediately within the frame of the monarchy some of the aims of classical republicanism, and that he hoped that a reformed monarchy, for all that he professed to think that it might last for a long time,[65] would prove but a step to a full republican system.

We may now ask to what extent such ideas as he advanced represented the aims of the Whigs in general. The Whig party of the early 1680's, like the party which overthrew Charles I, was essentially the product of a combination between the commercial classes of the cities, the Puritan squires of the House of Commons, and a group of great land-owning and Protestant houses. In the last of these categories were such families as the Cecils, Russells, Montagues, Sydneys, Cavendishes, and Holleses, who had for the most part risen to great estate in the sixteenth century, who had in the 1640's usually either remained aloof from, or been hostile to, the cause of Charles I, and from whom came the Denzil Lord Holleses who opposed alike the first and second Charles and the protectorate of Cromwell. In the early 1680's they supplied the Lord William Russells, Earls of Essex, and Algernon Sydneys of the struggle with Charles II, and it may be noted, parenthetically, that their descendants became the great Whig oligarchs of the eighteenth century. All of the groups who coalesced to form the Whig party by no means had identical aims. It was the object of the great land-owning families to make themselves the real rulers of England. Whether this would be done in terms of the domination of a narrow or a broad aristocracy was a question not yet decided, for Nevill's contention that the balance of power had passed to the "popularity" was an over-statement of the situation.[66] But the Whig aristocrats saw clearly that such a system would have to rest on a broad national basis. To secure this, though they were very far indeed from proposing any such nineteenth-

[62] P. 229.   [63] P. 227.   [64] P. 292.   [65] P. 229.
[66] See below, p. 185.

century program as a vast extension of the suffrage, they did attempt to gain, and in a large measure were successful in gaining, the support of the non-conformists, among whom was many an old republican, by espousing or at least defending the cause of religious dissent.[67] It was the easier for them to succeed in this aim because, like the dissenters themselves, they were opponents of what the age called "arbitrary power," because such power meant in the seventeenth century royal power, and because it was not as apparent to Englishmen in 1680 as later that the power of a ruling aristocracy could be quite as arbitrary as that of any monarch. Opposition to arbitrary power was the bond which drew all varieties of Whigs together and gave the group what unity it possessed in 1680. As to what they would have in place of arbitrary power, Whig opinion varied among those who wanted a domination of the Commons, a domination of the Lords,[68] and among those who wished one or the other of these things within the frame of the monarchy, those who were prepared to pursue them outside that frame, if necessary, and those who desired to do so. There was furthermore a division of opinion, as we have seen, between those who were exclusionists and those who were not, and between those who looked to Monmouth as their hope and those who were already looking ahead to the accession of William of Orange.

This being the somewhat heterogeneous character of the Whig party under Charles II, we cannot suppose that the ideas of Nevill represented anything like what we may call *the* program of the Whig party. But some things are clear; for instance, that Nevill's professed program may be taken as a fair statement of the aims of those Whigs who were not exclusionists and who wished to permit the accession of the Duke of York but under limitations which would render him largely powerless. In the second place, the project of making the king, whoever he might be, like a Duke of Venice as far as the exercise of power was concerned, was one which cannot but have been greeted by approval, not only by those who agreed with Nevill on exclusion, but by exclusionists and other varieties of Whigs as well. The third thing which is clear is that though they were no doubt a small minority, there were enough republicans active in Whig circles to make it correct to say that the republican element in Nevill's thought was representative of a certain amount of republi-

---

[67] See Lord John Russell's comments in his *Life of Lord William Russell* (London, 1820, 3rd ed.), I, 271; II, 13; and Louise Fargo Brown, *The first Earl of Shaftesbury* (New York and London, 1933), pp. 306–07.   [68] See below, p. 185.

canism which was present in Whig circles. Nor was this republicanism limited to those who were anti-exclusionists. It was present among the exclusionists themselves. If this was not the case, at least the Tory pamphleteers were persuaded to a man that it was. It was charged that there was a "phanatical plot" among the Whigs,[69] that Monmouth was merely a tool in the hands of the exclusionists,[70] and that their real object was the complete subversion of the monarchy on the death of Charles II. The "main incentive" of the"Republicans," declared the author of *Religion and loyalty supporting each other*, was "their hopes, that the breaking of the succession [by the Exclusion Bill] would upon his present Majesties death break the Monarchy to pieces and restore their beloved Commonwealth."[71] Another pamphleteer set forth the republican danger by asserting that a "Republick (were there any possibility of settling one) would destroy all our present Peace, and Felicity, ruinate our Trade and Traffick, involve us in a Field of Blood, alarm all our Neighbours, make our best Allies our bitterest Enemies; and probably draw upon us the united force of Christendom to crush the Embryo."[72]

There was another respect in which Nevill was representative of Whig aims. It is clear that not only the project of making the king like a duke of Venice was in the air, but that the heightened interest in that republic which we have observed in the 1670's had resulted in its figuring in various ways in Whig thought. An anonymous poem of 1682, *The impartial trimmer*, concludes with a contrast between England's wretched plight and

> happy Venice, whose good Laws are such,
> No private Crime the publick Peace can touch.[73]

---

[69] *A narrative of the phanatical plot, setting forth the treasonable designs which they have been carrying on against the king and government.* By John Zeale, Gent. (London, 1683).

[70] *A seasonable address*, p. 14. The charge long continued to be made. See *A caveat against the Whiggs*, p. 101.   [71] (London, 1681), p. 5.

[72] *The interest of the three kingdoms with respect to the business of the black box* (London, 1680), p. 15. This tract consists in part of passages adapted to the situation in 1680 but otherwise quoted verbatim from a tract sometimes attributed to Sir Roger L'Estrange which had appeared in 1660 as *A plea for limited monarchy as it was established in this nation before the late war.* For further charges that a republic was aimed at by the Whigs see *An address to the freemen and free-holders of the nation* (London, 1682), p. iii; *A seasonable address*, pp. 15, 17; *The present interest of England; or a confutation of the Whiggish conspirators anti-monyan principle* (London, 1683), pp. 4, 35; *The power of parliaments in the case of succession* (London, 1680), *passim.* Like the charge that Monmouth was merely the tool of the Whig leaders, the charge that they aimed at a republic long continued to be made. See *A caveat against the Whiggs*, p. 101, and the character of "The republican Whig Jacobite" in *The character of a Whig under several denominations* (London, 1700), p. 89.   [73] *Poems on affairs of state*, I, 168.

Nostradamus's prophecy, another political poem which may quite possibly belong to this period rather than to Marvell, to whom it has often been assigned,[74] praises Venetian liberty.[75] Still a third poem, *Oceana and Britannia*, though it attacks Nevill from the exclusionist point of view, mentions Rome, Sparta, and Venice as the states which will be excelled upon the institution of a Harringtonian state in England by Monmouth.[76] *The third part of no protestant plot*, one of the series of tracts which appeared in 1682, celebrated the famed justice of the Venetian republic and called on Charles II to imitate it.[77] A Tory tract of the same year testifies to the prominence of the Venetian model by arguing that a government of the Venetian sort without a king would not insure freedom from arbitrary power.[78] There was a great deal of interest in the Venetian secret ballot, which was doubtless a culmination of the interest which we have observed developing anew in it in the previous decade. The best evidence at once of this fact and of the fact that Nevill's interest in Venice was representative of a general interest in it in the Whig groups is afforded by a tract which appeared early in the 1680's as *The benefit of the ballot, with the nature and use thereof; particularly in the republick of Venice*.[79] Actuated by the same desire to avoid political parties which Harrington had worked under, the author proposed the introduction of the Venetian ballot into England and suggested its use, as in Venice and Oceana, in Parliament itself.[80] But he had other aims also. Thoroughly under the influence of the ideas of classical republicanism and apparently intent on realizing them, and possessed of all the notions associated with admiration of Venice, such as its continuing for centuries under its "ancient Rules" and its prospective immortality, the writer proposed that a Grand Council of life members be set up, consisting of the two houses of Parliament, and that these should elect by the ballot a "Council Di Stado" of thirty members, fifteen from each house, who would rotate through one-third retiring each year.[81] Great officers of state would be chosen out of the Grand Council, also by the ballot.[82] That the author was a Harringtonian is obvious, but it is equally clear that he was drawing his ideas directly from the Venetian

[74] See above, p. 126.
[75] L. 48. The poem is available in both Grosart's and Margoliouth's editions of Marvell.
[76] Ll. 49–51. This poem makes the prediction also that the state so instituted will last forever.   [77] P. 66.   [78] *An address to the freemen and free-holders*, p. iv.
[79] This tract was reprinted in 1693 in *State tracts; being a collection of several treatises relating to the government. Privately printed in the reign of K. Charles II*, pp. 443–46, from which I quote.   [80] Pp. 443–44.   [81] P. 444.   [82] P. 445.

model itself, a fact which is demonstrated by his citation of the collection of descriptions of the ballot of Venice in Ray's *Observations* and the description of the ballot with which the tract concludes.[83] About the same time, the activities of William Penn afford still further evidence of the importance of Venice in Whig thought, for it was in the early 1680's that he was busy with those activities as the Lycurgus or law-giver of Pennsylvania which resulted in a plan of government for that colony. This plan, with its Great Council or Senate, its Assembly, its four committees of the Senate rotating with one-third retiring each year, and its secret ballot, contained much that came doubtless from Venice through Harrington, but it is clear that the ballot came directly from Venice, and the provision for Penn's having two votes in the legislature bears the unmistakable impress of an imitation of the Venetian practice of giving a double vote to the Doge in the Grand Council.[84] This constitution is the more significant as showing the interest in Whig circles in Venice as a model because it was the product, not of Penn alone, but of a group of friends, among whom was possibly Algernon Sydney.[85]

The variety of the evidence is such as to enable us to say with certitude that Venetian precedents were in the minds, not merely of men like Nevill who proposed no violence, but of Whigs generally and in particular of those who were seen by the Tories as involved in a plot to subvert the government, and who in the period after Charles's sudden dissolution of the Oxford Parliament at the end of a few days and his triumph over the exclusionists, when it was widely believed that he would never call another parliament—he never did—resorted to plans for an insurrection.[86] But when a political reputation becomes associated with a partisan political program, as that of Venice

[83] P. 446.

[84] See the discussion of this constitution in Russell Smith, *op. cit.*, pp. 167 ff. Penn was a true classical republican who had traveled much on the Continent and was as familiar with Venetian practices at first hand as Harrington himself. He proposed also the use of the ballot according to the "method of the Venetians" in his plan for an European union (*The peace of Europe: The fruits of solitude, and other writings* [London and New York, n.d.], p. 11).

[85] See Smith, pp. 170 ff., for an excellent account of the activities involved in the framing of this constitution. Sydney's participation has been both asserted and denied. It is accepted by Smith, p. 170. For Sydney's own very clear interest in Venice see below, p. 158.

[86] Dalrymple, I, 76 ff. The Oxford Parliament was dissolved at the end of March, 1681. Shaftesbury, the most furious of these intriguers, was in custody from the beginning of July to December 1. His release marked his resumption of those intrigues and plots which culminated in his flight to the Continent in December, 1682, and his death there the following month.

so obviously had, it will not long go without attack. This truism
had been illustrated before, at the time of the Restoration, and it was
now again to be. The results of the attack on the two occasions
were, however, quite different. The earlier one, as we have seen,
had been ineffective and had done no real damage to the political
reputation of the republic. The assault which now developed dealt a
powerful blow at the vision of the ageless, perfectly-functioning state
which a long line of panegyrists had conjured up. There were several
reasons for this development. The favorable, or what we may now
call the Whig, view of Venice was based on accounts of the republic
which were derived from the works of Venetian champions like
Contarini and of political philosophers like Machiavelli who dated
back to the sixteenth century. These, as we have seen, were the first
accounts of Venice to be translated or widely circulated in England,
and they were the sources, therefore, to which Englishmen went first
for information about the republic. There had developed, however,
on the Continent in the seventeenth century a strong counter-current
of criticism of the city. This arose largely from the anti-Venetian
propaganda carried on by papal champions and Spanish interests in
the great quarrel between Venice and Pope Paul in 1605–06, a quarrel
which had as its aftermath the Spanish plot against the republic
a few years later,[87] and which produced as its most interesting
literary document the notorious *Squittinio della libertà Veneta* (1612).
This anonymous work was probably written by Alphonso della
Cueva, Marquis of Bedmar,[88] the Spanish ambassador at Venice.
Its character may be surmised from Saint-Réal's statement that Bedmar wrote with the deliberate object of destroying "that respect
which all Europe had shown for so many ages to this republic, as

[87] On the quarrel between Venice and the Pope see above, p. 44. Sarpi's famous
History of the Council of Trent, which had editions of the English translation in 1620,
1629, 1640, and 1676, was a Venetian counterblast to the papal propaganda. Whether
the Spanish plot of 1618 was an actual conspiracy or an invention of the Venetians to get
rid of Bedmar, the Spanish ambassador, has been the subject of some dispute. If it was an
invention of the Venetians, it was a good one, for it accords perfectly with Spanish
foreign policy in this period. For the details of the plot see the Abbé de Saint-Réal's
Conspiracy of the Spaniards against the republic of Venice, which I use in the London edition
of 1823, to which all subsequent references refer; P. J. Grosley, *Discussion historique
et critique sur la conjuration de Venise* (Paris, 1756); von Ranke, *Ueber die verschwörung
gegen Venedig* (Berlin, 1837); and Horatio F. Brown, "The Spanish conspiracy; an epi-
sode in the decline of Venice," in *Venetian studies* (London, 1887).

[88] The authorship has been variously assigned. See on the question and on the evidence for Bedmar's claims Amelot de la Houssaye, *Histoire du gouvernement de Venise*
(Amsterdam, 1695), sig. Ii2r; and Saint-Réal, *op. cit.*, pp. 1–18. All subsequent citations
of Houssaye are to the 1695 edition.

the most free and ancient of states."[89] The author undertook to prove several propositions: that Venice did not originate as a free state; that it was from time to time under the rule of emperors and kings; that it had changed its government several times; and that it was a narrow oligarchy in which only the small minority of citizens who were nobles had any rights. Venice, in short, did not have liberty in its origin, it had not perpetuated it, and it did not have it at the time the author wrote. Those who spoke with warmth and admiration of its government were wholly in error.[90] The *Squittinio* is a scurrilous work, a malicious libel with misrepresentations as gross as any it attacked, but it had an appeal to historical fact which on some matters was hard to meet. The Venetian Senate wisely decided not to attempt a direct answer.[91] Amelot de la Houssaye declared that it was read by every prince and minister in Europe,[92] but he was a prejudiced witness who wrote a long time after the event, and his remark must be disregarded. The evidence which I have presented in Chapter II is incontrovertible that the two early seventeenth-century editions of the *Squittinio* were smothered beneath the chorus of Venetian praise which poured from presses all over the Continent. There is no evidence whatever that the tract was widely known in England in the first six decades of the seventeenth century; I have, in fact, found no reference to it by an English writer in that period. Indeed, as we have seen, the first, and for long the only, effect in England of the controversy between Venice and the Pope out of which the tract arose had been to increase the political reputation of the republic.[93] In the 1670's and 80's, however, circumstances at which we shall presently have to look resulted in the resurrection of the tract and a wide circulation of it which made it readily available to English readers.[94]

The political reputation of Venice suffered also from the appearance of another book, *The maxims of the government of Venice*, which came out under the name of Paolo Sarpi, the remarkable man to whose activities we have already called attention as the moving spirit in the Venetian resistance to the papal claims in 1606. This work purported to be the secret instructions drawn up by Sarpi at the order of the Senate for the future guidance of the republic. It is Machiavellian in character in the sensational sense of the word. That Sarpi wrote it is highly questionable; it is quite likely that it

[89] P. 16.   [90] I use the edition published with Houssaye's *Histoire*, p. 7.
[91] Saint-Réal, p. 18; Houssaye, sig. Ii2v.
[92] Sig. Ii2r.   [93] See above, p. 44 f.   [94] See below, p. 143.

is a spurious work designed to blacken both Sarpi's reputation and that of the republic, and as such is to be considered as arising out of the same campaign as that which produced the *Squittinio*. In any case, it contains much that could not but injure the traditional view of the republic. Not only are many of the purported maxims unscrupulous in their advice, but the extended criticisms of the defects of the constitution[95] ill accorded with the conception of Venice as a masterpiece of politics. This work was not published in an English version until 1689; it is clear, however, that it circulated before that time in manuscript both on the Continent and in England.[96]

But what really provided English champions of the king's cause with ample materials for the attack on those who would remodel England on the Venetian model was two phenomenally successful works which appeared in the middle of the 1670's and which, paradoxically enough, got translated into English in the upsurge of interest in the republic in that decade. These were the Abbé de Saint-Réal's *Conjuration des Espagnols contre la Venise en 1618*, and Abraham Amelot de la Houssaye's *Histoire du gouvernement de Venise*. The first of these came out in 1674 and was translated into English the following year.[97] Saint-Réal was not a political satirist. He was primarily interested in telling his story, and he did not himself attack the Venetian government, but his book contained ample materials for anyone wishing to indulge in such attacks, in his account of the charges made against the republic by Spanish propagandists.[98] Houssaye's *Histoire* made its appearance two years later. "J'écris," the author began, "l'Histoire du Gouvernement de Venise, qui est sans contredit le plus beau de l'Europe en son genre, puisque c'est une fidéle copie des anciennes Républiques de la Gréce, et comme l'assemblage de toutes leurs plus excellentes loix."[99] Elsewhere, he declared that Venice was "célèbre par la forme de son Gouvernement, qui est un Chef-d'oeuvre de Politique."[100] But the picture which emerges from the following pages is different indeed from what these statements would lead one to expect. The *Histoire* was the work of a man who had spent three years in Venice in a minor diplomatic capacity, and who had seen only too clearly the symptoms of the decadence of the great republic. Not only Venetian policies are condemned or criticized, but Venetian institutions. The Senate was not the repository of wisdom. It was so slow to act that it sometimes seemed to be asleep. Incompetence and irresolution were its leading

---

[95] (London, 1707), pp. 22 ff.   [96] *Ibid.*, p. vii.   [97] See above, p. 140.
[98] Pp. 16–18.   [99] P. 1.   [100] Sig. xxir.

characteristics. It produced evil counsels more frequently than good ones. It followed the maxim of honoring heroes openly and making away with them secretly lest they should overshadow the Senate's authority.[101] In the whole government, fools were more common than the wise men that republics were supposed to produce.[102] Everything was sacrificed to keeping a narrow oligarchy in power. The nobles poisoned or otherwise made away with those who curried the favor of the people. Those who were too intelligent or who had oratorical gifts were exiled.[103] The parsimony of the nobles was so great that they left the Arsenal empty and the state so unprepared that it was unable to meet foreign attacks when they came.[104] In their private lives the Venetians were abandoned to their pleasures and dissipations. The youth of the republic, instead of being brought up in that sobriety and virtue which free states were supposed to encourage, were the most debauched, insolent, and licentious in the world.[105] These and similar charges are common in Houssaye's book. The circumstances surrounding its publication helped to give it an enormous popularity. Giustiniani, the Venetian ambassador in Paris, made a strong protest which resulted in a brief imprisonment of the author. Further protests about a second edition brought the suppression of the work, but there followed within three years twenty-two editions and translations into several languages, among them English in 1677. Moreover, apparently with the object of justifying himself, Houssaye brought forth the *Squittinio* and the *Harangue* of Louis Hélian, a tirade against the Venetians which had been delivered before the Emperor Maximilian by the French ambassador in 1510. These were published separately by Houssaye at Rouen in 1677, and appear in most editions of the *Histoire* after the first.[106]

It was inevitable with such materials at hand as Saint-Réal and

---

[101] Pp. 453–61, 468.   [102] P. 460.
[103] Pp. 469–70.   [104] P. 465.   [105] Pp. 487–88.

[106] For all that Houssaye was imprisoned and the second edition suppressed, there are several circumstances which suggest that the book was not displeasing to the French government and that its phenomenal circulation may even have been aided by the connivance of that government. It appeared at a time when Franco-Venetian relations, never very smooth since the League of Cambrai, were particularly ruffled (see pp. 475–76); it was printed by the king's printer; and it was dedicated to Louvois. Houssaye's imprisonment was short, and may well have been intended rather to placate the ambassador than to punish the author. The printing of the *Squittinio* and the *Harangue* with the book is understandable, as I have pointed out, in terms of the author's desire to justify his work to the world; it is by no means clear that it was necessary to justify it to the government. Certainly, had it been desired to carry on a propaganda campaign against the republic for political reasons, a more effective weapon than Houssaye's omnibus would have been hard to find.

Houssaye provided, that they would be put to use by partisans of the crown. Early in 1682 they were put to use in Otway's *Venice preserved*, which was drawn directly from Saint-Réal's book.[107] This play has been called "the best tragedy out of Shakespeare"; the opinion is open to question. What is not open to question is that it is one of the most notable political plays in the language, but that its significance has usually been either misunderstood or not fully perceived.[108] The common explanation runs that Shaftesbury, the leader of the exclusion movement against York, is caricatured in Antonio, the absurd Venetian senator;[109] that Shaftesbury is also represented in the play by Renault, who is one of the conspirators;[110] and that the plot in the play is a covert allegory of the Popish Plot.[111] The first two of these statements are undoubtedly correct, but we shall encounter major difficulties in attempting to make any political sense out of the play if we accept the third. If the political plot represented in the play is wholly an allegory of the Popish Plot, then Venice becomes England, the plot becomes an actual and dangerous one from which the state was happily rescued, and those who were zealous in suppressing the plot, among whom was Shaftesbury, should be celebrated as saviors of their country. But these things are as contrary to the play and to Otway's well-established Tory sympathies as anything could well be.[112] Venice as it appears in the play is not a glorious state whose happy deliverance is celebrated; it is rather a state not worth saving. It is impossible to suppose that by the actual plot of the play Otway intended to suggest that the Popish Plot was a genuine danger. He shared the Tory view that it was largely a fabrication of the Whigs, devoting the first part of the Prologue to making

[107] For the close relation between the two works see Charles F. McClumpha's edition of *The orphan* and *Venice preserved* (Boston, 1908), pp. 304–26.

[108] The most extraordinary instance is afforded by Roden Noel in the Introduction to his edition in the Mermaid Series in 1888. He advances the curious opinion that Otway had no political sense and that *Venice preserved* exhibits this fact (p. xxx).

[109] The grounds for this universally-accepted identification are fully set forth by Thomas Thornton in his edition of the *Works* (London, 1813, 3 vols.), I, xviii; III, 7.

[110] See J. C. Ghosh's edition of the *Works* (Oxford, 1932, 2 vols.), II, 509; Roswell G. Ham, *Otway and Lee* (New Haven, 1931), p. 190; and Montague Summers's edition of the *Complete works* (London, 1926, 3 vols.), I, lxxxviii, III, 278. The identification is clearly indicated by ll. 23–28 of the Prologue.

[111] For a typical statement of this view see Thornton's edition, I, xviii. See also McClumpha's discussion, pp. 34–35. Ghosh refers in his notes on the play only to the Popish Plot. He does point out in his notes on the two epilogues that Whig conspiracies are referred to by them, apparently without seeing that this fact affords a clue to the real plot in the play.

[112] On Otway's Tory principles, see Thornton, I, xviii. They are clearly indicated in the Dedication of the play and in many places in his works (see Ghosh's notes, *passim*).

fun of its fantastic details and the second half to making clear that the political plot in the play was a *different* plot. As for Shaftesbury, there can be no mistaking Otway's intentions regarding him: he portrayed him clearly and unmistakably as Antonio, who is a fool, and Renault, who is a knave. Furthermore, the notion that the political plot of the play is explained by saying that it is an allegory of the Popish Plot creates difficulties when we encounter the fact that Shaftesbury appears in the play in two different rôles. It may possibly explain why that statesman in his character as Antonio is found among the Venetian senators, that is, among the suppressors of the plot, but it explains nothing else.

It helps considerably to have the suggestion that the political plot hatched in the play was intended to have reference not only to the Popish Plot, but to the Whig conspiracies which were in the air.[113] It helps considerably because it is not logical to assume that a man of Tory sympathies wrote a play with political implications at a time when rumors of Whig conspiracies were the sensation of the time and did not intend his play to have reference to them as well as to a plot which was something of an old story when the play appeared. It helps considerably also because it is clear that Otway leveled his attack at Shaftesbury, not primarily because he was a zealous suppressor of the Popish Plot, but because he was the leader of the exclusionist movement against York which was supposed in Tory circles to be the product of a plot to subvert the government. Moreover, the suggestion helps because it asks us to believe the thoroughly sensible proposition that when the Tories made the play into a sort of paean of triumph, when Charles II ostentatiously visited it on the poet's day, and when the Duke of York made his first public appearance at it after his return from exile,[114] they were celebrating, not the suppression of the Popish Plot, which would be absurd to suppose, but the royal triumph over the exclusionist movement which had been secured by the dissolution of the Oxford Parliament the preceding March. Finally, it may be noted of this suggestion that if it does not explain why Shaftesbury is in the play as Antonio, it does explain why he is there in his character as the conspirator Renault. The play, however, was not merely the celebration of a triumph, for though Shaftesbury's power had in fact been broken,

[113] This is best presented by Ham, pp. 188, 190. The suggestion appears also in Genest's *Some account of the English stage*, from which it is quoted in Gollancz's edition of the play (London, 1899), p. vii, and in Summers, I, lxxxviii. McClumpha also quotes from Genest, apparently without understanding the implications of the statement (p. xxxiv).

[114] Ham, p. 186.

he had been released from his imprisonment the preceding December and was embarked on the desperate courses which marked the end of his life. Moreover, the air was thick with rumors of other Whig conspiracies, intrigues of the sort which were to lead a little later to the suicide of Essex and the execution of Sydney and Russell.[115] At these plots as well as at the plot supposed to be behind the exclusion movement, *Venice preserved* was aimed.

We begin, therefore, to get a better idea of what the play meant to Otway's contemporaries when we see it in this light. But we still do not have the full implications of its political significance. If we did, there would have been every reason for representing the established government of Venice as a noble and glorious thing, for if the conspirators were the Whigs, the government of England would then seem to be represented by that of Venice. The same condition, in short, would prevail as if the plot represented merely the Popish Plot. But, as I have pointed out, Venice is not represented as admirable. Two things distinguish the treatment of the republic at Otway's hands. The first of these is that as the background of the action, it receives much fuller and more attentive treatment than dramatic exigencies alone required. The second is that the governmental system is presented in a most unfavorable light. Venice is "a wretched state," a place

> Where all agree to spoil the public good,
> And villains fatten with the brave man's labours.[116]

The senators are a corrupt and tyrannical oligarchy. They

> Cheat the deluded people with a shew
> Of Liberty, which yet they ne'r must taste of.[117]

Whomever they please, "they lay in basest bonds."[118] Those who have served the state are recompensed with ingratitude.[119] The famed justice of the republic is specifically denied; it is "lame as well as blind," and the laws are perverted to the ends of those who make them.[120] All the strength of the state is

> empty magazines,
> A tattered fleet, a murmuring unpaid army,
> Bankrupt nobility, a harassed commonalty,
> A factious, giddy, and divided Senate.[121]

---

[115] See above, p. 137.   [116] I, i, 208–09.   [117] I, i, 154–55.
[118] I, i, 157.   [119] I, i, 197.   [120] I, i, 212–13.   [121] II, 267–70.

The Venetians
> have neither safety, Unity, nor Peace,
> For the foundation's lost of Common Good.[122]

Such is the picture of government in Venice which emerges from the play. Two obvious explanations which suggest themselves are that conspirators naturally make speeches against the power that they are plotting to overthrow, and that Venice is presented unfavorably in the play because Otway found it so presented in his source. But neither of these explanations is fully adequate. It is not true that Saint-Réal himself gives an unflattering picture of Venice. He notes that the Senate levied heavy taxes during the war in which the state was engaged, that there was consequent discontent in the city, and that some senators were corrupt, but the general impression is hardly that of a state tottering from internal corruption, nor is the Senate pictured as foolish or futile. The state is represented as more than a match for its enemies, and as checkmating the Spaniards repeatedly.[123] It is true that Saint-Réal details Bedmar's charges against Venice in his private reports to Spain and in the *Squittinio*, but he refers to them as a libel.[124] He presented, in short, two views of Venice. That Otway should have chosen that represented by Bedmar's charges in composing the speeches of the conspirators in the play is adequately explained by dramatic exigencies, but no such explanation can account for the fact that the representation of the corruption of the Venetian government is not by any means confined to the speeches of the plotters. It rather runs through the whole play and finds its epitome in a meeting of the Senate itself.[125]

These considerations force us to one conclusion: that the representation of the Venetian government as vicious and corrupt was deliberate on Otway's part. Why it was deliberate should be apparent when we recall the prominence of the Venetian model in Whig thought. Venice as it appears in the play is a hostile, Tory representation, not of the England that the Whigs were accused of conspiring against, but of what is taken as the Whig ideal of a Venetian state. Otway thus aimed a double-barreled attack at the Whigs. He satirized them both as conspirators and as wishing to introduce a corrupt and vicious Venetian system into England. The conspirators of the play are the Whig conspirators; the Venice of it is a representation of what they would set up in England. In the Prologue to the play, Otway had suggested that the Popish Plot was largely

[122] I, i, 210–11.   [123] Pp. 1–4, 15–16.   [124] P. 16.   [125] IV, 106 ff.

a Whig invention; in the play the real "plot discovered"[126] was the Whig-republican-Venetian conspiracy of which the Tories accused their opponents. The perfect document to explain the spirit in which Otway wrote is afforded by a characteristic tract of the Tory reaction published in 1683 as *A narrative of the phanatical plot, setting forth the treasonable and wicked designs which they have been carrying on against the king and government*, which made fun of the "consecrated Knives, Black-Bills, Jago-Pilgrims, French Armies etc." of the Popish Plot, and accused the Whigs of using these things as a cloak to hide their own treasonable designs.[127]

If it be objected that this interpretation makes the conspirators of the play stand in the allegory for the system which they were plotting to overthrow, I answer that this need not bother us in a play in which Shaftesbury in his character as Renault plots to overthrow Shaftesbury in his character as Antonio, the Venetian senator, and that the explanation which I offer affords the only good reason that can be given for Shaftesbury's presence on both sides in the play.

[126] The alternative title of the play was *A plot discovered*.
[127] Sig. Ar.

CHAPTER SIX

THE OLD CAUSE

> *But where's his wandring spirit gone,*
> *Since here he suff'red martyrdom?*
> *To heaven? Oh! It cannot be,*
> *For heaven is a monarchy.*
> *Where then I pray? To purgatory?*
> *That's an idle Romish story.*
> *Such saint as he can't go to hell?*
> *Where is he gone, I pri'thee tell,*
> *The learned say to Achitophel.*
> —Anonymous "Elegy" on Sydney

His contemporaries agreed that Algernon Sydney was incorruptible. They found him also a man of "overruling temper and height" with principles of such austerity that he shot a horse belonging to him which Louis XIV wished to have because it had been "born a free creature, had served a free man, and should not be mastered by a king of slaves."[1] Admired by Milton during the Puritan Revolution, who found his name "indissolubly attached to the interests of liberty,"[2] he spent seventeen long years on the Continent after the Restoration. In 1677, on the last illness of his father, he secured a pardon from Charles II after protracted negotiation and returned to England.

Such was the man who, about the time that Nevill was writing *Plato redivivus*, was working on his *Discourses concerning government*. His avowed purpose was to answer that epitome of absolutist theory, the *Patriarcha* of Sir Robert Filmer, a work which, though it was composed, as were Filmer's other works, at the time of the Civil War, was not published until 1680.[3] In advancing his argu-

---

[1] "Memoirs of the life of A. Sydney," prefixed to J. Robertson's edition of the *Works* (London, 1772), p. 34. All citations of Sydney's works refer to this edition, the items of which are separately paginated.

[2] *P.w.*, I, 293.

[3] Whether Sydney wrote the *Discourses* largely or *in toto* at this time or merely revised a manuscript which he had long been composing is a matter of some uncertainty. He declared in his *Apology* (pp. 12, 22) that the parts used against him at his trial for treason were written "twenty or thirty years" previously. In the paper which he gave to the sheriffs before his execution, he asserted that the work was unfinished, would have taken a long time to finish, would most probably never have been finished, and that "so much

ment, Sydney specifically disclaimed any intention to attack limited monarchy. Absolute monarchy, he declared, "is all that I dispute against, professing much veneration for that which is mixed, regulated by law, and directed to the public good."[4] Yet he was an old republican who was widely regarded as a republican still.[5] Dalrymple asserts that Sydney undertook to show to Louis XIV through Barillon, the French ambassador, that the establishment of a republic in England would be less prejudicial to French interests than the accession of William of Orange,[6] and it is certain that Barillon, who was an astute observer, believed that it was Sydney's desire to see a republic set up.[7] These facts prompt us to inquire to what extent the *Discourses* are to be considered, first, as republican in character, and second, as reflecting the theories of classical republicanism.

That Sydney's statement should be disregarded as an expression of his real views is strongly suggested by the character of the arguments which he opposed to the *Patriarcha*. To Filmer's contentions that monarchy is the form of government appointed by God, that

---

as is of it was written long since, never reviewed, nor shown to any man" ("Memoirs," pp. 38–39). On the strength of these statements, A. C. Ewald in his *Life and times of the Hon. Algernon Sydney* (London, 1873, 2 vols.), II, 343, advances the theory that the work was begun shortly after the "usurpation" of Cromwell, largely completed during the years of exile on the Continent, and revised in the early 1680's. Against this view are important considerations. Sydney's statements appear in documents which not even his most ardent admirer can read without perceiving their evasive character. Furthermore, they are in part flatly disproved by references within the *Discourses* to events which occurred after the Restoration (II, xv, p. 137; xix, p. 158; xx, p. 165; xxv, p. 222; xxvii, p. 228; xxviii, pp. 240–41; III, v, p. 249; xviii, p. 366; xxxviii, p. 470; xlii, pp. 488–89; xlvi, p. 502). Such references, extending in one case to 1680 (III, xlii, p. 489), make it impossible to accept Sydney's statement that the work was "never reviewed" even if it was written "twenty or thirty" years previously. They make it difficult also to believe that any part of it dates from the period of the Cromwellian ascendancy. The assumption that the work was largely composed during the Continental exile is open to the objection that it asks us to believe that Sydney expended the great labor obviously involved in the *Discourses* to answer a work which existed and circulated only in manuscript and that he did this moreover at a time when the doctrines it presented were not an active issue in English politics. It seems much more likely to assume that he was writing to answer a published book at a time when its theories were being actively promoted by the king's supporters. Sydney refers in I, i (p. 2) to Filmer's book as published to the world. At the least this is incompatible with his statement that the *Discourses* were "never reviewed"; at the most it tends to suggest that he wrote the work from the beginning after Filmer's book had been printed. I incline to the belief that the "time of leisure" to which he refers as writing in (I, i, p. 1) was the period after the publication of the *Patriarcha* and before he had been drawn into Whig intrigues, and that the fact that the work is unfinished is accounted for by his finally throwing himself into those intrigues. It is quite likely that he made use of some older pieces of writing, but it seems probable that the *Discourses* were essentially a product of 1680–81.   [4] II, xi, p. 111.

[5] Dalrymple, *op. cit.*, I, 86; II, 116. See also Meadley's comments in his *Memoirs of Algernon Sydney* (London, 1813), pp. 183, 292.   [6] I, 353, 379.   [7] *Ibid.*, I, 357.

royal power is absolute because sovereignty is indivisible, that states originated out of the expansion of families, and that kings exercised their power by right of inheritance from the paternal power bestowed by God on the head of a family, Sydney replied that the people are sovereign and may set up any form of government they choose,[8] that government rests on a compact,[9] that a king is a king only as long as he observes the law,[10] that when he fails to do so he may be deposed and the people alter the government in any way they wish,[11] and that absolutism had no basis in the law of God[12] or nature[13] or the constitution of England.[14] These contentions remind one of nothing so much as Milton's arguments in the *First defense*. It is, in fact, no exaggeration to say that Sydney in these matters answered Filmer with the very theories with which Milton had replied to Salmasius. Such ideas, of course, were not inconsistent with the acceptance of limited monarchy, but they had been prominently associated in the past with republicanism, and they had a republican ring about them. Moreover, they contained a justification of republicanism if men chose to have a republic, and a vindication of the right to set up one even if doing so involved rebellion against an established monarchy.[15]

But if these contentions indicate that Sydney's statement that he

---

[8] I, vi, pp. 12 ff.; II, xxxii, p. 269; III, xlviii, p. 468. Cf. I, xx, pp. 54 ff.

[9] I, x, pp. 21–22; xi, pp. 22–23; II, v, pp. 76 ff.; III, i, p. 290.

[10] I, xvi, p. 39; III, xlii, p. 489.

[11] II, xvi, p. 140; xxiv, pp. 191–93. Cf. II, xxi, p. 166; xxxii, p. 268; III, i, pp. 277 ff.; xxxvi, p. 457.   [12] I, vi, p. 13; xvii, pp. 40 ff.; cf. I, xx, p. 55; II, v, p. 78.

[13] II, viii, pp. 99 ff.; I, xx, p. 55; II, xxix, p. 241.   [14] See below, pp. 158 ff.

[15] There is no doctrine in Sydney more explicitly or repeatedly set forth than this one. Civil war, he declared, was an evil, but it was not the worst of evils, and if gentle means failed in correcting a defective government, force was just (III, xl, p. 479). In III, xxxvi, he asserted that "the peace may be broken upon just grounds, and it may be neither a crime nor infamy to do it" (p. 458). In II, xxxii, we are told that the "damnable conclusion" that the people may not "correct or depose their magistrates" is a notion arrived at by "fools or knaves" (p. 268). In II, xxi, Sydney wrote: "Nations may at the first set up popular or mixed governments, or without the guilt of sedition introduce them afterwards, if that which was first established prove unprofitable or hurtful to them" (p. 166). In III, i, he declared that there was nothing in the nature or institution of monarchy "that obliges nations to bear the exorbitances of it, when it degenerates into tyranny" (p. 277). See further II, xxiv, pp. 191–93; II, xvi, p. 140. Sydney saw the right to change a government, by force if necessary, as the natural accompaniment of the sovereignty of the people. The law applied to individuals, but it could demand nothing from the whole people because they were the masters and source of it. "Though every private man, singly taken," he asserted, "is subject to the commands of the magistrate, the whole body of the people is not so." The whole body of a nation could not be "tied to any other obedience than is consistent with the common good, according to their own judgment" (III, xxxvi, pp. 457–59).

opposed only absolutism should be disregarded, there are others which leave no doubt that it must be. The *Discourses* abound in arguments which, ostensibly directed against absolutism, apply with equal force to all forms of monarchy. One of the most insistently urged of Sydney's points is that monarchies do not put the best man or men at the head of the state. Because of the hereditary principle, the head of a monarchy might be "a child, a fool, a superannuated dotard, or a madman."[16] "Those governments only deserve praise," he wrote, "who put the power into the hands of the best men."[17] Assuming that the head of the state would also be the head of the armed forces, he found monarchies especially defective in time of war.[18] Nor could a wise and good council supply the defects of young, foolish, or ill-disposed kings, for such rulers would choose men as foolish or corrupt as themselves. Even if wise and honest men were chosen, the situation would be little better, for there would always be a variety of opinions among them, and a weak or vicious prince would choose the worst of several proposed courses.[19] Good monarchs were rare, and when they were found, their virtues perished with them. History showed that greatness and goodness were not inherited by their descendants. In France at one time ten base and slothful kings had succeeded one another in a row.[20] Even the best constituted of states were broken by a succession of two or three weak or evil rulers.[21] Not only do such arguments apply to limited monarchy, but Sydney frequently could not restrain himself from pointing out that they apply. The defect that nature did not insure the transmission of a good king's virtues to his progeny was not only "a breach never to be repaired," but "a disease . . . not only in absolute monarchies, but in those also where any regard is had to succession of blood, though under the strictest limitations."[22]

It is, however, only when we come to Sydney's further remarks on the disruptive character of the hereditary principle that we grasp the full measure of his repudiation of monarchy. This principle he found uncertain in meaning and open to varying interpretations. It had been understood in at least five different ways in as many different countries.[23] Even when one of these was chosen, it was be-

---

[16] II, xxi, p. 186. [17] II, xv, p. 133.
[18] II, xxiii, p. 181. [19] I, iii, p. 8; III, xvi, p. 349.
[20] II, xxiv, p. 207; xxi, p. 169.
[21] II, v, p. 295. The baleful effect of a succession of two weak princes was a favorite idea of classical republicans. See Machiavelli, *Discourses*, I, xix.
[22] II, xxiii, pp. 180, 181. For other instances of the open extension of the argument from absolute monarchy to all forms of it, see II, xi, p. 115; xxiv, pp. 187, 201, 214.
[23] III, xviii, p. 363.

set by constant ambiguities, and hence was productive of an unending series of struggles over the succession. Wars over this matter had made the history of monarchies a record of civil strife. By consequence, monarchy as a form of government, whether absolute or limited, was lacking in stability. France seemed to Sydney to afford a striking illustration of his point, but the miseries of England from this cause surpassed all others. But it was not only wars made to secure the succession that disturbed the peace of monarchies; they were subject to civil wars between a reigning king and those who thought they had a right to his title. It was a nice question "whether the most frequent and bloody wars do arise from the quarrels of divers competitors for crowns, before anyone gain the possession of them, or afterwards, through the fears of him that would keep what he has gained, or the rage of those who would wrest it from him."[24]

A second fundamental thing which makes no less clear Sydney's rejection of monarchy is his remarks on the nature of man. "Man," he wrote, "is of an aspiring nature, and apt to put too high a value on himself. They who are raised above their brethren, though but a little, desire to go farther; and if they gain the name of king, they think themselves wronged and degraded, when they are not suffered to do what they please. In these things they never want masters; and the nearer they come to a power that is not easily restrained by law, the more passionately they desire to abolish all that opposes it."[25] Even when a prince was virtuous and began by desiring nothing more than the power allowed him by law, he was subject to greater temptations to invade the liberty of his subjects than human nature could be expected to withstand. "The strength of his own affections," Sydney declared, "will ever be against him. Wives, children, and servants will always join with those enemies that arise in his own breast to pervert him; if he has any weak side, any lust unsubdued, they will gain the victory. He has not searched into the nature of man, who thinks that anyone can resist when he is thus on all sides assaulted."[26] Monarchy, in short, by the very constitution of human nature, tended always to degenerate into tyranny. It was a defective form of government because in the most important place of all it was lacking in those adequate restraints on the defects of human nature which all the classical republicans saw as an essential of any well-contrived government.

[24] II, xxiv, pp. 185–216, especially pp. 187, 201, 203–16.
[25] II, xix, p. 159. Cf. the views of Machiavelli, Harrington, and the sonneteer who praised Venice as a place where "all corrupt means to aspire are curbed," above, p. 61.
[26] *Ibid.* Cf. III, vi, p. 298; xliii, p. 492.

The concomitant of this parade of the defects of monarchy is an idealization of republics. States in which magistrates were chosen by frequent elections became nurseries of great and able men. Any one of them had produced more eminent figures than all the monarchies in the world.[27] Republics were assiduous to promote virtue and discipline because their very existence depended on them.[28] They excelled monarchies in war, not only because they chose able men to command instead of leaving the matter to the accident of birth, but because popular governments best fostered the "increase of courage, number, and strength" out of which great armies were formed. Monarchies were often conquered in a single battle, republics never.[29] "Many great kings," Sydney declared, "have been overthrown by small republics."[30] Republics were less subject to internal strife than monarchies. When they did have civil wars, such struggles were usually devoted to correcting some abuse in the government, and hence were not reprehensible like those in monarchies which concerned only succession and often involved attempts to invade the liberties of the people. Internal strife in republics was less bloody than in monarchies and often was composed by a wise and good man of the sort in which free states abounded.[31] Republics were not subject to the influence of such "bawds, whores, thieves, buffoons, parasites . . . and vile wretches" as haunted Whitehall, Versailles, and the Escorial.[32] With such statements in mind, there can be no doubt of what Sydney meant when he declared in his *Apology* that he died willingly for "the Old Cause."[33] His profession in the *Discourses* that he wrote only against absolute monarchy is clearly to be viewed as an attempt—futile because he could not restrain himself from giving his unchanged republicanism overt expression—to guard

[27] II, xxviii, p. 233.

[28] II, xvii, p. 157; xxi, p. 169; xxv, p. 217; xix, pp. 155 ff.; xi, p. 110. It is not difficult to see why Milton praised Sydney. The parallels between the thought of the two men are nowhere more striking than on the matter of the relation of virtue, discipline, liberty, and government. Sydney's contentions that liberty can never be upheld except by virtue, a point on which he cites Machiavelli but might as easily have cited Milton; that it cannot be preserved if the manners of a people are corrupted; that tyrants foster corruption as a means of enslaving the people; that a people cannot be enslaved as long as they remain uncorrupted—every one of these is Miltonic in character. So also, it may be noted, was his definition of virtue as "the dictate of reason, or the remains of divine light, by which men are made benevolent and beneficial to each other" (II, xxvii, p. 229). Both men saw the grand problem in government to be so to contrive it that the evil in man would have no scope, and the good would be fostered and placed in control. They differed on the extent to which this problem could be solved.

[29] II, xxi, p. 181.   [30] II, xi, p. 110.   [31] II, xxiv, pp. 214–15.

[32] II, xxv, p. 222; cf. xi, p. 115.   [33] P. 29.

himself at a time when every circumstance urged him to caution.[34] The fact that he made the attempt at all suggests that his profession at his trial that the *Discourses* was a work of private amusement not intended for publication must probably also be taken as only a partial truth. So determined a republican, for whom caution was so difficult, in a purely private document would probably not have been concerned to attempt to guard his statements. I think it quite likely that Sydney began the work with the intention of publishing a reply to Filmer, but that as it progressed even he came to see that it could never be printed under the monarchy.

We may turn now to examine the extent to which Sydney's thought exhibits the characteristic features of classical republicanism. Though he was widely read in history and political theory and ranges in his illustrations over all countries and periods, no one can read the *Discourses* without becoming aware of the profound influence of the classical republics and their eulogists on his political ideas. He took his stand squarely on the theory of the mixed state. "There never was a good government in the world," he declared flatly, "which did not consist of the three simple species of monarchy, aristocracy, and democracy."[35] Though he applied this theory to good governments of all periods,[36] he was quick to point out that the monarchial element need not be a king,[37] and it is significant of the sources from which he derived the concept that the first examples he cites are the Greek states, Rome, and Venice.[38] We also observe marching with these examples "the government of the Hebrews, instituted by God," a fact which reminds us of a favorite idea of the classical republicans illustrated by Harrington's remark that the ancient Hebrews learned the principles of mixed government from God, and the Greeks and Romans from nature.[39]

Further light on the nature of Sydney's classical republicanism is

[34] His return was conditional on his refraining from political activity ("Memoirs," p. 34). From the moment when he set foot in England he was a marked man. The court viewed him with the utmost suspicion. Shortly after the discovery of the Popish Plot he was accused of being the head of a great non-conformist conspiracy. He asserted in his *Apology* that when he only looked over a balcony he was indicted for a riot and that he was no sooner back in England than he perceived that his life was in danger (p. 4).

[35] II, xvi, p. 138; see also II, xxx, p. 258; III, xxi, p. 390.

[36] III, xxi, p. 390.   [37] II, xvi, p. 139.

[38] II, xvi, pp. 138 ff. He also got the theory straight out of Polybius, whom he cites (I, v, p. 11).

[39] Sydney's view on this matter was, in fact, exactly that of Harrington. See his statement in III, vi (p. 299) that the "virtuous pagans" discovered the fundamental truths of government by "the light of nature" and his remark in II, xxx (p. 251) that the Spartan and Hebrew governments corresponded.

afforded by his indebtedness to Machiavelli. This is to be observed
not only in occasional citations of that writer,[40] but in some of the
most notable features of his thought. Though like all classical republicans he had exaggerated notions of the longevity of Sparta,
Rome, and Venice, he did not follow Milton and Harrington in
making these notions into an argument for supposing that it was possible to create a perfect and perpetually healthy state. He agreed
that to "constitute a government that should last forever" would
be the "noblest work" in which the wit of man could be exercised,[41]
but he had Machiavelli's overpowering sense of the imperfection of
all things human, and believed that even the best constituted states
were liable to corruption with the passage of time. Like that writer,
too, he made the fact into a major argument for the contention that
states periodically have to be reformed or renewed.[42] In these respects,
it may be said that Sydney merely returned to one of the starting-
points from which the utopianism of Milton and Harrington had soared.

Another notable Machiavellian feature of Sydney's thought is
the acceptance of the Florentine writer's distinction between commonwealths which were instituted for preservation and those made
for expansion. Sparta and Venice illustrate the former, as they do in
Machiavelli, and Rome the latter.[43] Like Machiavelli, too, Sydney
argued that the best governments were those made for increase.
"All governments," he declared, "whether monarchical or popular,
absolute or limited, deserve praise or blame as they are well or ill
constituted for making war."[44] "Peace is desirable," he wrote, "by
states that are constituted for it, who, contenting themselves with
their own territories, have no desires of enlarging them: or perhaps it might simply deserve praise, if mankind were so framed, that
a people intending hurt to none could preserve themselves. But the
world being so far of another temper that no nation can be safe
without valour and strength, those governments only deserve to be
commended, which by discipline and exercise increase both."[45]
Elsewhere he declared that only those could be safe who were strong,
and that the government God gave the Hebrews fitted them "for war

---

[40] II, xi, p. 110; xxvi, p. 225; xxix, p. 245; III, xvi, p. 350. Cf. also III, xxv, p. 406.
[41] II, xvii, p. 144.
[42] See III, xxv, p. 406, where he cites Machiavelli, though not by name, on this point.
For further expressions of his disbelief in a perfect state see II, xiii, p. 124; xix, p. 160;
III, xxvii, p. 419. For Sydney, as for Machiavelli, the difference between monarchies
and republics in this respect was one of degree.   [43] II, xxii, pp. 173–74.
[44] II, xxiii, p. 181. Note that the point constitutes one of Sydney's main arguments for
the superiority of republics over monarchies.   [45] II, xv, p. 131.

and to make conquests." The Romans flourished more than the
Venetians. Indeed, the "too great inclination of the Venetians to
peace is accounted to be a mortal error in their constitution."[46] If
Sydney did not expand such ideas into a full-blown Harringtonian
imperialism, it is clear that Machiavelli and Rome supplied him,
as they supplied Harrington, with all the bases for it.[47]

But it was not only his admiration of the contrivance of Rome
for war that Sydney shared with Machiavelli. It is only when one con-
templates his idealization of the ancient Roman republic in all
its features that one perceives at once his essential relation to the
political thought of Machiavelli and the real nature of his classical
republicanism.[48] He refers to Rome far more frequently than to
any other state. Just as he had no terms adequate to condemn it under
the empire,[49] he exhausted himself in superlatives in praise of it
under the republic. Few things in Filmer made him more angry
than the assertion that the greatness of Rome was achieved only
under the emperors. He dared to affirm that "all that was ever desirable, or worthy of praise and imitation in Rome, proceeded from
its liberty, grew up, and perished with it."[50] In the days of the
Roman republic, virtue was honored to such an extent that it had
never elsewhere been excelled.[51] Good men throve.[52] Except for Ma-
nilius Capitolinus, no eminent Roman was executed from the foundation of the republic to the time of the Gracchi.[53] The discipline, valor,
and strength of the people were such that they overthrew all the
ancient monarchies.[54] Their modesty was "not less than their power
or courage." They did not choose a plebeian consul until forty years
after they were authorized by law to do so. Their wisdom was
equally distinguished. In choosing consuls, they were never more than
three times mistaken.[55] Following Machiavelli, Sydney contrived
to make the tumults of the republic into a mark of its virtue. Since

---

[46] II, xxii, pp. 173–75.

[47] Sydney does, however, like Harrington and following Machiavelli, note the details
of the Roman colonial system and the three ways the Romans had of dealing with conquered nations. See II, xiv, pp. 127–28.

[48] One interes. ng relationship between Sydney's and Machiavelli's views is disclosed
by Sydney's references to the idea of a constitutionally provided dictator of the sort that
Harrington had accepted as essential and Milton had rejected. It seems clear that under
the influence of Machiavelli Sydney was brought to admit that such an institution might
have its uses in a well regulated state, but that not even the fact that it was employed
in ancient Rome could make him enthusiastic over it (II, xiii, pp. 124–25).

[49] II, xii, p. 121 f.; xvii, p. 143; xxiv, pp. 198–99.

[50] II, xii, p. 119. See also p. 118.   [51] II, xiii, p. 125; xxviii, p. 235; xxi, p. 170.

[52] II, xviii, p. 152.   [53] II, xiii, p. 124.

[54] II, xii, pp. 119–20; cf. xxv, p. 219; xxi, p. 170.   [55] II, xiii, p. 124.

"all human constitutions are subject to corruption, and must perish, unless they are timely renewed," he explained, the internal strife of the republic was desirable, for it was chiefly by such means that rectifications of the government were made.[56] When the republic was subverted, it was succeeded, first, by the execrable reigns of the emperors[57] and then by the kingdoms established by the barbarous nations of the north which enjoyed neither peace nor justice, and in which a miserable nobility and people were obliged to fight in the foolish quarrels of their kings.[58]

If Rome was the chief recipient of Sydney's admiration, it was not the only one among the states associated with classical republicanism. The circumstance that he did not approve of Venice's being a commonwealth for preservation did not prevent him, any more than Harrington, from admiring other features of the Venetian constitution. To the cursory reader, this fact may not be immediately apparent. Sydney does not mention Venice more frequently than he mentions France, but he almost never cites the latter with approval or the former without praise. It is clear that in various ways he accepted the idealized view of the city current among the classical republicans. To mention only one point, we find him praising the Venetian administration of justice.[59] The nobility were not to him a narrow and selfish oligarchy, but an illustration of the services which a powerful and able aristocracy could perform in a state. The noblemen of Venice, he declared, "who are born and bred in families that never knew a master," better understood the common concernments than "the great men of France or Spain, who never come to the knowledge of anything, unless they happen to be favoured by the king." The vigor and wisdom of the Venetian nobility had alone preserved the state when the powers of Europe had united against it at the League of Cambrai.[60]

With this review of Sydney's political principles and enthusiasms in mind, we may turn now to his analysis of English constitutional history. One striking feature of it which may be noticed immediately is his refusal to consider the Norman Conquest as more than in inci-

[56] *Ibid.*

[57] II, xvii, p. 143; xxiv, pp. 198–99; xii, pp. 121 ff. With Sydney's views on the "execrable reigns" compare those of Harrington, *Oceana*, pp. 39, 12. Both men saw Julius Caesar as one of the great villains of history.

[58] II, xvii, p. 143.   [59] III, x, pp. 316, 317.

[60] II, xxviii, p. 237. For additional references to Venice, see II, xvi, p. 138; xxiv, pp. 190, 191, 192; xxv, p. 222; xxviii, p. 237; xxix, p. 247; III, x, pp. 316, 317; xxi, p. 387; xxvii, p. 419; xxviii, p. 432; xxxi, pp. 445, 447; xxxiii, p. 450; xl, p. 477; xlii, p. 486; xliv, pp. 497, 498. Sydney spent some time in Venice while he was on the Continent.

dent of the national history. He refused to admit that it had brought about any fundamental constitutional changes; in pursuit of the point, indeed, he denied that it even existed. William the Norman, whom he refused to call the Conqueror, was offered the crown on the same conditions as his predecessors, and had the same liberty to accept or reject them. When he accepted, he was bound by them like any other English king.[61] Sydney's insistence on this point is understandable, for few matters were more hotly disputed in the seventeenth century than the effect of the Conquest, it being a common absolutist contention that if the patriarchal theory did not explain why the king's power was absolute, the fact that William subjugated the English people and passed on his rights of inheritance to his heirs did.[62]

It was a consequence of Sydney's views on the Conquest that he found the governmental institutions of England mainly derived from the Saxons. In Saxon times, the country was divided into two classes of people, "freemen or noblemen (who were the same) . . . exempted from burdens and reserved for war" and villains, who were "little better than slaves, appointed to cultivate the lands, or to other servile offices."[63] The latter of these classes consisted of the serfs, whom the Saxons had brought with them, and the Britons, whom they had conquered, the former of the Saxons themselves.[64] The Saxons having conquered in England a great country felt themselves ennobled by their accomplishment. They were all noblemen "ennobled by a perpetual application to those exercises that belong to noblemen, and an abhorrence of anything that is vile and sordid." They became a ruling and noble race, for "there are," Sydney declared, "noble nations as well as noble men in nations."[65] The nobility, then, consisted of the whole Saxon people, who alone had the right to participate in the government. The nobility and the people, in short, were identical; they were, furthermore, identical with the citizenship.[66] He compared their position and that of the villains with that of the Spartans, all of whom were lords with respect to their helots, and the Venetian nobility, who were at once the people or citizenship of the state and an aristocracy when considered in terms

---

[61] III, xvii, pp. 360–61; x, p. 325; II, v, p. 85. Cf. Nevill's statement that William made no conquest on anyone but Harold, that he came in by treaty, and that his coming produced "no change or Innovation in the Government" (*op. cit.*, p. 113).

[62] Locke also felt constrained to answer this argument. See the *Essay concerning the true original, extent, and end of civil government*, ch. xvi.

[63] III, xxviii, p. 430.   [64] III, xxviii, p. 432.   [65] *Ibid.*

[66] Cf. his statement that the barons and the freeman were identical (III, xxviii, p. 432).

of the whole population.[67] All this was thoroughly in accordance with Sydney's conviction that the true basis of nobility was virtue and services performed for one's country.[68] Among the Saxons, it was especially felt that those "who nobly defended and enlarged their dominions by war" were noble. In the fact that those who had distinguished themselves by their military prowess shared in conquered lands, he found the origin of the landed wealth of the nobility.[69] The fact that this nobility was hereditary accorded with his conviction that "by noblemen we are to understand such as have been ennobled by the virtues of their ancestors, manifested in services done to their country," and that "respect is due to such as are descended from those who have bravely served their country, because it is presumed, till they show the contrary, that they will resemble their ancestors."[70] Among the Saxons there was no such thing as a peerage. Such titles as duke, earl, viscount, and baron were not hereditary, and were only "titles of offices conferred upon those, who did and could best conduct the people in time of war, give counsel to the king, administer justice, and perform other public duties."[71] The nobility of England as thus defined in Saxon times was an "infinite multitude."[72] It was strong and able, resting solidly on worth, valor, and landed wealth.[73]

In the Saxon nobility-people all power resided. It was exercised through "micel-gemotes, which were general assemblies of the noble and free-men."[74] Sometimes, and especially in later periods when they became too numerous and scattered to get together easily, they sent delegates to "wittena-gemotes."[75] No essential change in the system resulted when this was the case. We find Sydney also rather vaguely speaking of "senators" in the Saxon governments.[76] The oldest kings among the Saxons were, as among the Britons, only "temporary magistrates chosen upon occasion of present wars."[77] The title of later kings rested entirely on the fact that they were chosen "*omnium consensu*." The assemblies abrogated their power when they pleased, and the hereditary principle did not prevail except as it was confirmed by the assembly.[78] Kings, therefore, derived

---

[67] III, xxviii, pp. 431–32.
[68] "Men are truly ennobled only by virtue" (III, xxviii, p. 426).
[69] III, xxviii, p. 428.   [70] III, xxviii, p. 425.
[71] III, xxviii, pp. 426–27.   [72] III, xxviii, p. 428.
[73] See further on Sydney's views on this matter the opening part of III, xxx, p. 437, which is an excellent summary of his opinions.
[74] III, xxviii, p. 423.
[75] III, xxviii, pp. 423–24. This distinction is not consistently observed. See p. 427.
[76] III, x, p. 323; III, xxxviii, p. 427.
[77] III, xxviii, p. 423.   [78] III, x, pp. 321–25.

their whole power from the people-nobility. As the Saxon polities developed, they gradually assumed the form of that variety of mixed government known as mixed monarchy. They were not, he declared, ill constituted, for they had a numerous and able nobility with preponderant power which enabled them at once to restrain the ambition of princes and the turbulence of the people. Without such a nobility, Sydney declared, no mixed monarchy could survive.[79] In other places, however, he did not take so favorable a view of the Saxon settlement. In his Twenty-seventh discourse of the Third book, he has the Saxons attempting to contrive a mixed state with a balanced equilibrium and not succeeding very happily. "Our ancestors," he wrote, "who seem to have had some such thing in their eye, as balancing the powers, by a fatal mistake placed usually so much in the hands of the king, that whenever he happened to be bad, his extravagances could not be repressed without great danger."[80] He went on to declare that this error had "in several ages cost the nation a vast proportion of generous blood" and was the ultimate cause of the commotions of his own time.[81]

Such, essentially, was Sydney's view of the ancient constitution of England. It owed much, no doubt, to the vast amount of antiquarian and historical research into early institutions which was one product of the dispute between absolutists and their opponents as each sought to prove that the contentions of the other had no basis in the original institutions of the land, but it is obvious that it was colored to some extent also by the theories of classical republicanism. This can be seen especially in the application of the theory of mixed government, and it is observable also when Sydney has the Saxons trying to construct a government with balanced parts, when he compares the Saxon nobility to that of Venice and Sparta, and when we find him remarking that the Saxon government was the same in principle as that of ancient Rome.[82]

[79] The Saxons knew, Sydney asserted, that "no other way of supporting a mixed monarchy had ever been known in the world, than by putting the balance into the hands of those who had the greatest interest in nations, and who by birth and estate enjoyed greater advantage than kings could confer upon them" (III, xxxvii, p. 463). Cf. Harrington's contention that a monarchy had to be supported by a nobility or an army (*Oceana*, pp. 30–31).

[80] III, xxvii, pp. 419–20. Cf. Nevill's statement that when the government was set up, great power was given to the king because the people did not foresee that kings would attempt to invade their liberties (*op. cit.*, pp. 111–13).

[81] III, xxvii, p. 420.

[82] III, xxvi, p. 415. Also significant of his tendency to see the constitution in terms of classical republicanism is his remark that "the dukes of Venice . . . have no other power, than what is conferred upon them, and, of themselves, can do little or nothing. The grants of our kings are of the same nature" (III, xxix, p. 436).

What had happened to the government since Saxon times? Like Harrington, Sydney found that it had degenerated. He dated its general impairment from the death of Henry V.[83] The process had been accelerated since the time of Henry VII, whom he stigmatized as a "Welsh adventurer," and who, he broadly implied, had taken the throne after the old royal lines had killed each other off.[84] For the corruption of the ancient polity, he assigned numerous causes. At times he asserted that the "fatal defect" of having placed too much power in the kings was the root of the trouble.[85] Again he placed the blame on the civil wars to which he held all monarchies to be peculiarly subject.[86] He assigned it also to the attempts of the "Welsh adventurer" to establish himself on the throne.[87] In other moods he found the cause to lie in the imperfection of all things human. Our ancestors, he declared, could not foresee and provide for all the contingencies brought by the passage of time.[88] But the explanation which he set forth most fully is based on his view of the fate of the Saxon nobility. "Through the weakness of some and the malice of others," those titles which among the Saxons referred only to offices became hereditary, became empty titles of honor, and were conferred on "those who have not the offices, and are no way fit for them" in return for "the greatest crimes and the meanest services."[89] The result was the rise of an incompetent titular nobility which usurped the place of the old without having the numbers, ability, or landed wealth to perform the functions which the ancient nobility carried out. The balance of the government was thereby broken and the superstructure toppled because the foundation had been removed. The ancient nobility were deprived of all privileges "except such as were common to them with their grooms," and not only brought under the name of commoners but driven into the same interest with them. This class having most of the wealth and worth of the nation in it, all power had come finally into the hands of the king and the commoners, and there was nothing to cement or form a balance between them.[90] In the light of Sydney's assertion that a mixed monarchy could not survive without a strong and able nobility, this explanation carried with it the implication that the monarchy was headed for inevitable dissolution. Nor could it be saved by re-

[83] III, xlv, p. 506.
[84] II, xxiv, pp. 205, 213. Cf. Harrington's views, above, p. 69.
[85] III, xxvii, p. 420.   [86] II, xxiv, pp. 212 ff.
[87] II, xxiv, p. 213.   [88] III, xxxvii, p. 463.
[89] III, xxxvii, p. 464. See also xxx, p. 438; xxviii, pp. 425–26. Sydney's denunciation of the peerage is couched in the most unrestrained terms.   [90] III, xxxvii, p. 464.

storing its ancient balance. He declared flatly that it was as impossible to restore this balance as for "most of those who at this day go under the name of noblemen, to perform the duties required from the ancient nobility of England."[91]

What was the remedy? It is clear from his account of the Saxons that to some extent he had idealized the Saxon system in its most ancient form. The circumstance suggests that he saw the solution in terms of a return to that system. Such a return was indeed suggested to him by his adoption of Machiavelli's views on the necessity of periodically renewing governments because of the tendency of all things human to degenerate, and he noted that this power was lodged in Sparta in the *Ephori* and Senate of Twenty-eight, in Venice in the *Pregadi*, and in northern nations in the General Assembly.[92] We find him talking also of returning to the intentions of the Saxon makers of the government.[93] Moreover, as we shall see, his conception of what he would like to have in England, especially with regard to a nobility-citizenry with a general assembly and senate, would be to some extent a duplication of what he saw as the oldest Saxon system. But one could hardly say that Sydney saw the answer to the ills of the time simply in a return to that system. No man so thoroughly imbued with the notions of classical republicanism would have been satisfied with so simple a solution. We are not compelled to rest this conclusion on supposition, however, for a number of things make supposition quite unnecessary. In the oldest Saxon system, there were either no kings or elected kings. We cannot suppose him to have approved of the former of these situations because under the Saxon system, when there was no king, the state had no magisterial element whatsoever. At least we hear of none in Sydney. This would be true even though there were two councils among the Saxons, an assembly of all the freemen and a smaller council of elders or wise men, for the latter could not be at once the aristocratic and monarchial element in the government. Such a system was simply out of harmony with those principles of mixed government which Sydney so flatly asserted were embodied in all good governments. Nor would Sydney approve of the situation in which there were elected kings chosen for such temporary periods as those involving wars, for this still would leave the state without a monarchial or magisterial element in time of peace. No more did he approve the situation in which elected kings were chosen for life, for nothing is more certain than that his sense of the frailties of human nature led him to reject kings

[91] III. xxxvii. p. 464.   [92] III, xxvii, p. 419.   [93] III, xxxvii, p. 465.

elected for life as definitely as hereditary ones. Men who seemed to be modest and virtuous in private life, he found, too often proved to be vicious and corrupt when raised to power, and he observed that "the violence, spite and malice of Saul was never discovered, till the people had placed him on the throne."[94] No form of the magistracy, then, in the oldest form of the Saxon polity, let alone its later form, would have met with Sydney's approval. We may observe also that Sydney's notions about "senators" in the Saxon system were so vague that it seems certain he would have turned to the usual sources of classical republicanism had he attempted to set forth a plan for a body of such men. What makes it the more likely is the fact, as we shall see, that he did turn to such sources for his conception of the ideal magistracy. But what most makes clear the fact that if Sydney thought of a resurrection of the oldest Saxon system, it was of that system remodeled in the light of ideas borrowed from other sources, is the fact that he himself did not advance his program, insofar as he suggested one, on the basis of a simple return to the customs of one's ancestors. Repeated statements in the *Discourses* show that by a renewal of the government he did not mean merely a return to original situations. We find him declaring that time conferred rectitude on nothing;[95] that laws and constitutions, however ancient, should be weighed and if bad abolished; that it was stupid to follow what one's fathers had done if it was evil; that "we are not therefore so much to inquire after that which is most ancient, as after that which is best"; that "we are not to seek what government was the first, but what best provides for the obtaining of justice and the preservation of liberty"; that the fact that there had been kings in the past did not forever oblige men to continue them; and that "there can be no reason, why a polite people should not relinquish the errors committed by their ancestors in the time of their barbarism and ignorance, and why we should not do it in matters of government, as well as in any other thing relating to life."[96]

With these considerations in mind, we may now turn to examine Sydney's program for England. His avowed purpose of answering Filmer point by point precluded any attempt to set forth an elaborate plan for the reform of the state; the consequence is that though what he did not want is clear enough, we cannot on all points be certain as to what he did want. Nevertheless, he was no more able to keep his views on such matters from creeping into the *Discourses* than he was to confine them to an attack on absolutism. It is clear that his

[94] II, xxv, p. 221.   [95] III, xxviii, p. 421.   [96] III, xxxvii, p. 469.

ideal was a mixed government, and one, moreover, which was republican in character rather than a mixed monarchy. We can be
certain also about what he thought the regal or magisterial element
of this government should consist of. His objection to kings elected
for life extended to all forms of life magistracy.[97] He found his ideal
in annual or at least rotating magistracies, which he declared were
superior to all others. "When the regal power," he wrote, "is committed to an annual or otherwise chosen magistracy, the virtues of
excellent men are of use, but all does not depend upon their persons:
one man finishes what another had begun; and when many are by
practice rendered able to perform the same things, the loss of one is
easily supplied by the election of another. When good principles are
planted, they do not die with the person that introduced them, and
good constitutions remain, though the authors of them perish."[98]
Elsewhere we find him talking of annual magistracies as the right
and usual practice of republics. "If any unworthy persons creep into
magistracies," he wrote, "or are by mistake any way preferred, their
vices for the most part, turn to their own hurt. The state cannot easily
receive any great damage by the incapacity of one, who is not to
continue in office above a year, and is usually encompassed with
those, who, having borne, or are aspiring to the same, are by their
virtue able to supply his defects, cannot hope for a reward from one
unable to corrupt them, and are sure of the favour of the senate and
people to support them in the defense of the public interest."[99]
Statements of this sort not only leave no question as to how Sydney
would constitute the magistracy in a state to his liking; they also
suggest that on these matters he drew his ideas from the practices
of that Roman republic which he admired so greatly. The amount of
power to be allowed to the magistracy is not so specifically set forth,
but it is clear that he wished it to be small. Noting with approval
the practices of the Spartans and the Romans on this point, he declared that those states most deserved praise who "endeavoured to
supply the defects, or restrain the vices of their supreme magistrates."[100]

The question of his views on assemblies is more complicated.
From his hostility to the peerage, his remark that he would willingly
see it "fall,"[101] and the implication that it was bound to go down in
the discourse in which he traced its history,[102] it seems obvious that

[97] II, xxv, p. 221.   [98] II, xxiii, p. 180.
[99] II, xxiv, p. 214. See also II, xxviii, p. 241.   [100] II, xxx, p. 261; cf. III, xl, pp. 477 ff.
[101] III, xxviii, p. 425.   [102] III, xxxvii, p. 464.

his ideal state would not contain a house of lords. In its place, we may gather from his references to the senates which he saw as characteristic of republics and the oldest form of the Saxon state, would be a senate, which would constitute the aristocratic element in the state.[103] He does not tell us how it would be constituted. It might be composed "only of the people's delegates" or of "men chosen for their virtue, as well as for the nobility of their birth."[104] Beneath it would be a general as embly of the delegates of the people. On the relation between the two bodies, Sydney is far from clear, but it is possible to make several observations. The general assembly would be the direct representative of the people, and as such would constitute the democratic element in the state. Inasmuch as in his view all power resided in the people, this body would in the last resort have the highest authority, and he notes that it was so in the government which God instituted among the Hebrews.[105] But there is much in his remarks to suggest that he looked with favor on a state in which the aristocratic element predominated in actual administration. He finds that the mixed government given by God to the Hebrews was of this sort because the Sanhedrim or Senate of Seventy was a permanent element in the state whereas the general assemblies which constituted the democratic element were not regularly provided for.[106] We find him observing that in mixed states headed by the aristocratic element, fewer mistakes were made in the choice of men and the purity of manners was better preserved than in states dominated by the democratic part. The best and wisest men among the ancients, he asserted, had favored a state with a dominant aristocratic element.[107]

The citizenship of Sydney's state would consist of all gentlemen, the freeholders, and certain classes from the towns. "When the nation became more polished," he wrote, "to inhabit cities and towns, and to set up several arts and trades, those who exercise them were thought to be as useful to the commonwealth, as the freeholders in the country, and to deserve the same privileges." Hence corporations were set up in which rights were exercised sometimes by all the inhabitants, as in Westminster, sometimes by the common hall, as in London, or by the mayor and other magistrates.[108] In at least one place, we find Sydney speaking of the freeholders and, by inference, of the classes added to them, as corresponding to the

---

[103] II, xxiv, p. 214; xxviii, p. 241; xxx, p. 258; II, ix, pp. 103–04.
[104] II, xxx, p. 259.   [105] II, ix, p. 104.   [106] II, ix, p. 104.
[107] II, xix, pp. 161–62.   [108] III, xxxviii, p. 467.

nobility-people of the Saxons.[109] The remark suggests that he saw the nobility in the widest sense in his own time as consisting of all who possessed the right to participate in the government, who were " 'cives,' members of the commonwealth, in distinction from those who are only 'incolae,' or inhabitants, villains, and such as being under their parents, are not yet 'sui juris,' "[110] and that therefore he envisioned for his own time a situation corresponding not only to Saxon England but, though on a far broader basis, to that in Sparta and Venice. But whether this was the case or not, it seems clear that Sydney also thought of the nobility in a more restricted, even if still broad, sense. For all that he thought that the peerage had usurped the place of the ancient nobility, and that that nobility had been reduced to the name and status of commoners, nothing is more certain than that he believed that there existed in England in his own day a very large, able, and wealthy true nobility descended from the ancient nobility and founded like it, in part, at least, on landed wealth. Cliftons, Courtneys, and Hampdens, he asserted, were as ancient and of the same dignity as any of those who went under the name of duke or marquis,[111] and he found that those called commoners in his own time were the equal of the "patentees" in birth and valor, had in many cases far greater possessions, and formed the strength and virtue of the nation. They were "the true noblemen of England."[112] To them, not of necessity, but in recognition of virtue, valor, and ability, he no doubt confidently expected the citizenship to turn in choosing both the general assembly, which would be the democratic element of the state, and the senate, which would be the aristocratic one.

Data so fragmentary do not perhaps permit of further conclusions, but if one more may be permitted, it would seem that what Sydney desired was not greatly different in broad, general features from what Harrington wished, though there is no evidence to lead us to suppose that he would have adopted Harrington's complicated procedures. It seems likely that both men had in mind a state in which the citizenship resting on a broad basis would give the strength of Rome, but in which an aristocratic dominance in procedures would secure the advantages of the aristocratic systems of Venice and Sparta, which both admired.

Did Sydney have any plan for putting his ideas into effect? A good deal of light on this matter is probably shed by a passage in which

---

[109] *Ibid.*   [110] III, xxxviii, p. 467.
[111] III, xxviii, p. 426.   [112] III, xxviii, p. 431.

he discusses the various ways in which mixed governments had reformed their kings. Some such governments, when they became incensed against their kings, abolished them. "Others, as Athens . . . and the Latins, did not stay for such extremities, but set up other governments when they thought it best for themselves; and by this conduct prevented the evils that usually fall upon nations, when their kings degenerate into tyrants. . . . The Romans took not this salutary course; the evil was grown up before they perceived, or set themselves against it." The result, he declared, was that the Romans had to recover their liberty from Tarquin by a hard war. Then he adds: "But it had been much better to have reformed the state after the death of one of their good kings than to be brought to fight for their lives against that abominable tyrant."[113] These words, I believe, give us a very real clue to Sydney's desires. He wished to see the government reformed, at least as far as the kingship was concerned, on the death of Charles II. The supposition is rendered the more likely when we recall the charge repeatedly made by the Tories in the early 1680's that the real aim of at least some Whig groups was the dissolution of the monarchy on the death of that monarch.[114] If such were Sydney's intentions, it is probable that he wrote the passage which I have quoted before the dissolution of the Oxford Parliament in May, 1681. After that date, it was apparent to him, as it was to all men, that peaceable means would not avail.

Sydney's further activities are obscure. There was nothing in the *Discourses* to make him refrain from resorting to violence; on the contrary, the work contains repeated justifications of the use of force and armed power in the remaking of a government. It is true that he found this right to reside in the whole people, and that he declared the individual bound to obey authority, but it has ever been characteristic of such men that they easily identify their own cause with that of the nation. After the Oxford Parliament, a group of Whig leaders which included Lord William Russell, the Earl of Essex, Hampden the Younger, and Monmouth, discussed plans for an armed uprising, and sought the aid of Shaftesbury and his ten thousand "brisk boys" in order to secure that leader's strength in the city.[115] If we accept Sydney's statement at his trial that he had not seen Shaftesbury for two years, he was not drawn into this conspiracy until after the flight of that leader in December, 1682. He was certainly one of the conspirators after that date if not before, and

[113] II, xvi, pp. 139–40.   [114] See above, p. 137.
[115] Dalrymple, *op. cit.*, I, 80.

was one of the Council of Six which continued plans for the use of force. If Sir John Dalrymple may be believed, those involved had varying aims. Monmouth sought to advance his own cause; Russell, Essex, and Hampden intended to go no further than to exclude York and fix the limits of the power of the crown with precision; Sydney— and the statement checks with everything that the *Discourses* would lead us to expect—"aimed at the destruction of monarchy, and on its ruins to found that republic, which in imagination he adored."[116] Such ventures involve great risks; for a man in Sydney's position, this was especially true. He was arrested on June 26, 1683, and sent to the Tower on a charge of high treason. At his trial, Lord Howard, one of the Six and a thoroughly unprincipled person, was the chief witness against him. The trial, moreover, presided over by Jeffreys, was conducted in a manner which makes it infamous in the history of legal procedure.[117] But to say this does not automatically prove Sydney's innocence. He was executed, not long after Lord Russell, the other great victim of the Tory reaction, on December 7, 1683.

[116] *Ibid.*, I, 79.
[117] For the details of the trial see "The trial of A. Sydney" in the *Works*, pp. 1–65: "Memoirs," in the *Works*, p. 35; and Dalrymple, I, 94–97.

CHAPTER SEVEN

THE LAST PHASE

C LASSICAL republicanism as an actively advocated program for the reform of the government perished on the scaffold with Sydney in 1683. It is true that there were those who wanted a republic in 1689, and all the old schemes were discussed at that time, but republican councils were weak and ineffective and not supported by great names. In the face of a clear indication from William of Orange that he had not come to England to institute a republic, they made a small enough showing.[1]

Outside the field of active politics, the century which followed was not without its classical republicans. There was, for example, Walter Moyle, a grandson of that John Moyle who had been the friend of Eliot. In his earlier days one of the wits who gathered at Will's Coffee House and a poet of abilities sufficient to attract the attention of Congreve, Dennis, and Dryden,[2] Moyle began his career as an ardent Whig, and was in Parliament from 1695 to 1698. At the end of the century, he retired to his estate in Cornwall and gave himself up to the study of law and government, varying his researches with activities as an amateur botanist and ornithologist. Among his compositions, which were collected a few years after his death and published in 1726 and 1727,[3] are an *Essay on Lacedaemonian government* and an *Essay upon the constitution of the Roman government*. The second of these is a remarkable production. The work of a man who was steeped not only in the classical historians and "declaimers," but in Machiavelli and Harrington,[4] it is a kind of epitome of the ideas of classical republicanism on the subject of ancient Rome.

Setting out to trace the stages by which the Roman government

---

[1] Republican sentiment showed itself in *Now is the time; a scheme for a commonwealth* in *Somers tracts*, X, 197. Cf. *Some remarks upon government* in *State tracts of William III*, I, 161. On the various schemes proposed for settling the state, see Swift, *Examiner*, No. 36; Sir John Reresby, *Memoirs*, ed. Cartwright (London, 1875), p. 430; Burnet, *History of his own times* (London, 1724–34, 2 vols.), I, 810 ff. Cf. von Ranke, *History of England principally in the seventeenth century* (London, 1875, 6 vols.), IV, 508.

[2] Four pieces by him appear in the translation of Lucian which Dryden superintended in 1711.

[3] Thomas Sergeant brought out the *Works* in 1726; Curll, the *Whole works* the following year. The *Essay on Lacedaemonian government* appeared first in Curll.

[4] *Works*, I, 113.

achieved ultimately, under the republic, "the best Constitution in the World,"[5] he found that it had been given a good start by Romulus, whom he saw after the manner of Dionysius of Halicarnassus as a Lycurgean legislator. The frame of government which Romulus established, had it been adhered to by him and his successors, "would have been the most Noble, as well as most Lasting Constitution of Limited Monarchy that ever was in the World."[6] This observation is followed by praise of the religious settlement of Numa and remarks on the way in which, if given an opportunity, prelates can upset the balance of a mixed government which might have been written by Milton.[7] Much as Moyle admired the Romulean settlement, however, he was far from considering it perfect. Accepting the Harringtonian principle that power follows the balance of landed property, he found that the primitive constitution was not established on a steady balance.[8] Eventually, the balance in land shifted to the people, establishing the condition which made certain the end of the monarchy. The history of Rome showed, he declared, that when the balance is in the people, a monarchy will die a natural death.[9] These observations are accompanied with remarks on the defects of hereditary magistrates and the virtues of elected ones which Sydney himself could not have improved upon.[10]

Moyle considered it strange that on the expulsion of the Tarquins the Roman people, who possessed the balance, consented to an aristocracy, which was the next form of government.[11] The resultant disparity between balance and institutions produced the strife between the nobles and the people which ended in "the Dissolution of the Aristocracy, and the establishment of an equal Commonwealth."[12] This was not achieved at a single stroke, however, but by a series of changes. The right of electing senators was conferred on the people; tribunes with a negative on the proceedings of the Senate were set up, together with other popular magistracies; the people secured the power of proposing and debating laws and finally of enacting them without the consent of the Senate; a body of laws was "collected from the wise Institutions of the Grecian Commonwealths"; an agrarian law confirmed the balance of power against the nobility; and a great increase in the numbers of the people was

[5] I, 135.   [6] I, 4–5.   [7] I, 27, 29, 38.   [8] I, 63, 68, 70–72.

[9] I, 68, 70. The idea was, of course, a favorite Harringtonian contention.

[10] I, 57–60. Moyle considered the making of the kingship elective one of the stages by which the early monarchy was changed into a republic. He was not certain at what stage this occurred. See p. 62.

[11] I, 76–77. He speculated at length on the causes of this anomaly.   [12] I, 80.

secured by manumitting slaves, the promiscuous naturalization of foreigners, and other devices.[13] The stability of the government so improved was secured by a series of further measures. Marriages between the people and the nobility were permitted and encouraged, with the result that the two orders were cemented together, and the commons obtained the right to elect officers other than tribunes, such as dictators and consuls. One of the chief of these measures was the Licinian Law, an agrarian measure which, by limiting the possession of land to five hundred acres, prevented any one man or group of men from becoming powerful enough to disturb the peace of the state. This, he declared with Harringtonian fervor, "established the great Ballance of the Commonwealth, and would have render'd it immortal, had the Law been effectually put in execution."[14] The *Leges annales* fixed the ages requisite for enjoying the various magistracies, and so curbed the ambition of young men. Canvassing and soliciting for places during elections was forbidden, and the freedom of elections thus secured. Wise measures provided for the rotation of offices, and prevented the accumulation of several magistracies in a single hand. Magistracies like that of the dictator which were unlimited in power were limited in time. The *Leges tabellariae* provided for voting by ballot.[15] When all these steps had been taken, the constitution arrived at a perfection unequalled in the history of the world, and there ensued a tranquillity and internal peace which, he declared, could be "parallel'd in no Monarchy whatsoever."[16]

Aside from this account of the evolution of the Roman constitution, the most notable feature of Moyle's essay is its Harringtonian vision of Roman imperialism. Under the kings, he found that Rome was not able to extend itself much beyond its own walls, nor did it succeed much better under the aristocracy, which "fell naturally into the defensive Maxims, which all Aristocracies do or ought to pursue."[17] The aristocracy embarked on wars, not for conquest, but simply to divert the clamors of the people, "chusing rather to be vanquish'd in the Field by their Enemies, than to have hard Laws imposed on them in the City by the victorious Tribunes."[18] "Conquest and Dominion," he wrote, "were reserv'd to

---

[13] I, 80–89.
[14] I, 89–91. Cf. the statement on p. 98 that when the republic was finally perfected, it was "immortal from all inward diseases."   [15] I, 93–97.
[16] I, 98, 115–16. Cf. his repetition of the old argument of the classical republicans that Venice had been entirely free from seditions for centuries (p. 112).
[17] I, 117.   [18] I, 118.

complete the Felicity of a free and impartial Commonwealth."[19] In less than a century the Romans were masters of Italy; during "the equality of the commonwealth, they subdu'd the Universe."[20] Their success in conquest Moyle attributed to the facts that Rome was free from domestic tumults, which would have divided and weakened it; that the counsels of popular assemblies are more bold and courageous than the resolutions of senators and princes; that Rome, like all republics, abounded in great magistrates and commanders whose example encouraged others to emulate them; that the military system was a model of perfection; and that the laws were favorable to, and produced, a mighty increase in the population.[21] Moyle found the most striking feature of the imperialism of the republic to be the colonial system, however. Following Harrington, he found that Rome in her "rise" proceeded by colonies, and in her "growth" by leagues. The Romans used colonies not only to enlarge their dominions and multiply their people, but to transplant poor citizens, prevent seditions, and reward veterans. They used them also most skillfully to defend their borders, for by uniting the interest of the colonies to that of Rome, they made it unnecessary to maintain in them large and expensive bodies of Roman troops.[22] Moyle's description of the leagues which he saw as characterizing the maturity of the republican empire is based on the same Roman practices which Machiavelli and Harrington had earlier described, and like those writers he tells us how the Romans bestowed on conquered peoples provincial governments; governments according to Italian right, which bestowed the privileges of citizenship except for suffrage; or governments based on Latin right, which included citizenship and the suffrage.[23] But what most distinguished the imperialism of the Romans was the fact that subjects lived under "the mildest Administration, and the gentlest Yoke in the World." With this system, the Romans were so successful that they scarcely ever had to surrender "one spot of Ground, of which they had once got the Dominion."[24]

Moyle concludes with a discussion of the causes of the dissolution of the republic. One of these, he found, was the failure to observe fully the excellent laws. With the corruption of manners consequent on human depravity, the Romans became careless about the maintenance of fundamental provisions of their constitutional system, a remissness which permitted the seven consulships of Marius, the

[19] I, 119.   [20] I, 117. See also p. 121.
[21] I, 121–25.   [22] I, 127 ff.   [23] I, 130.   [24] I, 131.

multiplied honors of Pompey, and the long continuance of Caesar's command in Gaul.[25] Partly, also, the failure to observe the laws arose from the fact that "the Government was not often enough reduc'd to its first Principles," a statement which we find accompanied with an exposition of Machiavelli's reasons for the necessity of such periodic reductions.[26] Though he had earlier spoken of the government as perfect and immortal, he found additional causes of its ruin in certain defects of its institutions. The tribunes were too numerous, and the fact that there were two censors, instead of one, produced rivalry and disagreement.[27]

It is clear that Moyle's sentiments were those not only of a republican, but of a classical republican, the last really authentic specimen of the tribe. Moreover, it is impossible to read this essay, with its strong Harringtonian cast, without seeing that it embodied in a very real sense Moyle's conception of an ideal government. He did nothing to bring it about, but through the posthumous publication of his works he must be numbered among those who disseminated the ideas associated with classical republicanism. In addition to the *Works* of 1726 and 1727, editions of *A select collection of tracts by W. Moyle* appeared at Dublin in 1728 and at Glasgow in 1750. The *Essay upon Roman government* was reprinted in 1796, and in 1801 translated into French and published in Paris by Bertrand Barrière. This list of editions can hardly have left eighteenth-century Englishmen unaware that there were, or had lately been among them, men whose political ideal was a republic constituted after the manner of the classical masters and masterpieces of politics.

But had Moyle's works not done so, the activities of a notable eccentric of the second half of the century would have. Thomas Hollis was a Londoner who inherited a large fortune from his father and his grand-uncle, the benefactor of Harvard College. He did not profess to be a republican. He was, he declared, only a "true Whig" who took Viscount Molesworth's Preface to his edition of Hotman's *Franco-Gallia*, with its glorification of the settlement of 1689, as his political creed.[28] He disdained to submit to the favor

---

[25] I, 138.

[26] I, 132–33. The word *reduction* as Moyle uses it is somewhat misleading. What he had in mind was periodic renovations by which obsolete laws and laws which through changed conditions came to defeat the purposes for which they were established, would be abolished, and good laws which had fallen into disuse would be reëstablished and enforced.

[27] I, 142–43, 146.

[28] At the end of the Preface in his copy of Hotman Hollis wrote in large letters, "My Creed." See *Memoirs of Thomas Hollis* (London, 1780), pp. 118–19, 92–93.

or engage in the servility which he considered necessary to gain a seat in Parliament, referring to elections for that body as then conducted as "the grand septennial riot."[29] He preferred to sit at home in his study with "the picture of the incomparable John Milton" on one side of him and that of the "incorruptible Andrew Marvell" on the other, and propagate his principles by a vast correspondence and extensive gifts of books and tracts not only among his acquaintances in England but in all parts of the civilized world, accompanying his donations to foreign countries with copies of Wallis's *Grammar of the English tongue*.[30] He was commonly considered a republican, and had the curious habit of decorating books and engravings with daggers and caps of liberty. Whatever his precise principles were, it is the books he chose to distribute and with the editing of which he was in one way or another connected which give him this brief notice in our story. Among the works which he invariably included in his donations were the *Prose works* of Milton,[31] and he was variously involved in editions of Sydney's *Discourses concerning government* (1763) and Nevill's *Plato redivivus* (1764).[32]

But it is not to retired men of the study like Moyle and Hollis that we must turn for an estimation of the real and final influence of classical republicanism on English thought. Many of the ideas of the classical republicans could be pursued almost as easily within the frame of the monarchy as in an outright republic. In this circumstance is to be found the explanation of the fact that these notions lived on after the collapse of Sydney's cause in 1683 among men who accepted, and were content to work within, the frame of limited monarchy. We have now to examine the ramifications of this in-

[29] *Ibid.*, p. 103.
[30] He sent collections of books to St. Petersburg, Stockholm, Leipzig, Uppsala, Göttingen, Bâle, Geneva, and Groningen (*Memoirs*, pp. 126–27 and *passim*). To Harvard College he sent in 1758 a collection of nearly fifty volumes, which were consumed in the fire of 1764 (*Memoirs*, pp. 73–4). He did not always confine to gifts of books his endeavors to propagate the right principles. When he heard that a bed supposed to have been owned by Milton was for sale, he bought it and sent it to Akenside with the hope that it would inspire him to "an ode to the memory of John Milton, and the assertors of British liberty" (*Memoirs*, p. 111).   [31] *Ibid.*, p. 73.
[32] To Moyle and Hollis we should perhaps add the name of "Citizen" John Thelwall, in whom traces of classical republicanism lingered on to merge with the new manifestations of republican feeling which arose with the French Revolution at the end of the century. In Thelwall's case, the latter influence was, of course, the major one, but that when he delivered his lectures on Roman history in 1795 to 1797, he was not wholly concerned with finding Roman parallels to Jacobin ideas, and drew inspiration as well as illustrations from his subject, we have the fact that he named his eldest son Algernon Sydney Thelwall, and that he was responsible for the 1796 edition of Moyle's *Essay upon the constitution of the Roman government* to suggest.

fluence, to investigate, in short, the way in which the ideas with which we have been concerned entered in one way or another into the thought of the great English political parties.

For one thing, the classical constitutions long continued to be cited by English political writers. Toland recommended to gentlemen "a careful perusal of the Greec and Roman Historians";[33] Viscount Molesworth cited approvingly the Greek and Roman practice of sending abroad for the laws of other nations.[34] Even Locke in the *Essay concerning the true original, extent, and end of civil government,* a work not distinguished for its allusions to historical precedents, could not keep free from allusions to Rome.[35] The *Ephori* of Sparta figured largely in the great debate over the Peerage Bill in 1719.[36] In the years before political exigencies led him to discover that he was a Tory, Swift wrote an elaborate *Discourse of the contests and dissentions between the nobles and the commons in Athens and Rome,* in which he endeavored to draw lessons for his own time from Greek and Roman experience; and even in *Gulliver's travels* he could not refrain from having Gulliver discover, when he called up the shades of a Roman senate on the magical island of Glubbdubdrib, that it was "an assembly of heroes and demigods" beside which modern assemblies made a poor impression.[37]

The continued influence of the Venetian model is no less strikingly illustrated. Though the Tory attack of the early 1680's and books like Houssaye's which furnished the materials for that attack dealt, together with the increasingly obvious decline of the Most Serene Republic,[38] a serious blow at its prestige, not a little of its political

---

[33] Preface to his edition of the *Oceana and other works* of Harrington, p. x.

[34] Preface to *An account of Denmark, as it was in the year 1692* (London, 1694), sig. a5v.   [35] Ch. viii.

[36] See *The town talk, The fish pool, The plebeian, The old whig, The spinster etc. By the authors of The tatler, Spectator, and Guardian. First collected in 1789* (London, 1790), pp. 249, 271, 293.   [37] Ed. A. E. Case (New York, 1938), p. 210.

[38] How these things operated can be seen in Addison, who declared in his *Remarks on several parts of Italy* (1705) that Venice had been more powerful than it was, and was likely to become less so. "The Venetian Senate," he wrote, "is one of the wisest councils in the world, though at the same time, if we believe the reports of several that have been well versed in their constitution, a great part of their politics is founded on maxims which others do not think consistent with their honor to put in practice. The preservation of the Republique is that to which all other considerations submit. To encourage idleness and luxury in the Nobility, to cherish ignorance and licentiousness in the Clergy, to keep alive a continual faction in the common people, to connive at the viciousness and debauchery of convents, to breed dissentions among the Nobles of the Terra Firma, to treat a brave man with scorn and infamy; in short, to stick at nothing for the publick interest, are represented as the refined parts of the Venetian wisdom" (*Miscellaneous works,* ed. A. C. Guthkelch [London, 1914, 2 vols.], II, 56–57; also see p. 58). Where these ideas came

reputation survived and long continued to be an element in English political thinking. Indeed, it would be rather strange had this not been the case, for we have observed the strong influence of Venice on Whig thought at the time in the early 1680's when the party was really taking shape. We have seen that at that time the project of making the king of England into a duke of Venice, as far as his power was concerned, was entertained in Whig quarters. This scheme had its antecedents in the plans of certain Independent leaders in 1648 to which we have alluded, and was even prefigured in the sixteenth century by Sir Thomas Smith's declaration that the King of England was like the Doge of Venice.[39] The Tory reaction which marked the last years of the reign of Charles II and that of James II only interrupted such schemes, and they flowered anew during the Revolution of 1688–89. It seems scarcely too much to say that the Venetian duke represented for the Whigs of that period what they would like to see the king become in the exercise of power. It cannot be said that if such were their aims, they were then achieved, for William III was hardly a figurehead, but the process begun in 1689 did in fact during the Whig hegemony of the first half of the eighteenth century reduce the king essentially to the position of a doge.[40] It is not likely that in the realization of this fact the Venetian model which had been so long connected with the ideal was ever lost sight of.

But it is not only in the matter of the position of the king that we can look for traces of Venetian influence in Whig politics. Houssaye's revelation that Venice was in fact a pure aristocracy or oligarchy scarcely made it less attractive to the great Whig oligarchs, who in fact established in England in the period from 1714 to 1760 a kind of oligarchy of landed wealth. Disraeli, indeed, saw the Whigs as motivated by Venetian notions through this whole period. The "Venetian polity," he asserted, had "ever been the secret object of Whig envy and Whig admiration."[41] With many a witty

---

from becomes clear when we presently find him quoting Houssaye (p. 58). With Addison's remarks compare those of Swift in *The sentiments of a Church of England man* (1708), in which we are told that the aristocracy of Venice had "in our age admitted so many abuses through the degeneracy of the nobles, that the period of its duration seems to approach" (*Prose works*, ed. Bohn, III, 65).   [39] See above, p. 46.

[40] On the Whig scheme for a king "with the limitations of a Duke of Venice," see Swift, *Examiner*, No. 36. Cf. Disraeli's statement that "had William the Third been a man of ordinary capacity, the constitution of Venice would have been established in England in 1688" (*The spirit of Whiggism* in *The letters of Runnymede* [London, 1836], p. 184). See also his statement in *A vindication of the English constitution* that after the Revolution the Whigs "commenced a favourite scheme of that party, which was to reduce the King of England to the situation of a Venetian Doge" (London, n.d., p. 169).   [41] *Letters*, p. 197.

thrust about the "people" of the Whigs not being the people but the
ten-pound freeholders,[42] he described the Whigs under George I
as "Venetian magnificoes."[43] He saw the Peerage Bill of 1719,
which proposed to limit the creation of new peerages to six above
the existing number, as also Venetian in inspiration, asserting that
had it been enacted, "the British House of Lords would have been
transformed into a Venetian Senate."[44] These statements were made
in the heat of party strife, and are no doubt exaggerations. Yet
Macaulay could find nothing so apt as Venetian parallels to illustrate
the political objectives of the third Earl of Sunderland, the champion
of the Peerage Bill,[45] and when we remember the prominence of the
Venetian model in Whig antecedents, it is hard to believe that where
Disraeli saw so much, there was not a modicum of truth.[46]

Evidences of other aspects of Venetian influence on English thought
are more concrete. In 1707 there appeared in London an edition
of the *Maxims of the government of Venice*, with a long preface.[47]
We have previously had occasion to point out that the attribution of
this work to Sarpi is probably spurious and that it contained much
hostile to the political fame of the city. The writer of the 1707
Preface, however, accepted the work as Sarpi's and contrived to find
it a work of wisdom. More than this, though he was well aware of

[42] " 'The people' of the Whigs is, in fact, a number of Englishmen not exceeding in
amount the population of a third-rate city" (*Letters*, p. 194). See further pp. ix, 21, and
Vindication, pp. 189, 95.   [43] *Vindication*, p. 174.

[44] *Letters*, p. 188. The parallelism would not, of course, have been exact, for the Lords
would lack the elective features of the Venetian Senate, but it is true, whether the bill
was conceived under Venetian inspiration or not, that had it been passed, the way would
have been opened for the development of a situation somewhat like that prevailing in
Venice. I say this because if the peerage had been closed, it might have been impossible
to control it politically through the creation or the threat of creation of new peers, which
is quite probably what the authors of the bill hoped, and the peers would then have been
in a position to make the attempt, at least, to reduce the ministry to that dependence on
them, rather than on the Commons, which characterized the Venetian system with its
signory dependent on the Senate rather than on the Grand Council. On this bill see Basil
Williams, *The Whig supremacy, 1714–60* (Oxford, 1939), pp. 164 ff.; and A. S. Turberville, *The House of Lords in the eighteenth century* (Oxford, 1927), pp. 169 ff.

[45] *The history of England from the accession of James II* (Philadelphia, 1873), V, 4–5.

[46] The relation of the Whig and Venetian oligarchies has been incidentally noticed by
a number of historians, especially by Turberville, *op. cit.*, pp. 484–88. Without noting
the similarities and without entering into the question of the influence of the one system
on the other, Trevelyan concerns himself with pointing out the differences (*England
under Queen Anne* [London and New York, 1934, 3 vols.], III, 320). See further Arthur
Hassall, *Life of Viscount Bolingbroke* (Oxford, 1915), pp. 194, 197.

[47] An old hand on the title-page of my copy attributes the translation to William
Strahan. An earlier version by W. Aglionby had appeared in 1689.

the decline of the republic,[48] his preface turns into an eulogy of the
Venetian constitution. Had Amelot de la Houssaye been better in-
formed, he declared, he would not have made some of the statements which he did.[49] "The Frame and Government of the Republick of Venice," he wrote, "is thought to be no less worthy of the
Curiosity of our Times, than the Commonwealths of Rome and Lacedaemon were of the attention of former Ages." The form of its
government was "a Master-piece of Politicks." The republic had
"gather'd together all the Political Maxims that were in vogue among
the Grecian Commonwealths, and it seems to have pick'd out the
Commonwealth of Lacedaemon for the Pattern which it delights
most to imitate in its Civil Administration. But the Republick of
Venice has this Advantage over all the antient Republicks, that it has
preserv'd itself longer than any of the most powerful Commonwealths
in former Ages. The Commonwealth of Lacedaemon did not last
above seven hundred Years; and the famous Commonwealth of
Rome, the Queen of the World, was hardly able to maintain her
Liberty full five hundred Years; whereas it is near thirteen hundred
Years since the Commonwealth of Venice had its first beginning."[50]
The writer had read Giannotti and hence knew that the constitution
had not continued unchanged since its institution,[51] and he did not
believe in the possibility of creating absolutely perfect institutions,[52]
but it is clear that he entertained many of the ideas associated with
the most laudatory view of the republic. The "Wisdom and Prudence of its Councils" were "wonderful in all the Parts of the Constitution."[53] The method of choosing officers, making laws, rotating
magistrates, providing a store of trained statesmen from whom to
draw them, and administering the foreign service especially exemplified this excellence.

But the writer of this Preface was not merely an admirer of
Venice. For all that he wrote that the monarchy of Queen Anne was
"the mildest and gentlest Government in the World,"[54] it is clear
that he intended in certain respects to hold the republic up as a
model for reform. On three specific matters, Venetian and English
practices are set up against each other, and in the case of at least one
of these, the author not only suggested but sought to show the necessity for reform. The first of these contrasts is developed in the discussion of the Venetian practices in choosing magistrates and other

---

[48] Pp. xv–xvi, xxxiv.   [49] P. vii.   [50] Pp. xv–xvi.
[51] Pp. xiv, xvi–xviii.   [52] P. xxxiv.   [53] P. xviii.   [54] P. xxxv.

officers. He found admirable the system of not admitting patricians to the Grand Council until the age of twenty-five, or permitting them to be eligible for the Senate until they were thirty, but allowing them to sit in the Senate and observe how it worked. In this manner, he thought, and by rotation of office and putting young nobles in the lower offices first, the republic assured itself of "a constant and uninterrupted Succession of able Statesmen."[55] "What a vast difference," he wrote, "there must needs be, between a new Ministry of this sort, where the Ministers are thus prepared by a previous Knowledge of everything relating to the Interest of their Country, before they are admitted to govern it; and a new Ministry, where the Ministers perhaps have never extended their thoughts beyond the Concerns of their Private Families, have never studied the Maxims of their own Government, nor inquired into the Interests of other Princes. Wherever such men are admitted into the Ministry, who are perfect Novices in all Political Affairs, let them be men of never so great Integrity, of never so prodigious natural Parts, yet the Commonwealth will always be in hazard of suffering by their Management, till they have acquir'd some Years Experience."[56]

The second contrast between Venetian and English practices as conceived by the writer concerns the framing of laws. He describes at length the manner in which Venetian laws were drafted by experts and the various stages through which a bill passed, finding the method "suitable to the Wisdom and Prudence that is requir'd in Lawgivers." "Here the laws," he continued, "are not huddl'd up in the hurry of Publick Affairs; the care of drawing them is not committed to Persons, who are altogether unacquainted with the subject matter of the new Law, or whose Thoughts are distracted with all the other publick Concerns of the Commonwealth. The Laws of this Republick are maturely weigh'd and consider'd before they are laid before the Senate; and they are fram'd by Persons whose business it is to be daily conversant in those matters to which the new law relates; by Persons who are most sensible of the Abuses complain'd of, and who best know the proper ways to remedy them. When laws are drawn up with this maturity of Counsel and Deliberation, when they are examin'd with this foresight and precaution before they receive the Publick Sanction; this is a most effectual Expedient to prevent all Inconveniences from new Laws, and it is the only way to make the Laws of a State durable and lasting."[57]

But it is when we come to the views on parties and factions in

[55] Pp. xxii–xxiii.   [56] P. xxiv.   [57] Pp. xxxi–xxxii.

the Preface that we see Venice most definitely proposed as a model of better practices. The writer had an overpowering sense of the dangers to the stability of a state which arose from faction and party strife. "The Experience of past Ages shews us," he declared, "that Parties and Factions in a state have always ended in the Ruin and Subversion of the Constitution." Factions naturally tended "to the Destruction of the Persons concern'd in them." Neither an aristocracy nor a limited monarchy could survive them. A nation that wished to preserve its "present Constitution of Government, can never be able to do it, without entertaining a perfect Union and Harmony among its members."[58] In the past, parties or factions in England had led to those "intestine Commotions" which ended in the murder of the king and the complete ruin of the government.[59] In all this, there is observable the same strong convictions which had convinced Harrington that political parties were an evil in government. It is understandable how a man living in 1707, in an age when the violence of party struggles was great, could have entertained these ideas. It was, moreover, not so many years since the Whig and Tory parties had taken form in a factional struggle, that over the Exclusion Bill, which was conducted with head-hunting and ended with heads rolling. The writer found the cure for the difficulty in the same Venetian practices that Harrington had found it in. Candidates in elections, he wrote, "do not send their Emissaries abroad to proclaim aloud in the Ears of the People, that their Competitors are *Rogues*, and *Villains*, and *Traitors* to their Country." To prevent "the fatal Consequences of such immoral and unchristian Practices in Popular Elections, the Venetians have made severe Laws against all manner of canvassing or making interest for Places. And besides, they have so contrived the way and manner of their Elections, that they have made it almost impossible for the Electors to form themselves into Parties for any Candidate whatsoever, because of the uncertainty to whose lot[60] it will fall to be Candidates for the Place. The Votes are likewise collected with so much secrecy, that it is impossible for one man to know how another has voted."[61]

That this looking to Venetian practices as a means of correcting the evils of the party system was not an isolated phenomenon is shown by several pieces of evidence. In 1701 there appeared in London a tract entitled *An enquiry into the inconveniences of public and the*

---

[58] Pp. xxvii–xxviii.   [59] P. 26.

[60] The allusion is to the combination of lot and election used in the Venetian and Harringtonian systems of choosing officers.   [61] P. xix.

advantages of private elections, with the method of the ballott. This was followed in 1705 by *The patriot's proposal to the people of England concerning the ballot, the best way of choosing representatives in Parliament.* Both writers saw in the tranquillity and supposed freedom of Venice from the disturbances of faction an ideal which they would realize in their own country, and both proposed Harringtonian elaborations of the Venetian ballot as the means by which they would achieve their aim.[62] There is some evidence that Swift was not untouched by such ideas. He filled one of his early tracts with disturbing parallels between the contests of the political parties of his own day and the class struggles which he found had ruined Athens and Rome,[63] and in Book I of *Gulliver's Travels* he mercilessly satirized, not merely the Whigs, who of course bear the brunt of the attack, but the activities of political parties in general. Moreover, we observe that the Brobdingnagian kingdom held up in Book Two as more or less a model for imperfect man, is a partyless state. It is, in addition, a balanced mixed monarchy equipped with a militia vaguely reminiscent in organization of Harrington's militia.[64] These facts perhaps give a special significance to the statement that the officers of the militia are chosen "after the manner of Venice by ballot."[65] If it be objected that my implication reads more into the passage than is justified or that it must be taken satirically, the least that can be said of it is that it shows that notions about the advantages of the Venetian secret ballot were still in the air.

The idea that the Venetian model had something to offer died hard. On May 13, 1766, there appeared in the London *Chronicle* the following:

> The senate of Venice have issued an ordinance enjoining all the ecclesiastical communities in that republic to make sale immediately of all the estates which have been left them for charitable uses: and it is thought that they will produce upwards of two million of ducats.—Quaere, if the church-lands here in England, with all the real estates belonging to hospitals, and other charities were likewise sold at public auction, and the money vested in the funds to the same uses, would it not prove of equal benefit to this kingdom?

[62] See especially *The patriot's proposal*, pp. 7–8.
[63] *Discourse of the contests and dissentions between the nobles and commons of Athens and Rome* (1701).
[64] Ed. Case, pp. 141–42.
[65] *Ibid.*, p. 142. This suggestion is not inconsistent with Swift's remark on Venice referred to above, p. 293, for that remark occurs in a passage in which the idea is advanced that even the best governments cannot survive the corruption of manners.

Nor did the extinction of the Venetian republic during the Napoleonic wars, when Wordsworth wrote so feelingly and with so great a sense of its magnificent past, bring an end. In the person of Benjamin Disraeli, the reputation of the city was to exert one final influence on English political thought even after that which had given it substance had passed away. Disraeli, he who saw the Whigs as having created in the eighteenth century a "Venetian oligarchy," was himself strangely attracted by Venice. He liked to cherish the idea that he was descended from Venetian ancestors,[66] he wrote a novel, *Contarini Fleming*, with a hero supposed to be descended from one of the first of Venetian houses, and it was in Venice, as one of his biographers has said, that he "received the vision of a maritime and trading empire bathed in romantic splendor."[67] It seems likely also that his ideas on the position of the Queen were not uninfluenced by the example of the Venetian doge.[68]

II

We may conclude our examination of the extent to which the ideas associated with classical republicanism lived on in English thought after republicanism itself was dead by investigating the way in which the concept of mixed government became incorporated in what may be called the Whig theory of the English constitution. This concept, as we have seen, was the invention of a group of classical political writers who stemmed from Polybius. Though not incompatible with the idea of monarchy, for from the beginning one of its favorite examples had been Sparta, it had developed strong republican implications in the works of such classical writers as Cicero and its great modern expositor and propagator, Machiavelli. Aside from Sparta, moreover, the examples with which it was associated historically were mostly republics. These republican aspects of the theory were developed and applied specifically to the English constitutional struggle by the classical republicans with whom we have been concerned. The fact, however, that it could be applied to a state with an hereditary kingship, together with the circumstance that it fitted easily with the facts of the English monarchy, had led earlier to its being appropriated and applied to the English constitution, with the result that we begin to hear in the sixteenth century, in writers like Ponet and Sir Thomas Smith, that England was a mixed monarchy, an idea which came in the seventeenth century to be sup-

---

[66] See *What is he? and A vindication of the English constitution* (London, n.d.), p. xv.
[67] D. L. Murray, *Disraeli* (London, 1927), p. 52.
[68] See Murray's comments, p. 53.

ported with a vast amount of antiquarian research produced by the exigencies of political controversy which led to the further conclusion that all northern states had been founded as mixed monarchies.[69] In this form, the theory was agreeable to men who opposed absolutism without being willing to go to republican lengths, and whose patriotic feeling led them to profess that they took their political ideas from original English institutions.[70] In this form, moreover, the theory was revived and so repeatedly set forth after the Restoration that it became inseparably connected with Whig views of the nature of the English constitution. Charles II, indeed, was not yet back in England when this process of adaptation got under way. A royalist pamphleteer of 1660, sometimes identified as Sir Roger L'Estrange, in a tract called *A plea for limited monarchy, as it was established in this nation, before the late war*, argued that England was a mixed monarchy in which all the advantages claimed for a free state by republicans were incorporated,[71] and the same argument appeared in G. S.'s *The dignity of kingship asserted*.[72] By 1676, Denzil, Lord Holles, was expounding the English constitution to a Dutch correspondent in this manner:

> England then is a Government Compounded and mixt of the three Principal kinds of Government. A King, who is a Sovereign, qualified, and limited Prince; and the three Estates, who are the Lords Spiritual and Temporal, compounding the Aristocratical part of the Government; and the Commons in Parliament with an Absolute delegated power, making the Democratical part.[73]

After this date, ideas of this sort are found everywhere in writers with Whiggish inclinations.[74] Ultimately, after the Revolution

---

[69] Hunton, *op. cit.*, pp. 24–25, 35. The antiquarian research of the "Gothicists" and the political notions connected with it are treated by S. L. Kliger in an unpublished dissertation in the Northwestern Library.

[70] Hunton is a good example. The idea that England was founded as a mixed monarchy appears also, of course, as we have seen, in the classical republicans.

[71] P. 16; cf. p. 14.   [72] Pp. 64–65.

[73] *A letter to Monsieur Van—— B[euningen] de M——at Amsterdam, written Anno 1676, by Denzil Lord Holles concerning the government of England*, p. 4.

[74] Toland, *op. cit.*, p. viii; James Tyrrell, *Bibliotheca politica* (London, 1718), pp. 241, 248. Locke also belongs among the theorists who saw the English monarchy as mixed by virtue of his seeing the legislative power, which he held to be the supreme power in a constituted state, as divided among king, lords, and commons (*op. cit.*, ch. xix). From the discussion of political fundamentals in Swift's early and Whiggish *Discourse of the contests and dissentions between the nobles and commons in Athens and Rome*, it is clear that he saw the English government as a mixed monarchy (see especially ch. i). How completely the idea had permeated Whig thinking is shown by the fact that in the great dispute over the Peerage Bill of 1719, both sides agreed that England was a mixed monarchy (see *The town talk* etc., pp. 301, 249, 258–60, 284). For Sir Robert Walpole's ideas on the mixed nature of the English monarchy see Cobbett, *Parliamentary history*, IX, 473.

of 1688–89 had made Filmerism impossible even for the Tories, the theory was taken over by them also.[75] Indeed, so thoroughly was the idea of mixed government naturalized in England that its classical origin was not infrequently wholly lost sight of, and Englishmen began to think of the idea that government was best when it was mixed of the three simple kinds as their own or at least a northern contribution to politics. In 1701, Swift felt compelled to protest against the prevalence of the notion that the idea of mixed government was of Gothic origin.[76]

But it was not merely the idea of mixed government which was appropriated and incorporated into the Whig view of the constitution. Along with it went the notion with which it had been associated from the start—that balance was the grand secret in government. The idea that the success of a mixed government depended on the establishment and maintenance of an equilibrium among the parts appears everywhere in the works of the mixed monarchists; and as the republicans before them had used it to show why kings had to go or why the democratic or aristocratic element should predominate in the state, so the mixed monarchists applied it to the problems they had not yet settled. In 1676, Lord Holles, who wished to aggrandize the power of the peers or the aristocratic element of the government, and who earlier had disliked Cromwell for disliking lords, complained that the balance of the government had been at its best before Henry VII, when it had resided in the peerage, and that the government of his own time was weak because preponderant power lay in the popular part or the Commons.[77] The great controversy toward the end of the century over a standing army also turned on the idea of balance. It was a favorite contention of one group of Whig writers that such an army was inconsistent with mixed government because it gave the king power to oppress or overthrow the other two elements of the state, and thus break the equilibrium.[78] Similar arguments were used by Swift in the defense of Lord Somers and other Whig Lords when they were threatened with impeachment by the Commons, Swift declaring that the history of Greece and Rome showed, not

[75] Bolingbroke supplies a perfect illustration. See his *Works* (Philadelphia, 1841, 4 vols.), II, 381. Cf. I, 306–07, 331, 333; II, 114.

[76] *Discourse of the contests and dissentions*, ch. i.

[77] *Op. cit.*, p. 4. The identification of the Commons with the popular element of the state is Holles's own.

[78] See Moyle's and Trenchard's tract *An argument showing that a standing army is inconsistent with a free government, and absolutely destructive of the English monarchy* (London, 1697) and Lord Somers's *Letter ballancing the necessity of keeping a land-force in times of peace.*

only that the people when impeaching the nobility were usually wrong or guided by bad motives, but that doing this was a popular encroachment which would upset the balance of the Constitution.[79] In the Peerage Bill controversy of 1719, the idea of the equilibrium of the government played a very large rôle indeed. Those who like Addison supported the measure, maintained that it was necessary to keep the balance of the constitution, since without it, the monarchial and popular parts of the government represented by the King and Commons could, through the creation of new peers, destroy the influence of the aristocratic part, the Lords.[80] Those who opposed the bill, Steele among them, declared that a bill making impossible the creation of more than six additional peers would upset the balance by making the aristocratic element independent and would create a pure aristocracy.[81] Later in the century, Walpole opposed a bill to reduce the terms of members of the House of Commons from seven to three years on the ground that it would "destroy that equal mixture, which is the beauty of our constitution."[82] The ultimate development of this Whig adoption of the notion of equilibrium is perhaps its most interesting aspect, for, the principle being applicable to other divisions of government than the regal, aristocratic, and democratic parts, it afforded a basis for the doctrines of the separation of executive, legislative, and judicial powers with checks and balances which Locke and, more perfectly, Montesquieu elaborated.[83]

[79] *Discourse of the contests and dissentions*, ch. iv.

[80] *The town talk* etc., pp. 258–60, 268, 279.

[81] For Steele's views see *The town talk*, pp. 301, 241–43, 247, 249, 373, 380. The controversy provided the final breach between Addison and Steele. In a speech in the Commons, Walpole advanced the same views as Steele (*ibid.*, p. 399). For additional discussions of the relation of the bill to the balance, see *Considerations concerning the nature and consequences of the bill now pending in Parliament* (London, 1719), p. 17; *The constitution explain'd; in relation to the independency of the House of Lords* (London, 1719), pp. 2, 8; cf. pp. 19, 22, 45; [John] Asgill, *The complicated question divided: upon the bill now depending in Parliament relating to the peerage* (London, 1719), p. 8.

[82] Cobbett, *op. cit.*, IX, 474–75.

[83] Though Locke advocated the separation of powers to a degree, it is when we turn to Montesquieu that we can see exactly how the idea of balance connected with the theory of mixed government developed as one of its natural elaborations the idea of the separation and balance of powers. Though Montesquieu, unlike Locke, omits mixed government from his classification of the forms of government in Book II of *The spirit of laws*, he none-the-less had the substance of the theory and embodied it in the famous chapter on the constitution of England (XI, vi). It appears first in his conception of the nobility as moderating between the magisterial and popular powers—in this there was nothing new. What was new was a line of reasoning which proceeded as follows. In every government, whatever the ultimate source of all power may be, there are three kinds of powers, executive, legislative, and judicial. There can be no liberty when these are not separated from one another. It is natural to put the executive power in one magistrate

Along with the acceptance of the principle of balance went that of the Harringtonian theory that power depends on landed property, and that the balance in politics will follow its distribution. This theory was pleasing to Whig landowners who conveniently forgot Harrington's conclusion that the principle made necessary legislation to limit holdings in land, but not the corollary that such holdings could be protected by legislation.[84] Declaring that "the Foundation of this Government was first built and stood upon . . . the Ballance of Lands" and that "England being a Kingdom of Territory not of Trade, it always was, and ever will be true, that the Ballance of Lands is the Ballance of Government," Lord Holles, in the *Letter* of 1676 to which we have several times referred, proceeded to give a very Harringtonian account of the way in which the agrarian legislation of Henry VII had upset the old dominance of the peers.[85] In the dis-

(the kingly part of government) since administration can be better performed by one man than several; the legislative power belongs in the hands of the people (the popular element) or, in a numerous state, their representatives, since in "a country of liberty, every man who is supposed a free agent ought to be his own governor." However, there being in every state persons distinguished by birth, riches, or honors, who if they had no political powers other than those of all men, would find the common liberty their slavery, part of the legislative power should be bestowed on a senate of hereditary nobility (the aristocratic element), checked from using its powers corruptly by having only the power of veto in all laws relating to supplies. Though liberty would be lost were the executive to share in the "resolving" part of the legislative power, it is proper that he should share in it to the extent of the veto power to prevent the legislative elements from encroaching upon the executive, in which case liberty would also be lost. The judicial power should also be separate, though here again three exceptions were necessary: nobles should be tried only by the house of nobles to secure a fair trial; this house should serve as a court to moderate the severity of the law; and it should try impeachments brought in by the lower house. Montesquieu concludes this exposition of what should be by identifying it with the English constitution: "Here, then, is the fundamental constitution of the government we are treating of. The legislative body being composed of two parts, they check each other by the mutual privilege of rejecting. They are both restrained by the executive power, as the executive power is by the legislative." The fact that the English constitution as described by Montesquieu did not correspond with what the English constitution actually was even in his own time is true, as it is of the mixed monarchists generally, but irrelevant to the point we are here concerned with: that Montesquieu not only saw the English government as mixed, but in the process of idealizing it elaborated out of the notions of the mixed monarchists the concept of the balance of the *kinds* as well as the *exercisers* of power. Montesquieu, in short, saw in the English constitution a system of balances. That in doing so he elaborated ideas which became an important basis of the separation and balance of powers in the Constitution of the United States is not only true, but affords the link for establishing the connection between the kind of balance seen in that constitution and the kind traditionally associated with the idea of mixed government.

[84] Cf. Steele's assertion that if the Peerage Bill passed, it would be followed by a bill to prevent the lords from alienating their lands and that the basis for a pure aristocracy would then be established (*The town talk*, etc., p. 248).

[85] *Op. cit.*, pp. 4-5.

pute over the Peerage Bill, the idea was almost as prominent as that of mixed government itself,[86] Addison declaring that "of all maxims, none is more uncontested than that power follows property."[87] But even before this, as Russell Smith has pointed out, the Harringtonian principle that property did rule supplied the basis of the Lockean elaboration of the notion that it should rule.[88]

We come to perhaps the most striking relationship of the theories of the classical republicans and Whig thought when we examine the development of British imperial policy. It is an arresting fact that among the Whig mixed monarchists who were most definitely influenced by classical republicanism, we find men who were active in advocating an increased rôle in world affairs. Declaring that "the eyes of most part of the World are now upon us, and take their measures from our councils," Viscount Molesworth in 1694 condemned the late kings for isolationism and found that under William III England was taking its natural place in the world.[89] A few years later, Toland, who declared that the Revolution of 1688 had "settl'd the Monarchy for the future . . . under such wise Regulations as are most likely to continue it forever"; who asserted with far more justice than the pamphleteer of 1660 that England was a republic within the frame of the monarchy; and who found that London *was* the "new Rome in the West"—Toland declared that it deserved "like the old one, to becom the Soverain Mistress of the Universe."[90] I do not wish to imply that the classical republicans were the cause of the expansion of the British Empire, which doubtless would have occurred had they never lived. But the fact remains that they did live and that they did draw from classical examples, and from the political theory to which those examples gave rise, ideas which led them to embrace an expansionist position. The distinction between states made for "preservation" and those made for "increase," with the accompanying notion of the desirability and even necessity for a constitution of the latter type, was an idea of this sort. It seems clear that these were ideas which were not without their influence after classical republicanism itself was dead. Moreover, no one can contemplate the development of British imperial policy without believing

---

[86] *The town talk* etc., pp. 248, 304–05, 266–69, 277–78.   [87] *Ibid.*, p. 266.

[88] *Op. cit.*, p. 141. See pp. 143–51 for further evidence of the wide diffusion of the idea. Locke declared that government "has no end but the preservation of property" (*op. cit.*, ch. vii). The fact that he included lives and liberties as well as estates in his definition of "property" did not lessen the force of his statements in the minds of Whig landowners.

[89] *Op. cit.*, sig. a7r.   [90] *Op. cit.*, p. iv.

that the Roman-inspired imperialism of Harrington was an important determinant in the intellectual pedigree of that system of colonies, dominions, and "leagues" by which Britain came in time in truth to give "law unto the Sea."

As these appropriations from the theories of the classical republicans were made and incorporated into the theory of mixed monarchy, the way was prepared for the transference of the chorus of praise which the classical republicans had lavished upon Rome and Venice. It started early. A royalist pamphleteer of 1660 found the mixed monarchy of England the most "exquisitely composed" and "equally tempered" government in history.[91] By Toland's time it was in full voice. To that writer, the commonwealth-within-the-monarchy was "the most free and best constituted in all the world."[92] Steele took his stand in the Peerage Bill controversy on the ground that the balance of the constitution was perfect; Addison, his on the contention that it was almost so.[93] In 1734, Sir Robert Walpole spoke of the perfection of the constitution in words that might have been written by Polybius: "Ours is a mixt government, and the perfection of our constitution consists in this, that the monarchical, aristocratical, and democratical forms of government are mixt and interwoven in ours, so as to give all the advantages of each, without subjecting us to the dangers and inconveniences of either."[94] As a perfectly balanced machine, though not always with the same idea of what constituted its components, the constitution was seen by the great procession of panegyrists—Blackstone,[95] De Lolme,[96] and Montesquieu[97]—who followed later in the century. These writers spread its fame to the world as the masterpiece of mixed government. How through them, through Swift and Bolingbroke, this fame was transmitted to John Adams, to whom the English constitution was "the most perfect model that has yet been discovered or invented by human genius and experience,"[98] the "most stupendous fabric of human invention,"[99] and to others of the founding fathers of the United States; how the theory of the superiority of mixed government influenced those who

[91] G. S., *The dignity of kingship asserted*, p. 64.   [92] *Op. cit.*, p. viii.
[93] *The town talk*, pp. 249, 260.   [94] Cobbett, *op. cit.*, IX, 473.
[95] *Commentaries*, I, 50–51; 154–55. The fact that Blackstone, like Bolingbroke before him, was a Tory is illustrative of how completely the idea of mixed government had conquered English thought.
[96] *The constitution of England* (London, 1781, 3rd ed.), pp. 387, 428, 420, 451–52, 210. This once celebrated work first appeared in French at Amsterdam in 1771; the first English edition came out the following year.
[97] *The spirit of laws*, XI, vi. The first edition was at Geneva in two volumes in 1748.
[98] *Works*, ed. C. F. Adams (Boston, 1856), IX, 622.   [99] *Ibid.*, IV, 358.

met at Philadelphia to make the Constitution; and how the principle of the separation and balance of powers which Locke and Montesquieu had elaborated as an ultimate development of the idea of the balance of mixed government became incorporated in the Constitution of the United States—these things are another story and one that has already been well told.[100]

---

[100] By C. M. Walsh in *The political science of John Adams: a study in the theory of mixed government and the bicameral system* (New York and London, 1915), and Gilbert Chinard in "Polybius and the American Constitution," in the *Journal of the history of ideas*, I (1940), 38–58.

A NOTE ON THE THEORY OF CLIMATIC INFLUENCE

(See p. 91)

BODIN considered the influence of climate of such importance that he devoted a whole chapter to it (V, i). He divides the peoples of the northern hemisphere into inhabitants of the warm or "burning" regions situated in the first thirty degrees north of the equator; inhabitants of the temperate regions situated in the next thirty degrees; and inhabitants of the cold regions situated in the third band of thirty degrees (p. 547). Those who lived in the north were courageous, forceful, and hardy, but dull-witted, and, though lovers of freedom, lacking in political competence (pp. 548, 550, 554, 561, 563, 567). They were deficient in eloquence and learning and were designed by nature for "labour and manuall artes" (pp. 561, 559). The people of the "burning" regions were exceedingly subtle and quick-witted, and excelled in philosophy, mathematics, and the contemplative sciences, but were deficient in force and courage (pp. 550, 548, 561). The inhabitants of the temperate regions "had more force than they of the South and lesse policie: and more wit than they of the North, & lesse force"; they were more fit "to commaund and governe Commonweales." The "politique sciences" had come out of the temperate regions, and almost all the great empires of history had been situated therein (p. 550; see also p. 561). But Bodin was not content merely to put civilized men into three great divisions, for he subdivides each of these. Thus in the temperate region, those who lived in the southern half tended to be more like the inhabitants of the hot districts, whereas those who lived in the northern half tended to have the characteristics of northern peoples (p. 547). Moreover, within each of these subdivisions, peoples differed from one another as they were more northern and more southern in their situation. The English, for example, had less force than the Scots, but more than the French, whom they usually defeated in battle. The French, however, being more southern and hence possessed of greater subtlety, usually won the peace treaties, but were in turn outwitted by the Spaniards and Italians (pp. 550, 553).

Botero's treatment covers the first nineteen pages of his *Relations* in the London edition of 1630. It is notable for the detailed manner in which it works out the theory in terms of the influence of climate on the four humors of the body. Like Bodin, Botero finds northerners strong of body and courageous, but retarded in the development of their mental powers; southerners physically weak, but subtle, contemplative, and supplied with "extraordinarie gifts of minde"; and those of the middle regions masters of politics and government and founders of great states and empires. He classifies England in the group of northern nations, as, indeed, did Englishmen themselves. Note, for example, Milton's reference in *Of education* to Englishmen as "far northernly" and as dwellers in the "cold air" (*P.w.*, III, 468).

Bodin's and Botero's tripartite division was not only Aristotelian in precedent, but must be considered in some sense as a concession to patriotism, resulting as it did in the placing of France and Italy in the temperate zone. Even in this form, the theory was not very flattering to Englishmen. Other writers who had less regard for national sensibilities developed it in even a less flattering form. Ignoring the tripartite division altogether, they considered that Italians and Spaniards were inhabitants of warm regions, and were possessed of the characteristics of dwellers in both Bodin's and Botero's southern and middle regions, and that all to the north of them were inhabitants of cold climates and possessed of the characteristics of dwellers in such regions. Thus the author of a curious tract on the Italians which was originally written in France, but which was translated into English and published in London in 1591 under the title of *A discovery of the great subtiltie and wonderful wisedome of the Italians*, tells us that he wrote to "purge the Septentrionall and Occidental peoples of a grosse humour ingendred in them, by reason of the grossnes, and coldnes of the aier wherin they live, which letteth them for seeing so clearly into matters of state, and the government of this world, as doe the nations which are more Meridionall" (sig. A2v). What emerges out of the three representative writers to whom I refer is the idea that the inhabitants of the colder northern countries of Europe tended to be deficient in two notable fields of activity, the arts and learning, and politics, a fact which was emphasized in Milton's case by the circumstance that his references to the climatic theory show clearly that he thought of it in a form which was closer to that in *The discovery of the subtiltie of the Italians* than to that in Bodin and Botero.

THE DATE AND AUTHENTICITY OF MILTON'S *CHARACTER OF THE LONG PARLIAMENT*

(See p. 93)

THE *Character of the Long Parliament* was posthumously published in 1681 and attributed to Milton with the statement that it originally formed part of the Third book of the *History of Britain*. It is time that Miltonic scholarship freed itself from the influence of Masson's ill-considered treatment of this work in the sixth volume of his *Life of Milton* (pp. 806–12). Although constrained to admit that the *Character* is thoroughly Miltonic in style and that Milton could have written it in the late 1640's, Masson inclined to the view that it represented a "doctoring" of Milton's *History* by the licenser in 1670 when that work was being prepared for the press, and that Milton refused to assent to it and struck it out. The ground on which Masson urged this far-fetched hypothesis was that the *Character* had a "positively renegade" note about it and a certain "anti-Miltonism" in the sentiments. This anti-Miltonism turns out on examination of Masson's treatment to consist of two aspects of the work, its severe criticism of Parliament and its view on the political competence of Englishmen. But there is not a word in the criticism of Parliament which cannot be duplicated in other works of unquestioned authenticity (see above, pp. 111 ff.). As for the idea that Englishmen were lacking in political competence, we have seen that this notion was an implication of the climatic theory and that Milton was at times strongly influenced by this theory. It is likely enough, therefore, that at a time when he was disappointed in Parliament he would have produced just such charges as the *Character* contains.

Once the Miltonism of the sentiments is agreed upon, the date of composition offers no great difficulty. The statement in the 1681 edition that the *Character* originally formed part of the Third book of the *History of Britain* points clearly to the late 1640's, for Milton tells us that the first four books of that work were complete when, between March 13 and March 20, 1649, he was invited to become Latin secretary (*P.w.*, I, 261; see also Masson, IV, 79–83). The date thus indicated corresponds with the sentiments in the *Character*, for at this period Milton was angry with, and disappointed in, the Presbyterians, who controlled Parliament until Pride's Purge at the end of 1648. If we take the *Character* as an expression of Milton's feelings in the late 1640's, all difficulties about at least its approximate date and its Miltonism disappear.

The 1681 edition tells us that the work was "struck out" of the *History of Britain* when that book was being prepared for the press in 1670. I agree with Sir Charles Firth, not only in his acceptance of the genuineness of the *Character* and in his dating of it, but also in his suggestion that it was struck out by Milton himself, not because it was a "doctoring" of the licenser, but because Milton was unwilling to give his enemies the comfort of seeing him condemn the failures and shortcomings of those with whom he had once been associated (*Essays, historical and literary* [Oxford, 1938], p. 98).

POLITICAL IMPLICATIONS IN
PARADISE REGAINED

(See p. 105)

I N *Paradise regained* Satan is clearly represented as a dictator created by the general assembly of devils. This conception appears
first in the representation of the situation created by the appearance of Christ as a national emergency. It is so described by Satan in
his speech to the council at the beginning of the action, when he asserts that it "admits no long debate" and must "with something sudden be oppos'd" (Bk. I, ll. 95–96). In this view of the matter the
devils acquiesce, and thereupon, by Milton's own specific statement,
they make Satan dictator:

> Unanimous they all commit the care
> And management of this main enterprize
> To him their great Dictator . . . (Bk. I, ll. 111–13).

The conception is, moreover, carried over from the first Satanic
council to the second one in Book II, Satan's report on this occasion
making clear that his powers were extraordinary. He has acted, he
declares, as he undertook and

> with the vote
> Consenting in full frequence was impowr'd (Bk. II, ll. 129–30).

That his powers were also temporary may be deduced from his care
to have them renewed at the second council (Bk. II, ll. 233–35).

Now, in his rôle as dictator, Satan is presented as most ineffective.
Granted extraordinary powers by the first council, he is driven back
on the council for assistance after the first temptation, as his speech
to the council in Book II makes perfectly clear (ll. 143–46).
Given aid and securing a renewal of his dictatorial authority, he
goes forth a second time, and, after trying the utmost of which he is
capable, succeeds no better. The career of Satan as a dictator is a
career of unrelieved failure. The theme required that Satan should
fail; it did not require that he should be represented in failure as a
dictator. The implications, I believe, are clear and unmistakable.

Considered from the point of view of its political meaning, *Paradise regained* is an expression of Milton's lack of faith in dictatorship as it was conceived in seventeenth-century political thought. A constitutional dictator of the sort that so many commonwealth-planners wished to provide for, Milton would tell us, is a futile refuge when ordinary institutions break down in time of crisis. Thus there emerges out of the poem a point of view thoroughly consistent with that in *The ready and easy way*, in which Milton had put his full faith in the adequacy of perfectly-contrived institutions to meet all situations whether of peace or crisis. His political thought is thus seen to be bolder even than that of Harrington. He conceived the grand problem in government to be, not providing a dictator to take over authority when institutions perfectly adequate to performing the tasks of peace broke down in time of crisis, but the creation of absolutely perfect institutions as sufficient unto themselves in times of emergency as in ordinary periods. In the state which he had in mind, a constitutional dictator would be wholly supererogatory.

APPENDIX D

THE DATE OF MILTON'S *PROPOSALLS*
FOR A FIRME GOVERNMENT

(See p. 115)

I N THE eighteenth volume of the Columbia *Milton* is printed, possibly for the first time, a little-known prose work of the poet's of which the full title is *Proposalls of certaine expedients for the prevention of a civill war now feard, & the settling of a firme government.* The Columbia editors, Professors Mabbott and French, who are apparently the only ones who have dealt with this document, do not discuss its date, directly, although the slender evidence which they present to suggest that it may have been printed as a separate tract in 1659 leaves the reader to infer that it was composed sometime during that year (p. 501; cf. their earlier observations in *N. & Q.*, CLXXIII, 66, 24 July, 1937). I believe it is possible to show that the *Proposalls* was written between October 20 and December 26, 1659.

On the former date, Milton addressed to an unknown friend the *Letter concerning the ruptures of the commonwealth.* The *Proposalls* is like this letter in containing the suggestion that the principal army chiefs be given life tenure, a suggestion which appears in neither edition of *The ready and easy way* nor in the *Letter to Monk,* which cannot be earlier than February, 1660 (see E. M. Clark's edition of *The ready and easy way* [New Haven, 1915], pp. xff.). The idea was clearly a concession to the demands of the situation which prevailed in the last months of 1659, when the army régime was dominant in London after Lambert's coup on October 13. It was no essential part of Milton's political philosophy, as the *Letter concerning the ruptures of the commonwealth* itself makes clear, and with the collapse of the army régime in the last days of the year, we hear no more of it. Hence the *Proposalls* is earlier in date than either *The ready and easy way* or the *Letter to Monk.* Indeed, it must be more than a month earlier than *The ready and easy way,* since on December 26, 1659, Parliament resumed its sitting, and Milton's suggestion that the Parliament be again treated with to sit, shows conclusively that he was writing before this event occurred and even before it became obvious that it was going to occur.

On the other hand, the *Proposalls* contains an emphatic statement that members of the grand council should have life tenure. This principle is a central feature of both *The ready and easy way* and the *Letter to Monk*. It appears also in the *Letter concerning the ruptures of the commonwealth*, and there can be no question that it represented Milton's real opinion during this whole period and one toward which he had been long traveling. But in the *Letter* there is observable a willingness to compromise which is much greater than in *The ready and easy way*. In the *Letter*, indeed, Milton went so far as to say that "whether the Civil Government be an annual Democracy, or a perpetual Aristocracy, is not to me a Consideration for the Extremities wherein we are," but in *The ready and easy way* he would admit as an alternative to life tenure only a restricted rotation, and he argued against this with all the resources at his command. Clearly, the movement of Milton's thought from October, 1659, to February, 1660, was in the direction of an increasing unwillingness to compromise on the principle of life tenure. The views on this matter in the *Proposalls* are those of *The ready and easy way* rather than of the *Letter concerning the ruptures of the commonwealth*, and it would seem therefore that the *Proposalls* was written after that letter. I conclude that it was written between October 20 and December 26, 1659, and certainly some days removed from either extreme.

BIBLIOGRAPHY

This bibliography contains works cited in the text and notes, and the more important of the additional materials used.

ADAMS, JOHN. *Works*. Ed. with a life of the author, notes, and illustrations by Charles Francis Adams. Boston, 1850–56. 10 vols.

ADDISON, JOSEPH. *Miscellaneous works*. Ed. A. C. Guthkelch. London, 1914. 2 vols.

ALLEN, J. W. *English political thought, 1603–44*. London, 1938.

———. *A history of political thought in the sixteenth century*. New York, 1928.

An address to the freemen and free-holders of the nation. London, 1682.

Antidotum Britannicum: or, a counter-pest against the destructive principles of Plato redivivus. London, 1681. Dedication and Preface signed W. W.

The apostate protestant. A letter to a friend. 1682.

Aristotle. *A treatise on government*. Trans. William Ellis. London and New York, 1912. Referred to as *Politics*.

The arraignment, tryal, and condemnation of Algernon Sidney, Esq. London, 1684.

ASCHAM, ROGER. *The scholemaster*. Ed. Edward Arber. London, 1897.

ASGILL, [JOHN]. *The complicated question divided: upon the bill now depending in Parliament relating to the peerage*. London, 1719.

AUBREY, JOHN. *Brief lives*. Ed. Andrew Clark. Oxford, 1898. 2 vols.

AVITY, PIERRE D'. *Estates, empires, and principallities of the world represented by the description of countries, maners of inhabitants . . . with the beginning of all militarie and religious orders*. Trans. E[dward]Grimstone. London, 1615.

BARCLAY, JOHN. *The mirrour of mindes: or Barclays Icon animorum*. Trans. Thomas May. London, 1631.

BARKER, ARTHUR. *Milton and the Puritan dilemma, 1641–1660*. Toronto, 1942.

BAXTER, RICHARD. *A holy commonwealth, or political aphorisms, opening the true principles of government: for the healing of the mistakes, and resolving the doubts, that most endanger and trouble England at this time*. London, 1659.

BEMBO, PIETRO. *Historiae Venetae libri XII*. Venice, 1551.

BLACKSTONE, SIR WILLIAM. *Commentaries on the laws of England*. Oxford, 1765–69. 4 vols.

BOCCALINI, TRAJANO. *The new-found politicke, wherein the governments, greatnesse and power of the most notable kingdomes and common-wealths of the world are discovered and censured . . .* London, 1626.

———. *The politicke touchstone*. Trans. Henry Earl of Monmouth. London, 1674. Third ed.

199

BODIN, J[EAN]. *The six bookes of a commonweale.* Trans. Richard Knolles. London, 1606.

BOLINGBROKE, HENRY SAINT JOHN, VISCOUNT. *Works.* Philadelphia, 1841. 4 vols.

BORDE, ANDREW. *The first boke of the introduction of knowledge.* Ed. F. J. Furnivall. London, 1869–70.

BOTERO, GIOVANNI. *Relations of the most famous kingdomes and common-wealths thorowout the world . . . now once again inlarged . . . with addition of new estates and countries.* Trans. R[obert] J[ohnson]. London, 1630.

——. *Treatise concerning the causes of the magnificencie and greatnes of cities.* Trans. Robert Peterson. London, 1606.

The bounds and bonds of publique obedience. Or, a vindication of our lawfull submission to the present government, or to a government supposed unlaw-full, but commanding lawfull things. . . . London, 1649.

BROWN, HORATIO FORBES. *The Venetian republic.* London, 1902.

——. *Venetian studies.* London, 1887.

——. *Venice; an historical sketch of the republic.* London, 1895. Second ed.

BROWN, LOUISE FARGO. *The first Earl of Shaftesbury.* New York and London, 1933.

——. *The political activities of the Baptists and Fifth Monarchy men in England during the Interregnum.* New York, 1912.

BROWNE, SIR THOMAS. *Works.* Ed. G. L. Keynes. London, 1928–31. 6 vols.

BURCKHARDT, JACOB. *The civilization of the Renaissance in Italy.* Trans. S. G. C. Middlemore. London, 1892.

BURNET, GILBERT. *History of his own times.* London, 1724–34. 2 vols.

BURTON, THOMAS. *Diary . . . now first published from the original autograph manuscript. With an introduction, containing an account of the Parliament of 1654; from the journal of Guibon Goddard, esq.* Ed. and illustrated with . . . notes by John Towill Rutt. London, 1828.

Catalogue of the pamphlets, books, newspapers, and manuscripts collected by George Thomason. London, 1908. 2 vols.

A caveat against the Whiggs. In a short historical view of their transactions. London, 1714. Fourth edition.

The censure of the Rota upon Mr. Milton's book, entituled, The ready and easie way to establish a free common-wealth. London, 1660.

Chaos: or a discourse, wherein is presented to the view of the magistrate, and all others who shall peruse the same, a frame of government by way of a re-publique. London, 1659.

The character of a Whig under several denominations. London, 1700.

CHINARD, GILBERT. "Polybius and the American Constitution," in *Journal of the history of ideas,* 1 (1940), 38–58.

CHURCH, W. F. *Constitutional thought in sixteenth century France.* Cambridge, Mass., and London, 1941.

Cicero. *De re publica, De legibus.* Trans. Clinton W. Keyes. London and New York, 1928.

Clark, G. N. *The seventeenth century.* Oxford, 1929.

Cobb, Edith H. "Bibliography of Venice," in *Bulletin of bibliography,* III (1902), No. 3, 40.

Cobbett's Parliamentary history of England. From the Norman Conquest in 1066 to . . . 1803. [Edited by William Cobbett and J. Wright.] London, 1806–20. 36 vols. Title altered after vol. XII to *The parliamentary history of England, from the earliest period to the year 1803.*

A collection of poems on affairs of state by A—— M——l esq.; and other eminent wits. London, 1689.

A collection of scarce and valuable tracts, on the most interesting and entertaining subjects: but chiefly such as relate to the history and constitution of these kingdoms. . . . Revised, augmented, and arranged by Walter Scott. London, 1809–15. (*Somers tracts*)

A collection of state tracts publish'd on occasion of the late revolution in 1688 and during the reign of King William III. 1705–07. 3 vols. (*State tracts of William III*)

A collection of the rights and priviledges of Parliament, together, with the true and just prerogatives of the kings of England. London, 1642.

Considerations concerning the nature and consequences of the bill now pending in Parliament. London, 1719.

The constitutional documents of the Puritan revolution, 1625–1660. Ed. Samuel R. Gardiner. Oxford, 1906.

The constitution explain'd; in relation to the independency of the House of Lords. London, 1719.

The Constitution reconsidered. Edited for the American Historical Association by Conyers Read. New York, 1938.

Contarini, Gasparo. *The commonwealth and government of Venice . . . with sundry other collections, annexed by the translator, for the more cleere and exact satisfaction of the reader. With a short chronicle in the end, of the lives and raignes of the Venetian dukes, from the very beginninges of their citie.* London, 1599. (I have regularized the author's name, which appears on the title page as Gaspar Contareno.)

Coryate, Thomas. *Crudities; hastily gobled up in five moneths travells in France, Savoy, Italy, Rhetia commonly called the Grisons country, Helvetia alias Switzerland, some parts of high Germany and the Netherlands; newly digested in the hungry aire of Odcombe in the county of Somerset, and now dispersed to the nourishment of the travelling members of this kingdome.* Glasgow and New York, 1905. 2 vols.

Critical essays of the sevententh century. Ed. J. E. Spingarn. Oxford, 1908. 3 vols.

Crivellucci, Amadeo. *Del governo popolare in Firenze, 1494–95, secondo il Guicciardini.* Pisa, 1877.

Cromwell, Oliver. *Writings and speeches.* Ed. Wilbur C. Abbott. Cambridge, Mass., 1937–.

DALRYMPLE, SIR JOHN. *Memoirs of Great Britain and Ireland. From the dissolution of the last Parliament of Charles II until the sea-battle off La Hogue.* London, 1771–88. Second ed. 3 vols.

DANIEL, SAMUEL. *Complete works in verse and prose.* Ed. Alexander B. Grosart. London, 1885–96. 5 vols.

DAVIES, GODFREY. "The army and the downfall of Richard Cromwell," in *Huntington library bulletin,* VII (1935), 131–67.

———. *Bibliography of British history, Stuart period, 1603–1714.* Oxford, 1928.

DELATTRE, FLORIS. "La conception politique de Milton," in *Revue de l'enseignement des langues vivantes,* XXX (1913), 65–74.

A dialogue at Oxford between a tutor and a gentleman, formerly his pupil, concerning government. London, 1681.

DIODATI, GIOVANNI. *Pious and learned annotations upon the Holy Bible: plainly expounding the most difficult places thereof.* . . . London, 1648. Second ed.

DIONYSIUS OF HALICARNASSUS. *The Roman antiquities.* Trans. Earnest Cary on the basis of the version of Edward Spelman. Cambridge, Mass., and London, 1937–.

A discovery of the great subtiltie and wonderful wisedome of the Italians, whereby they beare sway over the most part of Christendome, and cunninglie behave themselves to fetch the quintescence out of the peoples purses. London, 1591.

DISRAELI, BENJAMIN, EARL OF BEACONSFIELD. *The letters of Runnymede.* London, 1836.

———. *What is he? and A vindication of the English constitution.* London n.d.

DUNNING, WILLIAM ARCHIBALD. *A history of political theories, ancient and medieval.* New York and London, 1902.

———. *A history of political theories from Luther to Montesquieu.* New York, 1905.

DWIGHT, T. W. "Harrington and his influence on American political institutions," in *Political science quarterly,* II (1887), 18.

An enquiry into the inconveniences of public and the advantages of private elections, with the method of the ballott. 1701.

EWALD, ALEX. CHARLES. *The life and times of the hon. Algernon Sydney.* London, 1873. 2 vols.

FAY, C. R. "The political philosophy of Milton," in *Christ's college magazine,* XXIII (1908), 81–92.

FEILING, KEITH. *A history of the Tory party, 1640–1714.* Oxford, 1924.

FERNE, HENRY. *A reply unto severall treatises pleading for the armes now taken up by subjects in the pretended defence of religion and liberty.* Oxford, 1643.

FIGGIS, J. N. *The divine right of kings.* Cambridge, 1896.

FILMER, SIR ROBERT. *The free-holders grand inquest, touching our sovereign lord the king and his parliament. To which are added Observations upon forms of government.* London, 1684. "Fourth impression."
———. *Patriarcha; or the natural power of kings.* London, 1680.

FINK, ZERA S. "The date of Milton's *Proposalls for a firme government,*" in *Modern language notes,* 1940, 407–10.
———. "Milton and the theory of climatic influence," in *Modern language quarterly,* II (1941), 67–80.
———. "The political implications of *Paradise regained,*" in *Journal of English and Germanic philology,* L (1941), 482–88.
———. "The theory of the mixed state and the development of Milton's political thought," in *Publications of the Modern language association,* LVII (1942), 705–36.
———. "Venice and English political thought in the seventeenth century," in *Modern philology,* XXXVIII (1940), 155–72.

FIRTH, SIR CHARLES H. "Anarchy and the Restoration (1659–1660)," in *Cambridge modern history,* IV, 539–59. Cambridge, 1906.
———. *Essays, historical and literary.* Oxford, 1938.
———. *The last years of the Protectorate, 1656–58.* London, 1909. 2 vols.

FOUGASSES, THOMAS DE. *The generall historie of the magnificent state of Venice. From the first foundation thereof untill this present.* Trans. W. Shute. London, 1612.

GAILHARD, JEAN. *The present state of the princes and republicks of Italy, with observations on them.* London, 1668.
———. *The present state of the republick of Venice, as to the government, laws, forces etc. of that commonwealth.* London, 1669.

GARDINER, SAMUEL R. *History of the Commonwealth and Protectorate, 1649–56.* London and New York, 1903. 4 vols.
———. *History of the great civil war, 1642–49.* London, 1886–91. 4 vols.

GEFFROY, A. *Étude sur les pamphlets politiques et religieux de Milton.* Paris, 1848.

GIANNOTTI, DONATO. *Libro de la republica de Vinitiani.* Rome, 1548.

GIERKE, OTTO VON. *Natural law and the theory of society, 1550–1800.* Trans. E. Barker. Cambridge, 1934. 2 vols.

GILLETT, CHARLES R. *Catalogue of the McAlpin collection of British history and theology.* New York, 1927–30. 5 vols.

GIUSTINIANI, BERNARDO. *Historia . . . dell'origine di Vinegia, & delle cose fatte da Vinitiani.* Venice, 1545.

GIUSTINIANI, PIETRO. *Le historie Venetiane. . . .* Venice, 1576.

GODDARD, THOMAS. *Plato's demon; or, the state physician unmaskt. Being a discourse in answer to a book called Plato redivivus.* London, 1684.

GOOCH, G. P. *The history of English democratic ideas in the seventeenth century.* Cambridge, 1898. (Cambridge historical essays, No. X.) Rev. ed. with notes by H. J. Laski, Cambridge, 1927.

————. *Political thought in England from Bacon to Halifax.* London, 1914–15.

GOUGH, J. W. *The social contract: a critical study of its development.* Oxford, 1936.

The grand problem briefly discussed: or considerations on the true nature and limits of obedience and submission to governours. By a divine of the Church of England. London, 1690.

GROSE, CLYDE LECLARE. *A select bibliography of British history, 1660–1760.* Chicago, 1939.

GROSLEY, P. J. *Discussion historique et critique sur la conjuration de Venise.* Paris, 1756.

GUICCIARDINI, FRANCESCO. *Historie conteining the warres of Italie and other partes, continued for many yeares under sundry kings and princes. . .* Trans. G. Fenton. London, 1579.

————. *Opere inedite . . .* illustrate da G. Canestrini e pubblicate per curia dei Conti P. e L. Guicciardini. Florence, 1857–67. 10 vols.

HAILLAN, BERNARD DE GIRARD DU. *De l'estat et succez des affaires de France. . .* Paris, 1580.

HALLAM, HENRY. *Constitutional history of England, from the accession of Henry VII to the death of George II.* London, 1846. Fifth ed. 2 vols.

HAM, ROSWELL GRAY. *Otway and Lee, biography from a baroque age.* New Haven, 1931.

HANFORD, J. H. "The chronology of Milton's private studies," in *Publications of the Modern language association,* XXXVI (1921), 251–314.

The Harleian miscellany. A collection of scarce, curious, and entertaining pamphlets and tracts, as well in manuscript as in print. Selected from the library of Edward Harley, second Earl of Oxford. With notes by William Oldys and Thomas Park. London, 1808–13. 10 vols.

HARRINGTON, JAMES. *Oceana.* Edited with notes by S. B. Liljegren. Lund and Heidelberg, 1924.

————. *Oceana and other works.* With an account of his life by John Toland. London, 1700.

HASSALL, ARTHUR. *Life of Viscount Bolingbroke.* Oxford, 1915.

H[AWKINS], R[ICHARD]. *A discourse on the nationall excellencies of England.* London, 1658.

The history of the league made at Cambray, between Pope Julius the Second, Maximilian the First, emperor of Germany, the kings of France and Arragon, and all the princes of Italy against the republick of Venice. London, 1712.

HOBBES, THOMAS. *Leviathan.* Ed. A. D. Lindsay. London, 1914.

HOLDSWORTH, SIR WILLIAM. *A history of English law.* London, 1931–38. Second ed. 12 vols.

HOLLES, DENZIL, LORD. *A letter to Monsieur Van——— B[euningen] de M——— at Amsterdam, written anno 1676, concerning the government of England.* 1676.

The horrid sin of man-catching. The second part. Or further discoveries and arguments to prove, that there is no Protestant plot. London, 1681.

HOTMAN, FRANCIS. *Franco-Gallia.* Trans. Viscount Molesworth. London, 1721.

HOUSSAYE, ABRAHAM NICOLAS AMELOT DE LA. *Histoire du gouvernement de Venise.* Amsterdam, 1695. 3 vols. English trans. London, 1677.

H[OWELL], J[AMES]. ΔΕΝΔΡΟΛΟΓΙΑ. *Dodona's grove, or, the vocall forest.* London, 1644. Second ed.

————. *Familiar letters.* Ed. Joseph Jacobs. London, 1892. 2 vols.

————. *Instructions for forreine travell, 1642.* Ed. Edward Arber. London, 1895.

————. *A survay of the signorie of Venice, of her admired policy and method of government.* London, 1651.

HUNTON, PHILIP. *A treatise of monarchie.* . . . Done by an earnest desirer of his countries peace. London, 1643.

The interest of the three kingdoms with respect to the business of the black box, and all the other pretentions of his grace, the Duke of Monmouth discuss'd and asserted. London, 1680.

JONES, RICHARD FOSTER. *Ancients and moderns: a study of the background of "The battle of the books."* St. Louis, 1936. (Washington University studies, new series, language and literature, VI.)

JORDAN, W. K. *The development of religious toleration in England.* London and Cambridge, Mass., 1932-40.

Jus populi, or a discourse wherein clear satisfaction is given, as well concerning the rights of subjects, as the right of princes. London, 1644.

LASSELS, RICHARD. *The voyage of Italy, or compleat journey through Italy, with characters of the people, description of the chief towns . . . and instructions concerning travel.* Paris, 1670.

L'ESTRANGE, ROGER. *A account of the growth of knavery under the pretended fears of arbitrary government and popery. With a parallel betwixt the reformers of 1677 and those of 1641 in their methods and designs.* London, 1681.

————. *No blinde guides, in answer to a seditious pamphlet of J. Milton's, intituled Brief notes upon a late sermon.* London, 1660.

————. *A plea for limited monarchy, as it was established in this nation before the late war; in a humble address to his excellency General Monk, by a zealot for the good old laws of his country . . .* London, 1660. This work appeared anonymously; it is commonly assigned to L'Estrange.

A letter from a gentleman in the city to one in the country; concerning the bill for disabling the Duke of York to inherit the imperial crown of this realm. 1680.

The leveller: or, the principles & maxims concerning government and religion, which are asserted by those that are commonly called levellers. London, 1659. (Reprinted in *Harleian mis.,* VII).

LOCKE, JOHN. *Of civil government; two treatises.* With an introduction by William S. Carpenter. London and New York, 1924.

LOLME, JEAN LOUIS DE. *The constitution of England; or an account of the English government.* London, 1781. Third ed.

LUDLOW, EDMUND. *Memoirs.* Vevey, 1698–99. 3 vols.

MACAULAY, THOMAS BABINGTON MACAULAY, LORD. *The history of England from the accession of James II.* Philadelphia, 1873. 5 vols.

MACHIAVELLI, NICCOLÒ. *Discourses upon the first decade of T. Livius . . . with some marginall animadversions noting and taxing his errours.* Trans. E[dward] D[acres]. London, 1636.

———. *The prince and other works including Reform in Florence, Castruccio Castracani, On fortune, Letters, Ten discourses on Livy.* New trans., introductions, and notes by Allan H. Gilbert, Chicago, 1941.

———. *The prince and The discourses.* With an introduction by Max Lerner. New York, 1940.

———. *The works of the famous Nicolas Machiavel.* Trans. [Henry Nevill]. London, 1675.

MACK, J. F. "The evolution of Milton's political thinking," in *Sewanee review*, XXX (1922), 193–205.

MAITLAND, FREDERIC WILLIAM. *The constitutional history of England.* Cambridge, 1931.

MARVELL, ANDREW. *Complete works.* Ed. Alexander B. Grosart. 1872–75. 4 vols. (Fuller worthies' library)

———. *Poems and letters.* Ed. H. M. Margoliouth. Oxford, 1927. 2 vols.

MASSON, DAVID. *The life of John Milton; narrated in connexion with the political, ecclesiastical, and literary history of his time.* London, 1859–94. 7 vols.

MAUROCENI, ANDREA. *Historia Veneta ab ano MDXXI usque ad annum MDCXV.* Venice, 1623.

The maxims of the government of Venice. In an advice to the republick; how it ought to govern it self both inwardly and outwardly, in order to perpetuate its dominion. By Father Paul [Paolo Sarpi]. Trans. [William Strahan (?)]. London, 1707. The attribution of this work to Sarpi is probably erroneous.

McCLELLAN, GEORGE B. *The oligarchy of Venice.* Boston and New York, 1904.

MEADLEY, GEORGE WILSON. *Memoirs of Algernon Sydney.* London, 1813.

Memoirs of Thomas Hollis, esq. London, 1780.

Mercurius politicus; comprising the summ of all intelligence, with the affairs and designs now on foot . . . in defence of the commonwealth. 12 Sept., 1650–12 April, 1660. Title altered after No. 254 for 26 April, 1655 to *Mercurius politicus, comprising the sum of foreine intelligence with the affairs now on foot in the three nations of England, Scotland, and Ireland.* Marchamont Nedham was the editor and the author of most or all of this paper.

[MICANZIO, FULGENZIO]. *The life of the most learned Father Paul of the order of the Servii. Councellour of state to the most serene republicke of Venice.* London, 1651.

MILTON, JOHN. *Prose works.* Ed. J. A. St. John. London, 1848–53. 5 vols. (Bohn ed.)

————. *The ready and easy way to establish a free commonwealth.* Edited with introduction, notes, and glossary by E. M. Clark. New Haven, 1915. (Yale studies in English, No. 51.)

————. *The student's Milton.* Ed. Frank A. Patterson. New York, 1933. Rev. ed.

————. *The tenure of kings and magistrates.* Edited with introduction and notes by W. T. Allison. New Haven, 1911. (Yale studies in English, No. 40.)

————. *Works.* Edited by various hands under the general editorship of Frank A. Patterson. New York, 1931–38. 18 vols. in 21. Index in 2 vols., 1940.

MISOPAPPAS, PHILANAX (pseud.). *A tory plot: or the discovery of a design carried on by our late addressers and abhorrers, to alter the constitution of the government.* London, 1682.

A modest plea for an equal common-wealth against monarchy. London, 1659. Variously attributed to Sir Henry Vane, William Spriggs, and others.

[MOLESWORTH, ROBERT MOLESWORTH, VISCOUNT]. *An account of Denmark, as it was in the year 1692.* London, 1694.

MONTESQUIEU, CHARLES DE SECONDAT, BARON DF. *The spirit of laws.* Berwick, 1770. Fifth ed. 3 vols.

MORE, SIR THOMAS. *Utopia with the Dialogue of comfort.* London and New York, 1910.

MORGAN, J. DE. *Milton considered as a politician.* London, 1875.

MORTIMER, C. E. *A historical memoir of the political life of John Milton.* London, 1805.

MORYSON, FYNES. *An itinerary . . . containing his ten yeeres travell. . .* London, 1617.

MOYLE, WALTER AND JOHN TRENCHARD. *An argument showing that a standing army is inconsistent with a free government, and absolutely destructive of the English monarchy.* London, 1697.

MOYLE, WALTER. *Whole works.* London, 1727.

————. *Works, none of which were ever before publish'd.* London, 1726. 2 vols.

MURRAY, D. L. *Disraeli.* London, 1927.

NANI, BATTISTA. *The history of the affairs of Europe in this present age, but more particularly of the republick of Venice.* Trans. Sir Robert Honywood. London, 1673.

NASHE, THOMAS. *Works.* Ed. R. B. McKerrow. London, 1904. 6 vols.

NEAL, DANIEL. *History of the Puritans.* London, 1937. 3 vols.

[NEDHAM, MARCHAMONT]. *The excellencie of a free state: or, the right constitution of a common-wealth.* London, 1656.

[NEVILL, HENRY]. *Plato redivivus: or, a dialogue concerning government.* London, 1681. Second ed.

NICOLSON, M. H. "Milton and Hobbes," in *Studies in philology,* XXIII (1926), 405–33.

No Protestant plot: or the present pretended conspiracy of Protestants against the king and government, discovered to be a conspiracy of the papists against the king and his Protestant subjects. London, 1681.

NOVELL, JOHN. *The seditious principle, viz. that the supreme power is inherent in the people.* London, 1662.

OGG, DAVID. *England in the reign of Charles II.* Oxford, 1934.

OTWAY, THOMAS. *Best plays.* Ed. with introduction and notes by Roden Noel. London, 1893.

——. *Complete works.* Ed. Montague Summers. London, 1926. 3 vols.

——. *The orphan* and *Venice preserved.* Ed. Charles F. McClumpha. Boston and London, 1908.

——. *Venice preserved.* Ed. Israel Gollancz. London, 1899.

——. *Works.* Ed. J. C. Ghosh. Oxford, 1932. 2 vols.

——. *Works.* Ed. Thomas Thornton. London, 1813. 3 vols.

A parallel of governments: or, a politicall discourse upon seven positions, tending to the peace of England. 1647.

PARKER, WILLIAM R. *Milton's contemporary reputation. An essay together with a tentative list of printed allusions to Milton, 1641-1674, and facsimile reproductions of five contemporary pamphlets written in answer to Milton.* Columbus, Ohio, 1940.

The parliamentary or constitutional history of England. London, 1751-66. 24 vols.

PARUTA, PAOLO. *The history of Venice.* Trans. Henry Earl of Monmouth. London, 1658.

——. *Politick Discourses.* Trans. Henry Earl of Monmouth. London, 1657.

The patriot's proposal to the people of England concerning the ballot, the best way of choosing their representatives in Parliament. London, 1705.

PEASE, THEODORE CALVIN. *The leveller movement.* Washington, 1916.

PENN, WILLIAM. *The peace of Europe: the fruits of solitude, and other writings.* With a life by Joseph Besse. London and New York, n.d.

PERKINSON, RICHARD H. " 'Volpone' and the reputation of Venetian justice," in *Modern language review*, XXXV (1940), 11–18.

A persuasive to a mutual compliance under the present government, together with a plea for a free state, compared with monarchy. Oxford, 1652.

PLATO, *The republic.* Trans. with an analysis, and notes, by John L. Davies and David J. Vaughan. London, 1920.

PLUTARCH. *The lives of the noble Grecians and Romans.* Trans. John Dryden; revised by Arthur Hugh Clough. New York, n.d.

Poems on affairs of state: from the time of Oliver Cromwell to the abdication of K. James the second. Written by the greatest wits of the age. 1697.

Poems on affairs of state: from the time of Oliver Cromwell to the abdication of K. James the second. Written by the greatest wits of the age. Now carefully examined with the originals, and published without any castration. 1703-07. Fifth ed. 4 vols.

POLLOCK, JOHN. *The popish plot; a study in the history of the reign of Charles II.* London, 1903.

POLYBIUS. *Histories.* Trans. Evelyn Shuckburgh. London and New York, 1889. 2 vols.

PONET, JOHN. *A short treatise of politike power, and of the true obedience which subjectes owe to kynges.* London, 1556.

The power of Parliaments in the case of succession. London, 1680.

The present interest of England; or a confutation of the Whiggish conspirators anti-monyan principle. London, 1683.

R., W. *The English ape, the Italian imitation, the footesteppes of Fraunce. Wherein is explained, the wilfull blindnesse of subtill mischiefe, the striving for starres, the catching of mooneshine: and the secrete sound of many hollow hearts.* London, 1588.

RALEIGH, SIR WALTER. *The cabinet council; containing the chief arts of empire and mysteries of state.* London, 1658.

———. *Remains.* London, 1675.

———. *Three discourses.* London, 1702.

———. *Works.* Oxford, 1829. 8 vols.

RANKE, LEOPOLD VON. *A history of England principally in the seventeenth century.* Oxford, 1875. 6 vols.

———. *Ueber die verschwörung gegen Venedig.* Berlin, 1837.

RAVÀ, BÉATRICE. *Venise dans la littérature française.* Paris, 1916.

RAY, JOHN. *Observations, topographical, moral, and physiological; made in a journey through part of the Low-Countries, Germany, Italy, and France.* London, 1673.

RAYMOND, DORA N. *Oliver's secretary: John Milton in an era of revolt.* New York, 1932.

RAYMOND, JOHN. *An itinerary contayning a voyage made through Italy, in the yeare 1646, and 1647.* London, 1648.

Religion and loyalty supporting each other. By a true son of the Church of England. London, 1681.

RERESBY, SIR JOHN. *Memoirs.* Ed. from the original manuscript by J. J. Cartwright. London, 1875.

REYNOLDS, BEATRICE. *Proponents of limited monarchy in sixteenth century France: Francis Hotman and Jean Bodin.* New York, 1931.

ROBERTSON, ALEXANDER. *Fra Paolo Sarpi.* New York, 1894.

ROGERS, JOHN. *A Christian concertation with Mr. Prin, Mr. Baxter, Mr. Harrington. For the true cause of the commonwealth.* London, 1659.

———. *Mr. Harrington's parallel unparallel'd: or a demonstration upon it . . . wherein it appears that neither the spirit of the people, nor the spirit of men like Mr. R. but the spirit of God, of Christ, of his people in Parliament and adherents to the cause, is the fittest for the government of the commonwealth.* London, 1659.

RONALDS, FRANCIS S. *The attempted Whig revolution of 1678–81.* Urbana, 1937.

RUSHWORTH, JOHN. *Historical collections of the great civil war*. London, 1721. 8 vols.

RUSSELL, LORD JOHN. *The life of William Lord Russell; with some account of the times in which he lived*. London, 1820. Third ed. 2 vols.

S., G. *The dignity of kingship asserted; in answer to Mr. Milton's Ready and easie way to establish a free common-wealth*. London, 1660. (Facsimile Text Society reproduction with an introduction by W. R. Parker identifying G. S. as George Starkey, New York, 1942.)

SABINE, G. H. *A history of political theory*. New York, 1937.

SADLER, JOHN. *Olbia, the new island lately discovered with its religion, laws, customs, and government*. Part I. 1660.

SAINT-RÉAL, C[ÉSAR] V[ISCHARD] DE. *The conspiracy of the Spaniards against the republic of Venice. To which some remarks are added on the use made of the history of the Abbé St. Réal, in the composition of Venice preserved*. London, 1823.

[SARPI, PAOLO]. *The history of the quarrels of Pope Paul V with the state of Venice*. Trans. [C. Potter]. London, 1626.

SAUMAISE (SALMASIUS), CLAUDE. *Defensio regia pro Carolo I ad serenissimum Magnae Britanniae regem Carolum II filium natu majorem, heredem, et successorem legitimum, sumptibus regiis*. 1649.

SCHMIDT, HENRICH. *Milton considered as a political writer*. Halle, 1882.

A seasonable address to both houses of Parliament concerning the succession; the fears of popery, and arbitrary government. 1681.

The second part of No Protestant plot. London, 1682.

SEELEY, J. R. "Milton's political opinions," in *Lectures and essays*. London, 1895.

SEYSSEL, CLAUDE DE. *La grande monarchie de France*. Paris, 1558.

SHERINGHAM, ROBERT. *The king's supremacy asserted, Or a remonstrance of the king's right against the pretended Parliament*. London, 1660.

SIDNEY, SIR PHILIP, AND HUBERT LANGUET. *Correspondence*. Ed. with notes and memoir of Sidney by Steuart Adolphus Pears. London, 1845.

SISMONDI, JOHN CHARLES LEONARD SIMONDE DE. *History of the Italian republics; being a view of the origin, progress and fall of Italian freedom*. London and New York, 1907.

SMITH, H. F. RUSSELL. *Harrington and his Oceana: a study of a 17th century utopia and its influence in America*. Cambridge, 1914.

SMITH, LOGAN P. *The life and letters of Sir Henry Wotton*. Oxford, 1907. 2 vols.

SMITH, SIR THOMAS. *De republica Anglorum. A discussion of the commonwealth of England*. Ed. L. Alston. Cambridge, 1906.

The social and political ideas of some great thinkers of the sixteenth and seventeenth centuries. Ed. F. J. C. Hearnshaw. London, 1915.

SOMERS, JOHN, LORD. *A letter ballancing the necessity of keeping a land-force in times of peace: with the dangers that may follow on it*. London, 1697. (*The balancing letter*.)

State tracts: being a collection of several treatises relating to the government. Privately printed in the reign of K. Charles II. London, 1689. New edition, 1693.

State tracts: being a farther collection of several choice treatises relating to the government from the year 1660 to 1689. London, 1692.

STEELF, SIR RICHARD AND JOSEPH ADDISON. *The town talk, The fish pool, The plebeian, The old Whig, The spinster etc. By the authors of The tatler, Spectator, and Guardian.* First collected in 1789. London, 1790.

STERN, A. *Milton und seine zeit.* Leipzig, 1877–79. 2 vols.

STERNE, LAWRENCE. *Tristram Shandy.* Ed. James A. Work. New York, 1940.

STUBBE, HENRY. *The commonwealth of Oceana put into the ballance, and found too light. Or an account of the republic of Sparta, with occasional animadversions upon Mr. James Harrington and the Oceanisticall model.* London, 1660.

SWIFT, JONATHAN. *Gulliver's travels.* Ed. with notes and commentary by Arthur E. Case. New York, 1938.

———. *Prose works.* Ed. Temple Scott with a biographical introduction by W. E. H. Lecky. London, 1897–1908. 21 vols.

SYDNEY, ALGERNON. *Works.* Ed. J. Robertson. London, 1772.

SYMONDS, J. A. *Renaissance in Italy.* Modern library ed. New York, n.d. 2 vols.

TEMPLE, SIR WILLIAM. *Works.* Edinburgh, 1754. 4 vols.

The third part of no Protestant plot: with observations on the proceedings upon the bill of indictment against the E. of Shaftesbury. London, 1682.

The Tory plot. The second part, or, a farther discovery of a design to alter the constitution of the government, and to betray the Protestant religion. London, 1682.

Tracts on liberty in the Puritan revolution, 1638–1647. Ed. William Haller. New York, 1934. 3 vols.

TREVELYAN, GEORGE MACAULAY. *England under Queen Anne.* London and New York, 1930–34. 3 vols.

———. *England under the Stuarts.* London, 1928. Fourteenth ed.

TURBERVILLE, A.S. *The House of Lords in the XVIIIth century.* Oxford, 1927.

TYRRELL, JAMES. *Patriarcha non monarcha, or the patriarch unmonarched.* London, 1681.

———. *Bibliotheca politica: or, an enquiry into the antient constitution of the English government. In fourteen dialogues.* London, 1718.

VARCHI, BENEDETTO. *Storia Fiorentina . . . nella quale principalmente si contengono l'ultime revoluzioni della repubblica Fiorentina, e lo stabilimento del principato nella casa de' Medici.* Florence, 1721.

VILLARI, PASQUALE. *Life and times of Girolamo Savonarola.* Trans. Linda Villari. London, 1899.

———. *Niccolò Machiavelli and his times.* Trans. Linda Villari. London, 1878. 4 vols.

Vox populi: or the peoples claim to their Parliaments sitting . . . humbly recommended to the king and Parliament at their meeting at Oxford, the 21st of March. London, 1681.

WALSH, CORREA MOYLAN. *The political science of John Adams: a study in the theory of mixed government and the bicameral system.* New York and London, 1915.

WERSHOFEN, CHRISTIAN. *James Harrington und sein wunschbild vom Germanischen staate.* Bonn, 1935.

WHITELOCK, BULSTRODE. *Memorials of the English affairs from the beginning of the reign of Charles the First to the happy restoration of Charles the Second.* Oxford, 1853. 4 vols.

WIEL, ALETHEA. *Venice.* New York and London, 1894.

WILLIAMS, BASIL. *The Whig supremacy, 1714–1760.* Oxford, 1939.

WITHER, GEORGE. *Works.* Spenser society ed. 1871–82. 20 vols.

WOLFE, DON M. *Milton in the Puritan revolution.* New York, 1941.

WOOD, ANTHONY À. *Athenae Oxonienses: an exact history of all the writers and bishops who have had their education in the . . . University of Oxford.* Ed. Philip Bliss. 1813–20. 4 vols.

WOODHOUSE, A. S. P. *Puritanism and liberty. Being the army debates (1647–9) from the Clarke manuscripts with supplementary documents.* London, 1938.

WOTTON, SIR HENRY. *Reliquiae Wottonianae; or, a collection of lives, letters, poems, with characters of sundry personages: and other incomparable pieces of language and art . . . by the curious pencil of the ever memorable Sir Henry Wotton.* London, 1672. Third ed.

WRIGHT, THOMAS. *The passions of the minde.* London, 1630. Second ed.

[WREN, MATTHEW]. *Considerations on Mr. Harrington's commonwealth of Oceana.* London, 1657.

———. *Monarchy asserted, or the state of monarchicall and popular government in vindication of the Considerations upon Mr. Harrington's Oceana.* Oxford, 1659.

ZEALE, JOHN (pseud.). *A narrative of the phanatical plot, setting forth the treasonable designs which they have been carrying on against the king and government.* London, 1683.

INDEX

213

Botero, Giovanni, 42, 92; on Venice, 36, 43; on climate, 192
Bounds and bonds of publique obedience, The, 101
Brabantio (*Othello*), 35, 42
Britannia and Rawleigh, 125 ff.
Browne, Sir Thomas, 91
Brutus, Lucius, 1, 7, 90, 105 f.
Burnet, Gilbert, 170
Burton, Thomas, 86, 132

C

Cabinet government, relation to classical republicanism, 132, 175 ff.
Caesar, Julius, 52, 158, 174
Cambrai, League of, 36, 143, 158
Capi di Dieci (Venice), 32
Carolina, plan for the government of, 125
Carthage, 2, 6, 37, 39, 57, 81
Castiglione, Baldassare, 39
Cato, 1, 90
Caveat against the Whiggs, A, 129, 137
Cecil family, the, 135
Censors, 174
Censure of the Rota, The, 1, 87 f., 115, 123 f.
Chaos: or a discourse, 86
Character of a Whig, The, 137
Character of the Long Parliament (Milton), 93, 110, 193 f.
Charles I, 24 f., 27, 68, 103, 135
Charles II, 123–30, 132–33, 135–37, 145, 149, 168, 177, 184
Charondas, 9
Charrier, Jean, 39
Checks and balances, in Venice, 34 f., 63; in Harrington, 63; in Milton, 121–22; relation to theory of mixed government, 2, 4, 34, 186
Christina, Queen, 92
Cicero, 26, 183; on Roman mixed government, 5–8, 10; relation to Polybius, 5; on Roman imperialism, 85
Citizens, of Florence, 16; of Venice, 30, 33, 34
Citizenship, Machiavelli on the closing of the, 16, 33; Sydney on the, 166
Claypool, Lady, 85
Climatic influence, theory of, in Milton, 91–94, 110, 192; forms of the, 191–92
Coke, Roger, 87
Collegio, the Venetian, 29
Colonial policy, Harrington on, 83–85; Sydney on, 157; Moyle on, 173; relation of English and Roman, 83, 189
Comedy of errors, The (Shakespeare), 43

Commissioners, 75 f.
Committee of Six, the, 169
Commonplace book, Milton's, 97 f.
Commons, the House of, 25, 75, 97, 128, 135 f., 185 f.
Commonwealth and government of Venice, The (Contarini), 28, 37 ff.
Commonwealth, Milton's free, regal element, 103–04, 108–09, 115; aristocratic element, 97, 98, 107; democratic element, 96, 116 f., 118–19; concilar magistracy, 103–04, 109, 115; Grand Council, 111, 112–15, 118, 121; Council of State, 103; rejection of constitutional dictator in, 105; mixed government in 120; classical models for, 114–16, 119; Venice as model for, 110, 114–16, 119; Sanhedrim as a model for, 115; institution of, 104–07; immortality predicted, 120–21; suffrage, 112, 114, 118; checks and balances in, 121–22; local government, 118; militia, 118; sovereignty in, 121; rotation in, 113, 115, 198; education in, 117, 119 f.; attacks on, 115; inspectors in, 112, 118; veto in, 118; minority rights in, 117; revenues, 112; perpetual governing bodies in, 112; life tenure in, 112 f.; use of armed force in attaining, 107
Congreve, William, 170
Conquest, the Norman, *see* Norman Conquest
Considerations concerning the bill in parliament, 186
Considerations on Mr. Harrington's Oceana (Wren), 44, 73, 85
Conspiracy of the Spaniards against the State of Venice, The (Saint-Réal), 125, 142
Constantinople, 77
Constitution explain'd, The, 186
Consuls, 4, 7, 75, 172
Contarini Fleming (Disraeli), 183
Contarini, Cardinal Gasparo, 10, 28–31, 34 f., 37–43, 47 f., 61, 63, 115, 119, 140
Contarini family, the, 37
Contarini myth, the, 38, 43, 54
Cornwall, 170
Coryate, Thomas, 44, 48
Council, councils, of Sixty-five, 15; of the Selected, 16; Grand, *see* Grand Council; in Utopia, *see* More, Sir Thomas; of Venice, *see* Venice; in Oceana, *see* Harrington; of state, 47, 103; Privy, 128, 131
Councilar magistracy, in Venice, 28 f.,

ADDENDUM FOR THE SECOND EDITION

The following additions and amplifications are correlated with the footnotes in the main text of this book, to which the page and note numbers heading each item refer.

Page 18, n. 70 In vaguely conceived forms more referable to Aristotle than Polybius and colored by the persistent Thomist attempt to assimilate the political ideas of Aristotle into religious conceptions, the idea of mixed government was not unknown even earlier. Two passages in Thomas Aquinas are relevant (*Summa theologiae,* II, i, q. 105, art. 1 and q. 95, art. 4), though whether he championed the theory, as Gierke and others have maintained, is questionable. The passage in q. 105, at least, is open to the suspicion of being an exegetical necessity, and he elsewhere, in the *De regimine principum* (I, ii) and in the *Summa* (II, ii, q. 50, art. 1), expresses conflicting opinions (see Ewart Lewis's comments in *Medieval political ideas* [New York, 1954], pp. 250, 352). John of Paris followed Aristotle and Aquinas, and both were quoted by conciliarists like d'Ailly and Gerson in support of their conception of the church as an organization of cooperating bodies, no one of which was supreme (d'Ailly, *De ecclesiae, concilii generalis, Romani pontificus et cardinalium auctoritate,* III, iv; Gerson, *Sermo habitus xxi die Julii,* 1415, III, ii; and cf. Lewis's comments, p. 273, on the vagueness of their conceptions).

Page 23, n. 93 Views similar to those of Ponet and with similar associations were expressed between 1533 and 1536 by Thomas Starkey in his imaginary *Dialogue between Reginald Pole and Thomas Lupset,* in which Pole, later Cardinal Pole, is the champion of the mixed state. "The most wise men, considering the nature of princes, yea, and the nature of man as it is indeed," Pole is made to declare, "affirm a mixed state to be of all other the best and most convenient to conserve the whole out of tyranny" (ed. Kathleen Burton [London, 1948], p. 165).

Page 23, n. 95 With Smith and Ponet must be grouped John Aylmer, like Ponet a Marian exile and later a bishop, who wrote: "England is not a mere monarchie, as some for lack of consideration think, nor a mere oligarchy, nor democracy, but a rule mixt of all these, wherein each one of these have or should have a like authoritie" (*An harborowe for faithfull and trewe subjects* [Strassbourg, 1559]). Starkey, Pole, Ponet, Aylmer, and Smith all studied in Italy, principally law at Padua and Venice, or elsewhere on the Continent. Pole was a friend of Contarini.

Page 23, n. 99 The Jesuit Robert Parsons in his *Conference about the next succession to the crowne of England* (1594) also describes the English monarchy as mixed.

Page 25, n. 104 See further Francis Osborne, *A persuasive to mutual compliance under the present government, and plea for a free state compared with a monarchy* (1652). Osborne, author of the celebrated *Advice to a son* and an admirer of Venice, also wrote *A discourse upon Nicholas Machiavel; or, an impartial examination of the justness of the censure commonly laid upon him*, in which he viewed *The Prince* as a minor work and protested against the distortion of Machiavelli's reputation by those who knew only that book. Osborne's republicanism got the first of the several posthumous collective editions of his *Works* into trouble in 1676, when it was brought to the attention of the House of Lords as a seditious and treasonable work. The *Persuasive* was omitted from at least most of these editions.

Page 42, n. 63 To this list should be added *The city and republick of Venice. In three parts. Originally written in French by Monsieur de S. Desdier* [A. T. Limojou de Saint Didier] (London, 1699).

Page 46, n. 84 See also *Venice looking glass: or, a letter written very lately from London to Rome by a Venetian clarissimo to Cardinal Barberini, protector of the English nation, touching these present distempers. Wherein, as a true mirrour, England may behold her own spots . . . faithfully rendered out of the Italian into English* (1648).

Page 46, n. 86 The idea antedates even Sir Thomas Smith. In Starkey's *Dialogue* (*ca.* 1533–36), Pole is represented as eulogizing the institution of the doge and declaring that if the King of England were like the Duke of Venice, the same internal tranquillity which had kept Venice without change for over a thousand years would be achieved (ed. Burton, pp. 163, 165, 167). The long-cherished, intermittent, often submerged, but persistent notion of making the king like a duke of Venice was a factor in English politics for a period of over two centuries (see also my comments on pp. 177–78).

Page 90, n. 5 Milton invoked classical precedent even in defending his divorce tracts. It is a source of never-ceasing chagrin to me that I did not think of lines 1 and 2 of his Sonnet XII in time to use them as an epigraph to this chapter:

> I did but prompt the age to quit their clogs
> By the known rules of antient liberty.

The "barbarous" noise that environed him on this occasion is an echo of the contrast drawn in the *Areopagitica* between "the old and elegant humanity of Greece" and the "barbaric pride of a Hunnish and Norwegian stateliness."

Page 141, n. 89 I have not been able to see a copy of *The sayings and doings of the ambassador Foscarini of Venice*, described as an anti-Venetian tract of about 1615 and attributed to Giovanni or Francesco

Biondi. It was perhaps related to the *Squittinio* in substance as well as in time. The *Squittinio* was answered by Dirk Graswinckel, *Libertas Veneta; sive, Venetorum in se suos imperandi ius, assertum contra anonymum Scrutinii scriptorem* (Leyden, 1634).

Page 170, n. 1 An additional tract relevant here is *Sidney redivivus; or the opinion of the late honourable Collonel Sidney as to civil government . . . by which the late proceedings of the nation against James the II are justified* (London, 1689).

Page 175, n. 32 It is a suggestive fact that the redoubtable Dr. Samuel Parr was given a copy of Polybius by Mackintosh Hooker.

Page 181, n. 58 The distrust of political parties long continued in English political thought. Halifax looked upon them as conspiracies of a part of the nation against the whole. In his *Maxims of state* he wrote: "Parties in a State generally, like Free-booters, hang out False Colours; the Pretence is the Publick Good; the real Business is to catch Prizes; like the Tartars, where-ever they succeed, instead of improving their Victory, they presently fall upon the Baggage" (No. 23); and in the *Cautions for the choice of members of parliament*, he devoted the whole fifteenth section to a warning against "Men ty'd to a Party." The attitude was widespread down to the publication in 1770 of Burke's *Thoughts on the cause of the present discontents*, a work notable for the recognition it gives to the role of political parties.

Page 185, n. 78 An *argument* states the issues in this lively controversy very clearly. Surveying Europe in their own day, Trenchard and Moyle found that under the French domination despotism had triumphed on the Continent; that this had happened though the Continental states, like England, had started out with mixed constitutions; and that everywhere the cause was the same—the development of standing armies made up of mercenaries. For such bodies they would substitute a militia made up of freemen—those who had property. The balance of a mixed state could "never be preserved but by the union of the natural and artificial Strength of the Kingdom, that is, by making the Militia to consist of the same Persons as have the Property; or otherwise the Government is violent and against Nature, and cannot possibly continue but the Constitution must either break the Army, or the Army will destroy the Constitution" (p. 4). "No Legislator," they asserted, "ever founded a free Government, but avoided this Caribdis, as a rock against which his Commonwealth must certainly be ship-wrack'd, as the Israelites, Athenians, Corinthians, Achaians, Lacedemonians, Thebans, Samites, and Romans; none of which Nations whilst they kept their liberty were ever known to maintain any Souldiers in constant Pay within their cities" (pp. 6–7). These contentions echo through the other tracts in the controversy: *To the annonimous author of the Argument against a standing army* (1697); [Andrew Fletcher], *A discourse concerning militia's and standing armies with relation to the past and present governments of Europe, and of England in particular* (London, 1697); [John Trenchard],

A letter from the author of the Argument against a standing army, to the author of the Balancing letter (London, 1697); *Remarks upon a scurrilous libel; called an Argument, shewing that a standing army is inconsistent with a free government etc.* (London, 1697); *The argument against a standing army, discuss'd. By a true lover of his country* (London, 1698); *The case of a standing army fairly and impartially stated in answer to the late History of standing armies in England; and other pamphlets writ on that subject* (London, 1698); *The case of disbanding the army at present, briefly and impartially consider'd* ([London], 1698); [John Trenchard], *A short history of standing armies in England* (London, 1698); and John Toland, *The militia reform'd; or an easy scheme of furnishing England with a constant land-force, capable to prevent or to subdue any forein power; and to maintain perpetual quiet at home, without endangering the publick liberty* (London, 1698).

Page 190, n. 100   Two recent works related to the ideas studied in this book are Charles Blitzer's *An immortal commonwealth: the political thought of James Harrington* (New Haven, 1960), and Caroline Robbins, *The eighteenth century commonwealthsman* (Cambridge, Mass., 1959).